From WAR to WESTMINSTER

From WAR to
WESTMINSTER

Stefan Terlezki CBE

Foreword by
Lord Howe of Aberavon

Pen & Sword
MILITARY

First published in Great Britain in 2005 by
PEN & SWORD MILITARY
an imprint of
Pen & Sword Books Limited
47 Church Street
Barnsley
South Yorkshire
S70 2AS

ISBN 1 84415 265 0

A CIP catalogue record for this book
is available from the British Library.

Designed and typeset (in 10pt New Baskerville)
by Sylvia Menzies, Pen & Sword Books Ltd

Printed and bound in Great Britain by
CPI UK

Pen & Sword Books Ltd incorporates the imprints of
Pen & Sword Aviation, Pen & Sword Maritime, Pen & Sword Military,
Wharncliffe Local History, Pen & Sword Select,
Pen & Sword Military Classics and Leo Cooper.

For a complete list of Pen & Sword titles please contact:
PEN & SWORD BOOKS LIMITED
47 Church Street, Barnsley, South Yorkshire, S70 2AS, England.
E-mail: enquiries@pen-and-sword.co.uk
Website: www.pen-and-sword.co.uk

To the memory of my dear mother, father and sister.
I only regret only that they did not live to see the
flag of freedom, the blue and yellow colours of
Ukraine, for which I have fought all my life,
flying over the country of my birth.

Contents

Foreword
by
Lord Howe of Aberavon

former Chancellor of the Exchequer,
Foreign Secretary and
Leader of the House of Commons.

I first met Stefan over twenty years ago, in June 1983, at a time when the Cold War between the Soviet Union and the Western Alliance was as cold as it had ever been. Margaret Thatcher had just asked me to move on, after four years as Chancellor of the Exchequer, to become Britain's Secretary of State for Foreign Affairs. And Stefan Terlezki, a Ukrainian born refugee, had just been elected – remarkably – as a Conservative Member of Parliament for Cardiff West. We were to get to know each other much better during the next year.

For Margaret Thatcher and I had decided that Britain should play a much more active part in trying to break the deadlock between East and West. So by July 1984 I was off to Moscow – the first visit by a British Foreign Secretary for seven years – and there to tackle the Soviet foreign minister, Andrei Gromyko (better known as 'Mister Niet') in his own den.

One of the important documents which I took with me to Moscow, and was able to leave with Gromyko, was a list of so-called 'reunification cases' – of families that had long been divided by the Iron Curtain and its inhuman formalities. One particularly moving example of these was Stefan Terlezki's, who had been trying to persuade the Soviet authorities to allow his aged father to visit him in the West. They had not seen each other for more than forty years. The Terlezki family were one of the two or three cases where Gromyko proved willing to accept my plea.

So I was able to share Stefan's surprise (and delight), when his father arrived in Britain – even if only for a short stay – just a few months later. And during the twenty years since then I have, of course, been able to hear enough of his quite astonishing life story to realize that this autobiography was bound to deserve commendation to the widest possible audience.

I had just one anxious reservation. Could this Welsh-accented, Polish-born Ukrainian, and sometime Red Army officer, actually write really readable English? I needn't have worried – on that or any other score. For this is a truly remarkable book, which tells an astonishingly gripping life story in crisp, beautifully crafted English. The spontaneity and recollection of language and mood is both evocative and convincing.

Stefan Terlezki gives us, as well as his own story, an equally fascinating and much broader insight into the turbulent history of the so-called nation states of twentieth century Europe. Begin, if you wish, with the tiny village east of the Carpathian mountains, Antoniwka, where he was brought up. Linguistically and ethnically part of Ukraine, Antoniwka was in Austrian Galicia until the break-up of the Austro-Hungarian empire at the end of the First World War. There followed twenty years of Polish rule, ending in military autocracy. In 1939, when Poland itself was partitioned under the Nazi-Soviet 'non-aggression' pact, Terlezki's homeland became part of the Soviet Union. 'If we thought we had suffered under the Polish flag' said Terlezki, 'it was as nothing compared to what happened to us under the red flag of Russia'.

But only at that stage for a brief two years, before Hitler's invasion of Russia brought Antoniwka under Nazi rule – the third brand of tyranny in thirty years. After two more years the tide of war had turned again. The Red Army had ousted the *Wehrmacht*.

Given the historic stability of our British background, I find it impossible to imagine what it must have been like to grow up, as Terlezki did, in the midst of such turbulence. Even before the final Russian 'conquest' his own father – a courageous citizen leader in a very poor but proud community – had experienced arrest and imprisonment. By the time Stefan was fourteen years old, he had himself been deported by the Germans and literally sold into slavery on an Austrian farm. Within three years, 'liberated' by Soviet forces, he found himself forthwith conscripted for action against the Japanese – and appointed a lieutenant in the Red Army. Astonishingly, he was able to desert and escape – and to retrace his perilous path back into what had become the British-occupied zone of Austria. By then fluent in Ukrainian, Polish, Russian and German, he somehow managed to make his way into employment in the catering services of the British Army and, much later, into mastery of the English language.

And so, eventually, to Wales and through the Cardiff College of Food Technology into the hotel industry, the chairmanship of Cardiff City football club and membership of the City Council. Election as a Conservative MP for the constituency which had previously sustained one of Wales' most admired Labour parliamentarians, Speaker George Thomas, must have seemed a fairly modest challenge, in comparison with those which had confronted Stefan Terlezki in the turbulence of his early life.

We native Britons seldom appreciate our historic privilege of living in a land for centuries unravaged by invading armies. This exciting book compels us to realize the full value of that blessing – and to admire the bravery and versatility of those who have had to struggle so hard to secure a share of the same.

Geoffrey Howe
April 2005

Acknowledgements

I am sincerely grateful to all the wonderful friends who helped me to tell my story.

Merric Davidson, my Literary Agent, was at all times extremely helpful. He gave me all the encouragement I needed to carry on writing with optimism and confidence. He helped me to improve the structure and clarity of my story.

I owe a special debt to Nick Powell, Head of Politics at HTV Wales, for unlimited time, effort and sound advice at all times. Without his extremely generous dedication, my memoirs might still be waiting for a publisher.

I would like to express my special thanks to Max Perkins, formerly HTV Wales Parliamentary Lobby Correspondent, for his considerable help with the story of my political career in local government and at Westminster.

My special gratitude is to David Melding AM, who read the manuscript and gave me sound advice, as well as encouragement that the book was worthy of publication.

I shall be forever grateful to Diane Hardy for transcribing my tape recordings. It was excellently done and I know she shed a few tears, listening to my words.

My heartfelt gratitude to Carol Christian for editing the transcript and putting it into shape.

My gracious appreciation to Sally Jones for her kind and appropriate advice at all times.

And last but never least my wife Mary, who endlessly typed pages and pages, as the chapters were given an uplift and not a put-down!

Stefan Terlezki CBE
Cardiff
March 2005

Preface

Ikept no diary; how could I? From the age of fourteen I was lost and blown in all directions by winds of horror, tragedy and uncertainty. I had no hope or future during and for long after the brutality which ended on 8 May 1945.

I was born in western Ukraine in the Stanislawiw region (now Ivano-Frankiwsk), when it was ruled by Poland. In 1939 we were told that the Russians were our liberators but we were soon subjected to the full horrors of Stalinist rule, including political indoctrination, oppression, collectivization and transportation of innocent people to Siberia. The Russians also held a rigged village election with bribery and intimidation in order to secure a bogus mandate for our forcible incorporation into the Stalinist system.

It was not plain sailing even to reach Great Britain in 1948. But my optimism never deserted me, neither did the will to succeed. My hope, like that of the rainbow's on the horizon, was that the sun would shine again.

Since 1948, I have lived in wonderful Wales amongst very hospitable people and made full use of the political freedom I have enjoyed in Britain. Regrettably we take our freedom so much for granted that we forget how precious it is until it is too late to defend it.

My diary was my head; a bank where, once you lock your memories, no one can take them out and destroy them. I kept them locked inside for decades but now I am delighted and honoured that they are published by Pen & Sword for all to read.

Chapter 1

1984
Reunion

'You were born in slavery, but I hope from the bottom of my heart that you will die in freedom.' Those were the last words my father spoke to me when I was forced to leave my homeland of Ukraine in 1942. I was one of the young people from our village taken away by train to become slave workers for the Germans. Since then, we had not seen one another for forty-two years.

It was now October 1984 and I was no longer a slave but a British Member of Parliament. I couldn't see him yet but my father was being pushed towards me in a wheel chair at Heathrow Airport. From the day I had gained the freedom that my father had wanted for me, I had longed more than ever to be reunited with him and my loving sister Lywosi.

When we were first separated, I had been taken by the Germans to Austria, where I had been able to exchange letters with my father, my other relatives and my school friends. That's how I had heard of my mother's illness, and ultimately of her death at the age of forty-two. She had never recovered from the day I was taken away from her by the Nazis.

Once the Nazis had been defeated and the Russians had regained control of my homeland the letters suddenly stopped, and although I wrote many times to my father and my relatives in my village, I received no reply. This went on for more than fifteen years and all the time I was desperate to know what had happened to my father and Lywosi. Were they dead? Had they been killed by the German army as it retreated from Ukraine? Had they been murdered by the Russian Red Army as it recaptured Ukraine? As letter after letter was sent out without any acknowledgement or reply I grew increasingly frustrated and apprehensive. Finally, I decided to write to the village chairman to ask him if he at least could tell me what had happened to my father and my sister. I knew, of course, that life had been very difficult in Ukraine ever since the Russians regained control. I waited and waited for a reply and eventually the letter came. When I opened the envelope all I could find inside was a very small piece of paper with what appeared to be my father's new address written on it – in Siberia! I stared at it in horror. There was no other message, no information of any kind. I was devastated by the news.

My father was still alive, presumably, but the circumstances didn't look good and that caused me the deepest pain. On top of that there was no mention of my sister – what had happened to her? I had yet another reason to worry. However, at least I had an address and could write to my father at his new home near Irkutsk in Siberia. I did so and, to my great joy, he wrote back. He was allowed to do so even though our mail was censored. I learned that he had to collect his letters from the post office where an official would have already opened and checked them. If there was anything they did not approve of in the letter it was burned. If I sent a parcel to Siberia, my father would have to travel eighty kilometres to collect it. Like the letters it would be opened first by the KGB who would help themselves to anything that took their fancy before they handed the package over. This censorship meant that my father could not tell me of the conditions in which he lived, but at least I knew that he was alive and well, and so was Lywosi.

Naturally, I desperately wanted to see my father and my sister, but I was sure that it wouldn't be safe to try to visit Communist Russia. I knew too much about the system and about the way the KGB treated people they suspected of being subversives. That included anybody who advocated freedom and democracy and then made the mistake of falling into their clutches. As an alternative I had tried repeatedly to get permission for my father to visit me but until now to no avail.

Our original farewells had been in public, and our reunion was to be equally public, this time in the full glare of publicity. The press had heard about this intriguing event – the arrival of a 'prisoner' from Siberia who was being allowed to come over simply as a goodwill gesture, without any exchanges or political strings attached. Press photographers flashed their cameras from all directions in their attempts to get a close-up. Journalists hovered, their pens and pads at the ready, to write down every detail of the reunion. Meanwhile hundreds of passengers were flooding into the arrival hall where friends and relatives were waiting for them. When they saw the media scrum frantically filming my wife and myself, they reacted in astonishment.

'Oh my God, what's this?' they were asking. 'Who on earth's coming? Is it a film star, or some sort of VIP? Are they here yet?'

Surrounded by all this feverish activity I stood there with a bouquet of flowers in my hands, my whole body trembling with anticipation and suspense – even the flowers were shaking. My lips were trembling and my eyes were red from tears of joy, which had been welling up ever since I'd heard the good news. My whole attention was now focussed on the doorway through which my father would soon appear. As I waited with my wife, Mary, the photographers and journalists were pointing me out to the increasingly curious throng of passengers and visitors. 'That's the VIP over there,' they would explain. 'He's a Member of Parliament and his father is just arriving from Siberia.' Even then I noticed some of the travellers taking a deep breath as they heard the news, exclaiming, 'Oh my goodness! Poor man! From Siberia!'

At last a courteous and friendly airport official came out to tell me that my father needed a wheelchair, but it wouldn't be long before we could see him. We waited, and then the official came back once again and apologized for the delay, saying that my father was almost ready to join us.

They say that drowning men see their lives flash before them. Now the excitement and shock of the day sent my mind racing back to my own early days. Once again I was a peasant boy, growing up with my family.

Chapter 2

1927-1938
Before the Storm

I was born in the village of Oleshiw, in the province of Halychyna or Galicia, on 29 October 1927. I was brought up in the nearby farming community of Antoniwka, which lies east of the Carpathian Range, in the fertile River Dniester valley. At that time western Ukraine was under Polish domination, having failed to secure its independence when the Austro-Hungarian Empire disintegrated at the end of the First World War. I lived with my father Oleksa, mother Olena and older sister Lywosi and my memories of early childhood are bathed in sunshine and happiness.

My father was a big, strong man, about 1.8 metres in height and 90 kilos in weight. I cannot remember him ever being ill. He worked as a manager at a brickworks and on our smallholding, which he farmed with the help of my mother and sister. He was upright in his physical posture and in his attitude to public life, a stalwart Christian, high principled and deeply aware of his responsibilities to his fellow men. He did not smoke or swear and rarely touched alcohol. Undoubtedly a stern disciplinarian, for it was no kindness to peasant children to overindulge them, he nevertheless had an irrepressible sense of fun and a lively sense of humour. If he was strict with me, it was in the hope that his only son would aim high, and come to enjoy advantages in life that he had never received. Despite his literacy and his qualities of leadership, he had left school to go to work at an early age.

My mother, Olena, was ambitious for me, too, but at the same time very loving. Of a frail, elegant build, in spite of the hard work in which she was always engaged, she was an excellent housewife, intelligent, sensible, and determined. As well as Ukrainian and Polish, which all of us spoke in those days, she spoke German, as she had served in her youth in the house of a Prussian noble family.

In addition to our immediate family, there were aunts and uncles living nearby; Uncle Roman, who also worked at the brickworks, and Uncle Dmytro, a farmer who produced most of our local musical and theatrical events. My grandfather, who lived with Uncle Dmytro, was the proud owner of a very fine quill pen. It was a souvenir of when he had served as secretary to the district governor in Tlumach, part of the Province of Stanislawiw (now Ivano-Frankiwsk) in the days of the Austro-Hungarian Empire. Having been a secretary, he dealt with private and legal matters for the village people who were unable to pay for a professional lawyer and who were very poorly educated or illiterate. In a way he was the equivalent of today's ombudsman. He was a good-tempered, warm-hearted old man, a mine of information for a boy since he had time to talk about all manner of things. Uncle Roman and Uncle Dmytro were my father's brothers. His sister, Aunt Paraska, and her husband, Uncle Danyelo, kept a general store in the heart of the village next to the church.

Our modest one-room home had walls of whitewashed mud and a thatched roof, and was subdivided by wooden partitions. The earthen floor was partly carpeted with home-woven carpets and our simple furniture, made by a friend of my father's, was carefully polished and greatly treasured. This house was on the edge of the village, in the shadow of high hills and beside the stream; all around us was farmland and orchards. A rough cart-track led from the far side of the stream into the centre of the village. In 1939, following the Polish retreat, I helped my father construct a bridge across the stream, using the chassis of a burnt-out army lorry. Before that, a few strong timbers had sufficed.

Life was simple: no gas or electricity, no bathroom or plumbing, no telephone or radio. A wood stove burned day and night to warm the house in winter. It provided hot water (a great luxury) for bathing, in a wooden tub in front of the fire, but the water had first to be drawn and carried from the village well, so we did not bathe often. Paraffin lamps and candles supplied a pleasant light; as I lay awake at night in a little alcove behind the partition, I was not in darkness. I could see the light and hear the conversations of my parents and their friends as they discussed the affairs of family and village, often becoming heated and angry at the injustice people suffered under the Poles. No one minded children listening, so long as they did not join in. That was strictly forbidden.

Much of the social life of the village revolved around our church, a few hundred metres down the road, one of the Greek Catholic churches to which most people in western Ukraine belong. Our church was very dear to our hearts, and we loved and revered our priest, Father Holowatyj, whom we shared with several other villages. Lywosi and I attended church four or five times a week, and I went to confession whenever I got into trouble at school or quarrelled with Lywosi. The priest would bless me and make me promise not to do wrong again. It didn't preserve me from further disobedience, thought I was sincere in my promises.

As with many country people, our year was marked out for us by the great church festivals. Christmas, celebrated on 7 January, was a time of heartfelt devotion, a wonderful festivity in every home. In each house, dishes of twelve different kinds, to represent the twelve apostles, would be prepared for the Holy Supper.

After the meal, the adults did the rounds of the village, drinking *horilka* (Ukrainian vodka) and singing Christmas carols. It was a romantic sight, with the glow of the lanterns on the snow, the colourful, elaborately-embroidered skirts and shawls of the women, and the soft light and sounds of singing issuing from all the houses.

Uncle Dmytro, who ran the local dramatic society, always organized a children's choir, with everyone dressed up as if for a Nativity play, and we, too, would go singing round the village, led by a boy carrying icons, a huge wooden star, and a large crèche filled with hand-carved wooden Nativity figures. Inevitably, I represented St Stefan, carrying a sack full of stones on my back. I don't remember whether I was aware at that time that he was stoned to death!

There was another traditional ceremony for the Feast of Jordan, the Blessing of the Waters, when the villagers, led by the priest in full vestments, went in procession onto the nearest frozen river. There we would find an altar and a cross cut out of the ice. The altar was dressed with cross and candles for the blessing service and everyone would take the holy water home, in bottles and jars, and keep it for the coming year.

Of all these celebrations Easter was the most joyous. Many charming customs had come down to us from pagan times, for instance the decorating of eggs goes back thousands of years and symbolizes the release of the earth from the shackles of winter, offering the promise of new hope, life, health, and prosperity. A decorated egg is said to be able to avert any evil, ensure good crops, and win young girls the bridegroom of their dreams. Easter brought colourful spring rituals full of singing, dancing, and merrymaking. It followed three days of fasting, when we were permitted only milk or water, and there was a thorough cleansing and whitewashing of our houses, inside and out.

The church, together with Uncle Danyelo's general store, the co-operative store, where produce was both bought and sold, and the village hall were the places where the hundreds of people in the village generally met to exchange news.

To buy liquor, people went to the shop kept by Uncle Maksym in the neighbouring village of Oleshiw. He was a distant relative but we called all the men and boys we had known all our lives 'uncle' and 'cousin'. Uncle Maksym sold beer and spirits and doubled as dentist to the village. He was a comical character with an unfortunate weakness for his own products, especially the local *horilka*. His wife would be driven to locking up the bottles in a cupboard to keep him sober but the story went that he had drilled a hole in the cupboard and could slip a straw through into a bottle when his thirst became too great! I don't know if he used the drill on anyone's teeth. He wasn't trained as a dentist and his dental equipment was minimal and primitive. Probably all he did was extract teeth when he was asked to. He was delighted to do that at any time of the day or night, drunk or sober, in return for a bottle of *horilka*. He performed a useful service as no one could afford to go to a real dentist. Uncle Maksym's service was also quicker and did not involve taking time off work.

Our medical treatments were as simple as our dentistry. Herbal remedies predominated, and leeches, or 'cupping', were much used to draw out blood and with it, one hoped, whatever ailed you. Once, when I was discovered to have intestinal worms, my father forced a half litre of a dark drink that he claimed was beer down my throat, holding my nose all the while. It was, in fact, paraffin, and I recall the treatment as nauseating, though it did the trick! However, I never quite forgave him for the deception.

Uncle Maksym's other claim to fame was that, having his own electricity generator, his was the only house to boast a radio. He allowed people into two rooms where they could listen to the radio direct but would also relay the sound to other rooms, if asked, and let people listen through earphones. They repaid him in kind, with eggs or vegetables, by doing repairs to his house, or by helping with the harvest. Mutual assistance was the order of things.

We grew up with a strong sense of national identity. No one in the village, or in the neighbouring small town of Nyzhiw, was prosperous, but we knew, almost from our birth, that the only thing standing in the way of our greater prosperity, in a land richly blessed by nature, was the Polish administration. Unlike eastern Ukraine, western Ukraine had never been part of the Russian Empire. Until the end of the First World War, it was part of Austrian Galicia. Then after a brief taste of freedom, it became a Polish Protectorate and up until 1939 was administered by the Polish military autocracy of General Pilsudski and, after his death, General Redzshmigel. It wasn't until 1939, when Poland itself was partitioned under the German-Russian 'non-aggression' pact that we were delivered into the hands of the godless Marxist tyranny of Russia.

The Terleckyjs had descended from nobility and had a family coat of arms. My father and his brothers were strong Ukrainian patriots, known to their friends and neighbours as actively striving for a politically independent Ukraine, though within the framework of the law. They lived in a country with plentiful resources but saw that, under a military regime, these were not exploited to better the lives of the ordinary people. The Poles enjoyed the best of everything. We were second-class citizens.

There was ample evidence of oppression. Ukrainians could be arrested and tortured by the Polish police – the *szandary* – without reason. It was enough for a *szandar* to say that the arrested man, or someone in his family, belonged to the Communists, Fascists, or Ukrainian Nationalist Party. People were taken in for questioning for nothing more than receiving correspondence from abroad, and this could be followed by prosecution and imprisonment. A Ukrainian could be imprisoned for up to twelve months for going into a forest owned by the local authority and collecting firewood. There were many such petty restrictions.

Attempts to instruct the young in the distinctive culture of their homeland – literature, arts music – were heavily discouraged. Ukrainians wanted to read newspapers and books in their own language, and give concerts and plays, and displays of their traditional dancing, arts, and crafts, but such things were censored and frequently banned altogether by the Polish authorities. Sometimes, when the *szandar* came to a village, ostensibly to look for underground literature and to question the villagers (permanently under suspicion) they simply burnt down houses, without producing any evidence whatsoever. We had no redress.

Many Ukrainians bore the scars of terrible beatings on their backs – scars that burst open when the beatings were repeated, and never healed again. Thousands of Ukrainians became permanent invalids because of the torments they suffered under interrogation, particularly those sent to a notorious prison called Kartuzka Bereza inside Poland itself.

Our country was not even referred to as Ukraine, but was called *Malo Polska*, 'Little Poland', while we were described as 'Little Russians'. This was an attempt, deeply resented by the people, to diminish Ukraine and wipe it from the map altogether. Those who resisted were quickly identified as political agitators and enemies of the state and had no mercy shown them. Yet people continued to stand up for themselves, putting their families in great peril. They had a compelling vision of a world in which Ukraine would be recognized as a free and independent nation, to the pride of coming generations.

I grew up acquainted with good times, but also with tragic situations in which innocent people were totally helpless. It was never a surprise to hear of pain and injustice inflicted on people we knew well. My Uncle Danyelo had petrol poured into the sweet jars and over the bacon and cheese in his shop by *szandar* who swore that he had failed to pay his taxes, though this was quite untrue.

The sale of produce from our small farm – we had about five hectares of farm land – was not enough to support the family, so my father worked sixteen hours a day in the brickworks at Oleshiw, several kilometres away. There was no machinery, just horses and carts to shift the heaviest loads, so the work was physically exhausting, and it was carried on almost without rest in order to fulfil the 'norms' necessary to ensure a reasonable rate of pay. I cannot remember him coming home without sweat running down his forehead. Since there was nowhere to wash at work, he was covered in dust; my mother kept a saucepan of water boiling on the wood stove ready for him when he came in.

My father's pay went on family necessities and it was a struggle to secure even those. If he managed to save any money, he would buy a few hectares of forest, fell the trees and clear it to enlarge the farm, since our survival depended on what we could grow.

These were years of political, social and economic depression and there was not much paid work about. Dismissals were frequent and there was no appeal if you were fired. My father was foreman at the brickworks, responsible to the management for getting the work done, so his job was comparatively safe. He was a hard worker and his masters knew that to dismiss him might cause trouble, yet he dared not miss a day's work, even through illness. If he had, he would have been replaced. His most determined attempt at protest, when I was eight or nine, ended in disaster.

I suppose my father was the nearest thing there was in Antoniwka to a trade union leader, in that he was continually trying to secure justice and some improvement in working conditions and wages for its people. Although he may not have achieved a very high standard of education, he was something of an intellectual, a radical thinker deeply opposed to the exploitation of the poor. His life revolved around providing assistance to relatives, friends, and neighbours, and supporting his forty or fifty fellow-workers at the factory. On one occasion, he presented a petition signed by the workmen asking for a shorter working day, and backed it up by organizing a week-long sit-in. The men stayed in the factory through the night because, if they had left it and gone home, other men would immediately have taken their places. They slept on the brick floor, with hay for their mattresses. They were not striking in the sense of withdrawing their labour. All they demanded was a fair deal, the kind of reasonable working conditions that could generally be guaranteed in western countries at that time.

Tip-toe as he might through the minefields of employment regulations laid down by the Poles, my father had gone too far this time. He and his fellow protesters were soon arrested for conspiracy against the state.

The first we knew of any danger was when five *szandar* came to our house saying that they were looking for subversive literature or weapons. I was terrified. My father was not at home and they would not answer my mother's questions. They ransacked the house, using bayonets to rip open pillows and mattresses and drawers full of clothing, and smashed a jar of eggs that my mother had ready for sale. All our best furniture and clothes, worked and saved for over the years, were broken or slashed. Then they went outside and started tearing the thatch off the roof, hoping I suppose, to find books or guns concealed there. They threatened to burn our house down – barn, stables, everything – unless my mother told them where our propaganda literature was hidden. She swore there was nothing. Eventually, after destroying a considerable part of the roof, they left saying that my father should report to the Police Station in Nyzhniw as soon as he got home. If he couldn't answer their questions, they warned us, we would never see him again.

When the police had gone, my mother pushed me out of the door, urging, 'Run, Stefan, as fast as you can, and tell Uncle Dmytro and your grandfather what has happened. Make them promise to be very, very careful. The *szandar* may go and search their house as well, if they haven't done so already.'

When I got to my uncle's house, my father was already there. I ran into his arms, crying and shaking as I told my fearful tale. He did his best to comfort me, but his face was grim and his voice contemptuous as he remarked to his brother, 'If they come here looking for subversive literature, tell them to search for it under the dog's tail!' His parting with his family was emotional. 'Pray God we meet soon, my dears, but it may not be for a year or two,' he warned them as we left.

Back at our own house, he stood with Mother, Lywosi, and me and wept as we stared at the devastation the *szandar* had wrought. Then he kissed us all and walked off to give himself up.

He was detained for several months. During the early part of that time, Mother and I went weekly to the police station, which was some four kilometres away, with a basket of food for my father, but we were always refused permission to see him. 'Woman,' the policemen would growl, 'take your son and go home.' We always left in tears, though we tried to make our presence known by shouting through a ventilation shaft high up on the wall outside.

Then, one day, I got a glimpse into the cell where a friend of my father's was being interrogated. Even so, it did not prepare us for the shock when we were finally allowed to visit Father in another prison building. When the *szandar* opened the door into his cell, it smelt worse than a cesspit and was desperately cold. It contained a bench and a bucket, and the blanket he had wrapped around his shoulders; that was all. Yet, in the ten minutes which was all we were allowed, my father was at last able to put his arms around us. Barefoot, thin, and complaining of stomach pains and headaches, he could not say much else because the *szandar* stood listening to every word. My father's chief anxiety was that he might be sentenced to remain in prison, or be refused permission to work if released. Either way, his family would be left destitute.

Unable to build up any real case against him, the *szandary* finally let my father go. I shall never forget how he looked the day he was released. It was as though he had come from the grave. A tall, strong man had been reduced to a skeleton and he looked as though his skin was the only thing that kept his bones from falling apart. He had been tortured by being hit in the face and kicked in the stomach. He had been suspended from the wall until he fainted and had cold water poured over him to revive him. All he could tell his gaolers was that he had been protesting about conditions in the brickworks, as he had done many times before without incurring official censure.

Although my father had not retracted his claim for better working conditions even under torture, he was reinstated. The sit-in had received some local publicity and the working hours were reduced, so it was not a complete waste. In the end, the men who had taken part in it were grateful at the outcome. They had families to feed and educate.

The importance that the parents of Antoniwka, some of whom were illiterate, attached to their children's education must have impressed itself on the children of the village, for we put great effort into our schoolwork, including homework. Older children seemed willing to help younger ones with their lessons. I was accepted at the village school before my fifth birthday, almost two years younger than usual.

The Dombrowska sisters who taught us were stout, kindly Ukrainian women with cultivated tastes and manners. Although well on in years, or so they looked to us, their devotion to children, combined with the ability to maintain order and discipline in the classroom, made them irreplaceable. Even at the infant level of education, they had to adhere strictly to a syllabus laid down by the Polish authorities, which allotted only about an hour a day to the teaching of the Ukrainian language and literature. Otherwise the language of instruction was Polish and the subject matter the same as it would have been in Polish schools. I loved school. Although there were fifty or more in a class, there was silence whenever the teacher spoke to us. Since there were only two teachers to three classes, one class always worked on its own, but we considered ourselves lucky to be there.

Few village children in western Ukraine at that time received more education than could be got in the three years they spent in the village school. After that they generally helped on the farm or earned money by hiring themselves out as labourers. I was luckier than most in that there were no younger children to be fed, and my aptitude for learning convinced my parents that I should go on to High School in Nyzhniw. My schooling would continue for another seven years. For a very few of the most able students, whose parents could afford it, it could even lead to a place at university.

My mother took me to call on the school's director, a man named Tzap. She was carrying gifts of a chicken, fruit, some butter and a small amount of money. Little could be accomplished, when calling on officials, if one arrived empty-handed.

As soon as he saw us he realized we were Ukrainian villagers and said that, although my school report was excellent, he regretted he had no vacancies. There was no desk or bench available.

My mother was no fool. She knew that if we had been Polish, or had come from a Polish-speaking professional background, the desk and bench would have presented no difficulty. Giving me a reassuring look, she told him with spirit, 'That's no problem then. I will buy him a desk and bench myself.' This apparently settled the argument, leaving Mr Tzap with no option but to accept me. I felt five metres tall, and my parents were equally proud. They would still have to provide money for textbooks and other school equipment, but they were prepared to make almost any sacrifice to ensure my continuing education.

A few friends from Antoniwka moved on to the same school with me, so I did not lack for companionship. Our walk to Nyzhniw took about an hour and in summer we walked on bare feet. In winter we went, wrapped up, on skis, sometimes in snow drifting to four or five metres deep. Classes started at eight in the morning and lasted till four in the afternoon, six days a week, and the only meal we had during the day was what we brought with us – in my case a chunk of bread and an apple.

There were some fifty boys and girls in my class and only one teacher. We were mainly Poles and Ukrainians, but there were also Jews. I don't recall any discrimination on grounds of race or nationality among the children, although we joked and teased one another about it. On the whole, we got on very well. I sat with three Jewish children, two boys and a girl, whose parents were shopkeepers, making them much better off than me, but I don't think they looked down on me, nor was I envious. I was also friends with two Polish boys, Janek and Franek, whose parents were good to me. With them, nationality and background were no great issue. Indeed, it seemed then that our generation was ready to break down the artificial barriers and divisions caused by class, wealth and nationality, and begin to build a better society.

Chapter 3

1939
Little Russians

In 1939, as summer was coming to an end, life in Antoniwka went on as usual. Preparations were made for the harvest of potatoes, corn and hay, and their storing for the winter. Fruit was ripening on the trees and vines and the fields of wheat and barley were turning gold. My mother and sister were busy pickling and bottling vegetables and making preserves. Yet life would never be the same for any of us ever again.

For months the political atmosphere in the country had been tense, putting inevitable pressure on the Ukrainian community. We had little communication with the outside world. There were few radios and no cinemas in rural areas, and whatever newspapers arrived had been heavily censored. Anyway, people had work to do, too much of it to spend time thinking about the outside world. However, when we asked permission to hold a fête, or put on a concert or play, it was noticeable that the Polish authorities had become more suspicious than ever. They vetted each application more severely than usual. We could see they were in a state of jitters.

A year before, after the fall of Czechoslovakia, Zakarpacka Ukraine, which had been ruled from Prague, declared its independence. It had elected its own parliament and president, Dr Voloszyn, and many Ukrainian nationals had wanted to go and fight for them, but the new republic was swiftly invaded and crushed out of existence by the Hungarians. Nothing, it seemed, ever came to anything. To whom were we to look for hope?

Slowly, inevitably, news of the political crisis in Europe filtered through to us from people who returned from abroad. We knew that Hitler's Nazi

Germany had gobbled up Austria and Czechoslovakia. Now there were signs that Poland would be next, and Poland's fate touched us even more closely.

Then, in early September, we heard that Germany had invaded Poland and the war had begun. Almost imperceptibly at first, then with gathering momentum, the attitude of the Polish government changed towards us. Our allegiance had become important to them. Poland could do little to resist the advancing troops of Nazi Germany without the support of the seven million people of western Ukraine. They needed our military and economic help and they began to demand our 'loyalty' in an emergency, which we felt was theirs alone.

We, who had never been recognized as a people, now began to hear ourselves described as 'Ukrainians' rather than as 'Little Russians' from *Malo Polska*, 'Little Poland'. The walls of our *tchytalnia*, the village hall, were suddenly plastered with propaganda posters:

'Ukrainians, help protect your Fatherland. Only by standing together can we turn back the German advance. Not even a soldier's button must fall into the enemy's hands!'

We were exhorted to enlist. Of course there were Ukrainians already serving in the Polish army. Now my father and other villagers received orders to stand by for a military call-up. One of my uncles was told to report within twenty-four hours of war being declared.

Such appeals to our patriotism were too much to absorb for people who had been treated as mindless drudges, without any of the rights of true citizens. There was much heart-searching among the men. If they fought, what would they be fighting for? If Poland won the war, would we be rewarded with independence for Ukraine? Would life be better for us, or worse, if Germany was defeated?

In retrospect it sounds naive, but the politically aware among us were placed in a most difficult dilemma. They felt we had nothing to lose from the overthrow of the Polish government. We had lived in a state of oppression, forced to deny our own past, to treat another country's history as ours and to speak its language. Our people had been second-class citizens, imprisoned and tortured by the Polish *szandary*. We did not view the coming of the Germans with the horror felt by the French and Belgians, Dutch, Danes and Norwegians, who had known freedom. It seemed possible that the Germans might be our liberators. After all, they called themselves 'national socialists'. Might they not offer us greater equality, even autonomy, for Ukraine?

History has shown how wrong we were! In their ultimate advance the Nazis were to occupy the whole of Ukraine and some 17 per cent of Russia. By the end of the war Ukraine, a major supplier of food and raw materials, had been hit harder than any single European country. Out of its then population of forty-two million, there were over three million military and well over five million civilian casualties, nearly nine million in all.

That September, however, we could be forgiven for responding half-heartedly to the call to arms. We were not aware of the bargain made between Russia and Germany. Some men felt they could have nothing to do with the fighting. Better to leave their homes and take to the hills and forests, while Poland and her military government defended the country as best they could. The majority, however, felt that this was no way to respond to an invasion. Our very homes were under threat and we had no quarrel with the Polish people, only with their rulers. They enlisted, however reluctantly, in the fighting forces.

The day that Germany invaded Poland was one of confusion. Our school closed, giving us a sense of being on holiday. We went home full of a strange mixture of excitement, expectation and foreboding. This cocktail of sentiment would soon become familiar: achingly so. No one among the civilian population seemed to have any idea of what was happening. People talked of train services being dislocated, and of military transport appearing on the roads and railways.

The next day we saw some Polish soldiers deserting from their units, making it evident that the Polish forces were already disintegrating. I watched one soldier from a neighbouring village disappear as if by magic right in front of my eyes, in the centre of Antoniwka. A crowd of villagers surrounded him and, when they broke up, he was nowhere to be seen, having become unidentifiable from the rest. His army uniform had been whisked off him and bundled out of sight and he walked away in civilian clothes, looking like everyone else.

My friends and I were not yet in our teens but we were mentally alert and mature for our age, having listened to the adults discussing politics for as long as we could remember. Meetings were frequently held in our house and in my family the children were never excluded from these discussions so long as they held their peace. Now the things the adults had talked about were beginning to happen. We could not help but be excited to find our quiet little village part of such momentous events. Suddenly there were cavalry and tanks swarming around, engaging in military exercises, no doubt, but rampaging across cultivated fields and destroying crops with no consideration whatever for our winter supplies.

One day we were sitting on the grass verge alongside the road watching a column of tanks in the distance when German dive-bombers appeared out of a calm blue sky like screaming vultures, letting loose their cargoes of death. We cowered, but stayed where we were, glued to the spot by the fascination of this grisly spectacle. Within minutes, the flame and the fury were over, the blackened tanks stopped in their twisted tracks and the planes gone. Destruction on a truly modern scale! We acknowledged then that the war had really begun.

As the bombing started, a number of Polish soldiers had been riding along the road towards us on bicycles. At the sound of the planes, they flung down the bikes at our feet and hared off for the hills. We could hardly believe our eyes. The bicycles were brand new and shiny; magnificent! They were supremely desirable to youngsters who had never possessed a bike. The minute the planes had gone, we grabbed them and rode off as fast as we could. Unfortunately, when we were not far short of the river crossing into our village, armed soldiers emerged from hiding and saw us. They came out from among the trees shaking their fists at us shouting, 'Hey! Where are you going with those bikes? Give them back!' We dropped them and fled, watching resentfully from a distance as the soldiers remounted and cycled away.

It was a sad fact, but the Polish army commanded little support in Galicia. People assumed the war had not begun, because we saw no soldiers with the heart and determination to oppose the German war machine. Within two or three weeks, Poland had fallen and there was a floodtide of refugees making for the Romanian border. That was how we learned that the Russians were advancing from the east to occupy our part of the country. To our horror, we found ourselves trapped between two foreign armies fighting on our soil. We had no wish to live under either of them.

As the days passed, the columns of refugees thinned and we heard stories of Polish deserters, renegade bands who were burning villages, looting and killing people as they roamed the countryside foraging for food. From villages further east came tales of mounting atrocities. Of the Germans we had learned nothing.

Then, at midday one Sunday, came the rumble of engines and the sound of tramping feet. Drawn to the centre of Antoniwka, as we always were when anything of importance happened, we saw an army approaching. The tanks that led the way were flying the second of my four flags, the red flag, with the hammer and sickle of the Russian Empire. Then I saw my first Russian soldiers. In tanks, on foot, and on horseback they arrived, with the officers riding in personnel carriers. Their uniforms were ill-fitting by comparison with those of the Polish soldiers, which were always smart looking. The troops, as they came abreast of us, reeked of sweat. Some officers, seeing us staring with unconcealed curiosity, stopped their car and came over. Their speech, though it sounded similar, was strange to our ears, but we accepted the loaves of white bread they offered. Then, realizing that we were Ukrainians, they asked us in our own language whether there were any Polish soldiers in the village and where any deserters might be hidden. We shook our heads. We could not answer because we did not know. Emboldened by the gift of bread, however, we asked if they had any sweets for us and, pleasantly enough, they replied that they had already given away their sweets to other children.

While we were talking, a dozen or more soldiers on horseback rode into the open field by the river which we used as a sports ground and meeting place. We were now told to alert our friends and neighbours to their presence and to invite everyone to come and meet the soldiers there and hear what they had to tell us.

Within half an hour, my father, Uncle Roman, our neighbour Petro and other villagers had passed the news around, so that most of the village was assembled. A table was produced and a Russian political commissar climbed onto it. He began his speech by reminding us, in Ukrainian, of the stirring words of Karl Marx: 'Proletarians in all lands, unite; shake off your chains and fetters.'

In declamatory tones, he went on to denounce Polish imperialism and the bourgeois oppression under which we had all suffered. Everyone nodded. He promised us that, in future, the working class would not be oppressed. We would all be equal partners in building a better society, and Stalin would ensure that, from this day forward, no one would be under-privileged. The rich farmers – the kulaks – and the political intelligentsia would be rooted out and liquidated so that we, the people, could enjoy prosperity in our own country and be masters in our own land. From our new friends would come practical help in the form of material supplies, up-to-date equipment and machinery, and the technical assistance we would need; all these, he assured us, Russia possessed in abundance and would provide. 'There will be land and freedom for all the people,' he declared.

Not surprisingly, there were roars of approval. Our hearts soared at the news that we were finally liberated from oppression and would henceforth have democratic control over our land, our industry, our schools and our entire way of life. Our destiny was henceforth in our own hands. Freedom at last!

The Russian commissar's address was fluent and highly polished. He had obviously delivered it many times before. As he finished, my father jumped up onto the table beside him to announce his wholehearted support. Everyone knew what my father had suffered at the hands of the Polish *szandary*. They knew him as a man who spoke up for the rights of ordinary people. Now he waxed eloquent about the new life we could create for ourselves under these changed conditions. Many people were moved to tears. Here was the first glimmering of light and hope at the end of the long dark tunnel of suffering and hardship we had endured under the Polish flag. That Sunday was to mark a new beginning. We strolled home full of wonder and gratitude.

Life soon returned to normal, with farmers harvesting what remained of their crops and schools re-opening. It was only to be expected that there would be Russian soldiers on the scene and Russian civilians beginning to fill the gaps left by departed Poles. Within a week or two, however, we were having second thoughts.

We had begun to think ourselves lucky that the partitioning of Eastern Europe between Hitler and Stalin had left us in Russian hands. What disturbed us now was the sheer size of their military operation. What was the point of such a vast build-up of soldiers, here in the west? Poland was defeated. From whom were we being defended? In Nyzhniw, there were thousands of soldiers where before the war there had been none. The Russian army had occupied many civilian buildings and taken over a large private estate.

In the stores it was business as usual. Our cooperative store appeared to have ample stocks of essential goods in hand, even if there were no luxury items for sale. Soon it became clear, however, that when these stocks ran out, they would not be replaced from Russia, as we had been promised. Quite the reverse, it was the Russian soldiers who were buying up consumer goods by the ton and sending them home to their families. They bought anything they could lay their hands on: food, clothing, cosmetics, toiletries, hardware. They descended on our stores like a swarm of locusts, leaving the shelves bare. Not only that; they were cheating the shopkeepers by paying not in roubles, which would have been equivalent to the Polish *zloty*, but in *kopek*, which were the equivalent of the *groszy*, or pennies. Village shopkeepers weren't to know the value of foreign currency.

Huge numbers of civilian personnel accompanied the Russian army, many from minority groups in the Caucasus or Central Asia. They looked very foreign to us, as well as shabby and ill-nourished yet, like the officers' families, they had large houses commandeered for their use. The owners, Poles for the most part, got no recompense and had no redress. Luckily, our house was small and off the beaten track, so we were left undisturbed. We lived largely off our own produce, and had our own firewood for the stove, so we could cook and keep warm, in spite of shortages; but suddenly there was no paraffin in the stores with which to fill our lamps, or soap to keep us clean. This was not what the Russian commissar had taught us to expect when he said Father Stalin would meet our needs.

Perhaps, we said to one another, it was just a temporary hiatus and, once transport was restored to normal, supplies of everything would be on their way.

Such optimism was sadly misplaced. Within a brutal and short space of time the social, political, religious and educational fabric of our society began to crumble. If we thought we had suffered under the Polish flag, it was as nothing to what happened to us under the red flag of Russia.

Perhaps we should have paid closer heed to that word 'liquidated' in the political commissar's inspiring address. It was not just a manner of speaking. In the months that followed, many prosperous farmers were liquidated. Furthermore, priests were imprisoned, and qualified teachers, professors, doctors, industrialists and engineers were deported to Siberia. Anyone suspected of being a Ukrainian nationalist was arrested, interrogated and often deported, never to be heard of again. We were not only denied equality, we were being denied the fundamental right of any human being to live; to have a free and independent existence. It was some time before we fully understood the enormity of the situation.

Some of the first casualties of the Russian occupation were the schoolchildren. The process of education became one of re-education. In Antoniwka, our dear teachers, Pani and Maria Dombrowska, quietly left. They were replaced by a former Protestant clergyman. He was evidently sympathetic to the Russian system and must have reached a certain understanding with the authorities to get the post. We could never understand how a man of God could accept a job under the Russians but, at the same time, we recognized that the Reverend Ostapowycz was a highly intelligent man and an excellent teacher. Perhaps, since he was not a Catholic, the Russians felt he would be more willing than the sisters to eschew Christian teaching and practice, as teachers were now obliged to do.

Russians, some with little experience of teaching, replaced many of our former teachers at the High School in Nyzhniw, but they were either long-standing members of the Communist Party or had volunteered to join it, knowing that they would be rewarded with a job. Religious instruction was banned from all schools and was replaced by the teachings of Marx, Lenin and Stalin. Geography and history were revised along ideological lines acceptable to the Russians. We were taught that socialism guaranteed equality, although even the most gullible could see that members of the Communist Party and those who worked for the Russian military and civilian authorities received any special privileges that were going.

The scarce, heavily censored Polish newspapers were now replaced by *Pravda* and *Izvestia*. *Pravda* means 'truth' but we called it 'liar' as neither newspaper ever wrote the truth. Portraits of Stalin, always referred to as 'Father Stalin', and of Lenin hung in our classrooms as symbols of proletarianism and liberty. One day I came home from school and said to my father, 'A teacher has told us that you are not my father; my father is Father Stalin'. He turned to my mother and said, 'Olenko, they are taking my son away'. They both wept in despair and disbelief. The process of indoctrination never ceased: children between twelve and sixteen were invited to join the Pioneers, and those over sixteen the Komsomol, or Young Communist Party. They could then wear the group's distinctive uniform when they marched in parades, carrying Red banners and portraits of Russian leaders, and singing Russian patriotic songs. Membership of either group had a strong appeal for us because it carried a definite cachet, bestowing honour and status in the new society.

My father quickly became disillusioned with our new masters, and was angry with himself for having been taken in by the political commissar's promises. To my intense disappointment, he forbade me to join the Pioneers. I felt I was missing out on something exciting but in retrospect I am glad I fell in with his wishes.

My father's judgment was based on frequent dealings with the Russian authorities on behalf of the community, for this was now his full-time occupation. By popular demand, he had given up his better-paid job at the factory to become *soltys*, or chairman, of the village council, replacing a man called Ivan, who had held that position under the Poles. In many towns and villages the chairmen deposed at this time were attacked, beaten up, or even killed, in revenge for the corrupt way they had run local affairs, but in Antoniwka Ivan had won the people's respect. He saw to it that if he could help it nobody would be put at risk of arrest and prosecution, so my father made it possible for him to live on in the village as an ordinary citizen. It was a measure of my father's tolerance and wisdom that he made a friend of the former *soltys* and was thus able to draw on his experience of getting things done.

At this time Father was serious and preoccupied. We seldom heard him laugh. He was always attending political meetings. He lived on a knife's edge, under constant pressure from the Russian commissars to take this action or that, yet determined to remain his own man. On occasion they even visited our home.

There were frequent meetings in the village hall, which we were ordered to attend. Even the sick and infirm were not excused. They had to drag themselves or be conveyed there somehow. Once assembled, we were subjected to barrages of propaganda from both military and civilian apparatchiks. We learnt how children must be educated, agriculture organized and industry run, and we were bombarded with Marxist slogans and Leninist propaganda.

Under the Poles, school had begun each day with prayer and the Polish national anthem. In spite of ourselves, we children dreamt of becoming *harzezy*, members of an elite cavalry unit who wore splendidly glamorous uniforms, though as Ukrainians we stood no chance of enlisting. Now portraits of Lenin and Stalin glowered down at us, we saluted the Russian flag, and there were considerable inducements to join Communist youth organizations.

With the help and cooperation of the villagers, my father did what he could to maintain a balance between the demands of the Russians and the requirements of the people for simple justice. He spoke out very forcibly at times. The Russians were set on the collectivization of farms but, after hearing the pleas of those who were going to lose their land without compensation, he managed to persuade our new masters that the time was not ripe for such a move. He was powerless, however, to secure anyone's exemption from military service, or to appeal against their being sent to parts of Russia as distant as Vladivostok or Irkutsk, popularly known as the place 'where the Devil says goodnight' – a hell from which there was thought to be no escape. Nor was there anything my father could do to prevent families being prosecuted for minor infringements of regulations and promptly deported, though this caused him great distress.

On one painful occasion, he was summoned in the early hours of the morning by the NKVD – dreaded forerunner of the KGB – and asked to accompany them to the village school, doubtless to lend legitimacy to their proceedings. There they arrested the clergyman turned teacher, Reverend Ostapowycz, whom we had begun to hold in high regard. Soldiers surrounded the school building while members of the NKVD went inside, woke their victim and dragged him from his bed. He was made to put his head against a brick wall and his hands behind his back, then move his feet a half metre back from the wall. In this position he could not get up, turn around, or see what was happening. They searched the classrooms and his flat without finding anything but schoolbooks and no reasons were given for his arrest. Nevertheless, they ordered him to get dressed and took him away.

Ostapowycz, we believed, would refuse to surrender, so the villagers refused to give up on his behalf. He spent months in prison without trial. Then, in response to a petition organized by my father and signed by the schoolchildren and their parents, Mr Ostapowycz was released and returned to the school. But it was only a brief respite; a week or so later he was re-arrested and taken away, and was never seen again. We assumed he was sent to Siberia, condemned without trial, like thousands of others, to the living death of a slave labour camp. Since he was, or had been, a clergyman, we wondered whether he might have been reported for telling the children stories in which there was some religious content. The school was closed down.

Father Holowatyj had also been spirited away, nobody knew where. The church became an office and ammunition store. Once a week, Russian soldiers lined up there to receive their pay. To lose our priest and our church was a grievous deprivation for our people at a time when the comfort and solace of their faith was more important than it had ever been. Now we had no one to whom we could confess, and from whom we could receive absolution, no one to whom we could go for spiritual guidance. Because of this, our burdens seemed that much heavier to bear.

The violent persecution of the Ukrainian Church, described by a church historian as a 'First Baptism of Blood' (the second was to follow after the war, when western Ukraine was again under the control of Russia) was hideous beyond belief. In 1941 the Metropolitan Archbishop of Lwiw reported to the Vatican that 250,000 people had been deported from his archdiocese, another 250,000 from the dioceses of Peremyshl and Stanislawiw, and that 6,000 corpses had been discovered in the prisons of Lwiw. We knew our own church was closed and our priest gone, but had no idea at the time that the suppression of Christian worship had reached such a pitch. It was plain enough, however, that the only religion tolerated, the new, all-embracing creed preached to us with fanatical fervour, was Stalinism.

There was no respite from raids on households by the NKVD and the military, often in the early hours of the morning when the occupants were asleep. The head of the house would be roused from his bed and told to identify each person living there. Then the entire house would be searched, the family told to take an axe, shovel and some clothes and go outside. They would be taken by lorry to a prison in some town – Stanislawiw, Tlumach or Buchach – and then, when there were enough of them, they would be herded aboard cattle trucks to be transported to camps in remote corners of Siberia. Within months, thousands vanished.

In the country it was smallholders and so-called *kulaks* who disappeared in this fashion. In the towns it was shopkeepers, local officials and anyone who had been reported to the authorities. Somehow we persisted in believing that we did not fit into those categories, but we suffered agonies in fellow-feeling for the victims as the terror spread.

Under instructions from my father, my friends and I used to wait by the railway line that ran through the village. Then, when particular trains passed through, we would collect the scraps of paper written by the condemned travellers and thrown out to us, so that my father could pass the messages on to their relatives. Any information at all was precious, not least the mere fact that someone they loved was still alive. In doing this, my father was defying the law and putting us all at risk, but we knew as well as he did that out of common humanity we could do no less.

Deep as the pain of all this touched us, it did not strike at the heart of our immediate family until the end of November 1939, when my father's brother, Uncle Roman, was arrested. Like my father, Uncle Roman was a radical liberal opposed to a class system which created vast discrepancies between the very wealthy – the Polish landowners, industrialists and professional people – and the great mass of illiterate poor. Though well-informed and active in the trade union movement, his own circumstances were humble. His farm and farm buildings were slightly superior to those of most of our community, but he was by no means a wealthy farmer.

Aunt Nastia came weeping to our house at 3:30 one morning with their six-year-old daughter Marusia, who was deaf and dumb, saying that the NKVD had taken her husband. Though it was still pitch dark, my father set off immediately for the prison in Tlumach, fifteen kilometres away, to ask the reason for his brother's arrest.

The inspector recognized him but could only say, 'We are investigating allegations that your brother employs slave labour on his farm, Comrade Oleksa.' The allegations had been made by villagers apparently ready to say anything in their anxiety to win favour with NKVD. My father was shocked by the groundless accusations:

'Roman does not employ anyone to work for him on his farm! He only owns five or six hectares of land! Roman works in the brickworks because his farm is too small to provide a living. The only time he employs labour is at harvest time, when he, like everyone else, needs a few extra hands to get the harvest in! He has no woodland or grazing land. His wife and sister-in-law look after his four cows, two pigs and the few dozen chickens and geese he keeps. He cannot possibly be classed as a wealthy farmer, a *kulak*. He earns his living where I worked and does what he can on the farm in the little time he has to spare, just as I used to do.'

But his protest fell on deaf ears, 'Are other farmers going to be arrested on this charge?' Father asked.

'You'll have to wait and see.'

Wagging a finger at my father in ominous fashion, the inspector went on:

'The collectivization of farms is going to go ahead, whoever tries to stand in its way, so you'd better go home and work out a system to get it going quickly, Comrade. Take my advice. Don't interfere in our legal matters. Don't keep enquiring about your brother. Just see to it that the *kolkhosp* (collective farm) comes into being soon.'

With that my father had to be satisfied.

Chapter 4

1940
Enemies of the People

Until the end of January 1940, Uncle Roman was in prison without trial in Tlumach. While he was there, many family members visited the prison but we were never allowed to see him. Such food and clothing as we took him were thoroughly searched. Loaves of bread were thinly sliced to ensure that no message or materials – needles, matches – were smuggled in. We learned later that clothing was picked apart at the seams.

We never saw my uncle to talk to. The only glimpse we had of him was through knotholes in a wooden fence that surrounded the prison yard. We watched him working with the other prisoners, sawing firewood or cleaning sleighs. We shouted news, but the only acknowledgement that he heard us was a slight nod of his head. Each time we called out to him the guards rushed up to the fence and yelled at us to leave. Sometimes they removed the prisoners from the yard.

I could hardly bear the sight of this tall man brought so low. Always full of fun, especially with children, he used to run races with me on stilts, much higher off the ground than I was, yet beating me hollow when it came to running up hills. He taught me to ride a horse bareback and barefoot, just holding onto the horse's mane. He would gallop ahead of me, shouting back over his shoulder, 'Faster! Gallop faster, Stefan! You will never make a Cossack warrior!' To which I would reply 'I will when I'm as big as you!' I was very fond of Uncle Roman.

Two of his friends, Stefan and Petro, who had been arrested at the same time, were badly beaten by the NKVD and were immersed in icy water up to their necks. Whatever was done to them, they had nothing to confess. Uncle Roman's tortures were meant to humiliate him. He had to kneel, hands together as in prayer, before his interrogator, who sat in a chair reading aloud from *Pravda*. Now and again, he would be kicked in the stomach or hit in the face so hard he keeled over. Then his tormentor would resume his reading, droning on in a monotonous voice, sometimes for hours at a time, in an attempt to break Uncle Roman's proud spirit.

In the months that my uncle was imprisoned, my father repeatedly risked his own safety by pleading his brother's cause and trying to obtain his release. After one appeal, the NKVD commissar raised my father's hopes by saying that they would like him to conduct his brother's trial himself. 'Since you are so strong on justice, this is your chance to see justice done, Comrade Oleksa. As Chairman of the tribunal you will be entitled to pass any sentence you like and it will be accepted, so long as it begins with the usual five years' hard labour.' This cynical offer so outraged my father, it provoked him to recklessness. 'If that is all you have in mind, arrest me, too!' he cried. Nevertheless, he remained at large for the time being. As chairman of the Village Council, with most of the village behind him, he was useful to the authorities.

The trial of Uncle Roman and two other prisoners is etched on my memory as if in acid. Instead of being held in Tlumach, as might have been expected, it was staged in the town hall at Nyzhniw, much nearer to our village, thus enabling local people to attend in large numbers. It was patently a propaganda exercise, demonstrating what could happen to us if we did not conform to Stalinist principles. At issue was not the size of the accused men's farms nor their treatment of hired workers, but their view of life. We persisted, however, in believing that it would be impossible to convict them. We were absolutely certain the evidence against them would be refuted.

The simple one-storey building serving as a courthouse was packed with people. Those who could not get in lined the road outside as twenty Russian soldiers brought the prisoners to the door in horse-drawn sleighs. Bitterly cold, the snow was driving down. Uncle Roman entered the hall, handcuffed to the other prisoners, and looked around for his family. As his eyes sought and recognized Marusia, his little deaf-and-dumb daughter, she ran towards him, a strange, strangled scream bursting from her throat. We could all see how much he longed to gather her in his arms, which he was prevented from doing by manacles. Powerless to comfort her, he broke down in sobs, and people in the court wept openly, feeling his humiliation as a father. Marusia, however, ignored the chains, flinging her arms around his waist and hugging him tight. For a dramatic moment, father and daughter clung to one another, tears pouring down their cheeks. Then a soldier abruptly shoved the child out of the way and the trial began.

In spite of the treatment meted out to him, we were full of optimism now that Uncle Roman's case had finally come to court. So many people were on his side! We had not reckoned, however, with human wickedness, which had become magnified in those brutal times. To our horror, the prosecution produced two witnesses from our very own village who testified to the fact that my uncle used slave labour on his farm and swore that they had been mistreated.   Everyone knew that they were lying and must have been threatened or bribed by the NKVD, so it still seemed that we had only to wait for evidence to the contrary. The prosecutor, however, refused to allow anyone to testify in favour of the accused men. The trial was a mockery, which continued throughout the day. We listened with mounting disbelief. When a number of people volunteered to speak for the prisoners, they were ruled out of order. Nor were the prisoners themselves given any chance to defend themselves by explaining why it was necessary to employ extra labour at harvest time, when everyone worked very hard. Each time they tried to speak, they were cut short by the prosecutor.

Finally the Russian judge rose slowly to his feet. We expected the usual long, tedious diatribe justifying the prosecution in the name of socialism and labelling the defendants 'Enemies of the People'. However, he did not even attempt to clothe his verdict in a cloak of justice. He said, 'In the name of Lenin, Stalin, and the Communist Party, I sentence each of the three accused to five years' hard labour in Russia,' and sat down with an impassive face.

Loud cries of indignation broke out in the courtroom. The soldiers hastily hustled the prisoners out through the door. Little Marusia, sobbing pitifully, made one last, desperate attempt to reach her father, but her way was barred. Even Aunt Nastia pleaded in vain for permission to kiss her husband goodbye. It was through a blur of tears that I saw the harrowed face of Uncle Roman as he was led away.

We walked home with the taste of salt on our tongues, through swirling snow. Inside our home, late that evening, I saw the terrible effect of the day's events on my father. Suddenly, he had lost confidence in himself; his dreams had been shattered. His waning hopes of a better world under communism had evaporated altogether when he saw the brother with whom he worked, whose political convictions he shared, callously convicted for a crime he had not committed.

'What will become of us all?' he asked my mother. 'Am I responsible in any way? Will we be next, Olenko?'

My mother tried to soothe and reassure him. She knew that the burden he bore as village chairman was heavy. She even suggested that, if the conflict within him was too great, he might resign his position and return to his job in the brickworks, but she added, 'You did all you could, Olekso.

Whatever happened, the people cannot blame you. They do not hold you responsible. Our friends understand, and things will change in time. Nothing's forever.'

Tears filled my eyes. Thoroughly overwrought from the scenes I had witnessed all day in court, I was further choked with distress at the sight of my father plunged into a pit of disillusion and despair. Suppose he, too, were to be arrested; what then? I would be the man of the family – but I was still only twelve. Not to upset him further, I crept off miserably to bed where I could cry into my pillow. Lywosi, in bed nearby, was weeping and praying to God. She got very worked up at any threat to either of our parents and continually worried about our mother's health.

Life grew harder every day. We had to swallow our resentment against the villagers who had brought the charges against Uncle Roman, grossly defaming a fair-minded man. They were clearly in the pay of the NKVD as informers and could as easily fabricate fresh lies against us. They and their children were simply distrusted and ignored. They became very isolated.

The cooperative store was nearly empty. Clothes were unobtainable. The wages my father received as village chairman were so meagre that he could barely provide a living for us, yet he was too scrupulous to seek any special privileges or preferment which might be seen as abuse of his position. He still had the confidence of the community and did everything in his power to alleviate the misery of the people, as one person after another was arrested and sent away; but the flame of hope had died within him. That vital spark, first kindled by his sincere belief that the just society promised us by the Russians might come to pass, had been extinguished.

A young Russian woman from Kyiv named Natasha, who now taught in our village school, increased his disillusion with our communist overlords. She enjoyed talking with my father, who was better informed than most villagers, and she spoke freely, if incautiously, about life in Russia. Her parents' letters were full of complaints about the lack of consumer goods. There were horrifying stories she told about the famine in eastern Ukraine years earlier, which had been artificially created by the collectivization of land imposed on the people by Stalin. It had resulted, in 1932-33, in the deaths of up to ten million men, women and children. She spoke of the death and deportation of landowners and the cream of the intelligentsia. She believed Stalin's aim was to crush the whole of Ukraine out of existence, convincing my father that those he had hoped would bring relief to his country had come to rape it instead.

I carried on with my schooling more determined than ever to change the system under which we lived. With my parents' approval, I concentrated on history, especially the history and social background of our own country, but declined to take part in any political or social activities wished on me by our Russian teachers. I had resolved not to be brainwashed into believing that Stalin was my father.

To help make ends meet – the trousers I wore to school had been patched so often you could not tell the original material from the patches – I picked up odd jobs that earned a little money. After school each day, I would go home for a bowl of soup and chunk of bread and then, with several friends, work for two hours clearing snow from the railway tracks before doing my homework for the following morning. We each earned about five roubles a day, enough to pay for ten grammes of the sweet known as halva and the writing materials we needed for school. I also shovelled snow at weekends. When the snow had gone, we chopped wood in the nearby forest. The pay was low but every rouble helped.

From then on, in the school holidays, my friend Fedir Kowaluk and I worked full-time felling trees, to clear the land for cultivation. It was hard and dangerous work, wielding heavy axes and saws, labouring alongside men who were more concerned with a high output, so as to earn as much money as possible, than with safety. They were impatient with youngsters who could not keep up with their gruelling work-rate. Nevertheless, we took home quite a few roubles.

Even leisure activities at school became permeated with political significance. Every performance by the choir began with songs extolling Russia's military might. Though my father was reluctant to have me join it, partly because it left me less time to earn money after school, I persuaded him there could be nothing political about the folk-dancing group! It would simply be lively and enjoyable. Dancing played a great part in our Ukrainian traditions: Cossack dancing, the *zaporozhets* and *kolomyika* and many others. We travelled to compete in neighbouring towns and villages, sleeping on the bare floors of local schools, and rising early next morning for the journey back to our own school by horse and cart.

I soon realized, however, that, although we were dressed in Ukrainian costumes and dancing national dances, everything my group performed was done in the name of Russia and the Communist Party. I considered resigning but was persuaded to continue because we were winning competitions which might take us through to a final in Moscow, performing in front of Stalin himself, and such dreams of glory were irresistible. Besides, it would be letting the team down if I dropped out. I remained with them until we were eliminated from the contest.

Everything we took part in contributed to the overall policy of either commandeering or wiping out our distinctive Ukrainian heritage. Ukrainians were being transported to Russia while Russian nationals increasingly occupied our towns and cities. In this way, the very roots of the people were being destroyed, their close-knit communities broken up and family members scattered, leaving us answerable only to the totalitarian regime.

My father and grandfather had always encouraged me to think for myself, so I seized every opportunity to question the validity of the things we were being taught. In the classroom I would enquire disingenuously, 'Why are we not learning more about our own country? In what sense is Stalin my father? Why do we, who are Ukrainians, sing only the Russian national anthem? Why is the Russian language given priority over our own language?'

The Russians were confiscating huge stores of grain and livestock for shipment to Russia and sending us, in return, matches and tobacco, which we did not need. This unjust traffic inspired a mutinous little chant which we used to intone under our breath. Using deep voices to represent the wheels of the heavily-laden trains that left Ukraine, and a high-pitched falsetto for the paltry shipments that came back to us, we would chant, 'Barley-wheat, barley-wheat, barley-wheat', to which the response was, 'Matches-tobacco, matches-tobacco, matches-tobacco'. These coded messages relieved our feelings and were childish enough to be tolerated by the authorities. It was not so for our elders.

Late in the spring of 1940, my cousin Wasyl, who had helped with my earliest schooling, was arrested by the NKVD along with two of his friends. Wasyl was now a twenty-year-old student at the University in Stanislawiw. The young men's crime? They were said to be politically motivated nationalists, and insufficiently appreciative of all that Father Stalin was doing for the good of our country.

Wasyl's family lived at the far end of the village on a smallholding adjacent to a sand quarry, which they owned and which provided much of their income. His mother was my father's sister and I used to play with Wasyl's younger sister and brother, Olenka and Dmytro. Sometimes we took our cows out to pasture together and whiled away the time playing the wooden flutes we whittled out for ourselves, with Olenka as soloist. Their education had finished with the village school, but Wasyl had done well at the High School and, thanks to the earnings from the sand quarry, his parents had been able to send him to university. He was their pride and joy.

Wasyl had promised his parents he would concentrate on his studies and steer clear of political activities instigated by the Communists. He was studying physics and was a quiet, diligent, introspective young man, with strong feelings for his family and country, but little interest in politics. A patriot, yes, but there was no way he could be called a revolutionary.

Once more my father felt compromised. First his brother, now his nephew, had been accused of crimes against the state, of which he was the local representative. This time he decided he would have to stand down as chairman of the Village Council. He resigned and called an election, making it clear to those who knew him best that he did not wish to be chosen again. To my mother he said, 'I will not walk the path of those who preach one thing and do another.'

On election day our cooperative store was stocked for the occasion by the Russian governor of our area in order to ensure a good turnout. Everyone could buy lemonade, white bread, salami and halva. After the votes were counted, my father was re-elected but immediately announced that he did not wish to carry on. Very reluctantly, because most villagers still felt he was the best man to deal with the Russians, they accepted his resignation. His deputy took over the next day, by which time the store's shelves were as bare as before. The consequences for the village were worse than anyone could have envisaged.

Petro Romaniuk was cast in a different mould from my father and quickly succumbed to Russian pressure. Within weeks, villagers found themselves repairing the roads and railway lines, and building an airfield at Stanislawiw. Two iron bridges over the River Dniester, which had been blown up by the retreating Polish army, were restored by our people, who did so without a scrap of recompense. Romaniuk controlled the selection of those compelled to work in this way and, anxious to fulfil the quotas laid down by the Russian authorities, made himself more and more unpopular. He ordered my father to send me to work on one of the bridges. It wasn't that I minded working at weekends but when we were so hard up, I did object to working without pay. Nor, of course, was I alone in this view. People spoke openly of 'meeting someone in a back alley'. It was not long before Romaniuk began to carry a revolver for his own protection. Bootlickers of his sort went at risk of their lives.

I visited Wasyl in prison but was never permitted to meet him face to face. On the day of his trial most of the village was up at five in the morning to begin the three-hour walk to Tlumach. When we reached the town, some of us younger ones went to the prison and yelled at the prisoners through cupped hands, 'We'll see you in court!' We heard the astonishment in their voices when they shouted back, 'Are you sure?' They had not even been told that it was the day of their trial.

At about ten in the morning, the three handcuffed prisoners were marched into the courthouse under armed guard. Only Wasyl was a university student. Of the other two, one was a blacksmith, a so-called capitalist who exploited the people, and the last one was an ordinary farm labourer.

Need I mention that the trial was as farcical as Uncle Roman's had been? The dock was an iron cage, in which the prisoners stood silent throughout the long, meaningless proceedings. No witnesses were called. The judge's statement accused the three men of subversion, of political activities undermining the Russian constitution – the usual charges. He quoted Article 12 of the constitution: Those who don't work don't eat, which seemed to have no bearing on the case at all. The only remarkable thing about the trial was the behaviour of one of the defendants. Wasyl and the blacksmith were both sentenced to five years' exile and hard labour. The third accused, of poor peasant stock, was given only three. It was stated that he had been misled by the other two defendants. He immediately objected. 'We were all charged with the same offence, and my friends received a sentence of five years. I believe I should serve five years, too,' he declared in fiery tones.

To our astonishment, the judge did not demur, though it was surely his prerogative alone to determine the length of sentences. 'So be it,' he agreed. 'If that is your wish, I sentence all three of you to five years in exile.'

Tears of pride stood in our eyes at this extraordinary act of courage, and the joy on the faces of the three young men stirred our hearts. It may have been a hollow triumph, given the punishment in store for them, but it seemed a triumph to us. The NKVD had not succeeded in demoralizing or dehumanizing them, in spite of all. The three prisoners were led away, forbidden even to shake our hands or say goodbye. They would never return. Many years later I learned that Wasyl died of cancer in the Urals. People sometimes returned from the slave labour camps, though the number of years to which they had been sentenced had little meaning. That day, we set out on the long walk home spared the burden of foreknowledge, but I felt worn down with rage and frustration and at least twice as old as my thirteen years. My smouldering resentment at our Russian overlords had reached a pitch of which I would hardly have believed myself capable. If Wasyl, a promising student and almost an older brother to me, could be sent into slavery at the age of twenty, what future was there for any of us?

My friends and I could no longer look forward to the religious feast days, which had once been such joyful occasions. Our churches were closed and our priests deported and murdered. These crimes, plus the confiscation of crops, of property, of farm animals – the forced labour and arrests in the middle of the night – were in complete contravention of all we had been taught was right. Our Christian beliefs had previously sustained us through many trials, so a small group of us from my school met occasionally to discuss how we should live in the light of those beliefs, and struggled to keep some spark of faith alive.

Most of the books in our village library were supplied by the Russians, so we could never find a book, magazine or newspaper that told the truth about the outside world. We had, however, one source of inspiration in the book *Kobzar*, written by the great Ukrainian poet and patriot Taras Shevchenko and banned by Poles and Russians alike because of its nationalist fervour. It passed from hand to hand in total secrecy. Long passages were memorized to recite among friends. It is still read by Ukrainians all over the world.

My father knew a lot about the political history of Russia and Europe between the two world wars. He had begun to treat me as an adult, who must be told the truth, and taught me things I could not have learned in any other way. He had once had great faith in socialism, though he was aware that conditions were better in western countries. Now he advised me to move westward if the occasion ever arose. At that time he still believed that Hitler was doing more for his country than the Russians for theirs, and he expressed admiration for the political system of Great Britain so that I absorbed a mental picture of Winston Churchill, short and square like a Ukrainian farmer, with a cigar permanently in his hand. My father warned me that Hitler might soon cast covetous eyes on Ukraine, which Stalin would certainly resist, so that, before long, we could be enveloped in a war between the two tyrannical dictators. In that case, I might have to enlist in one army or the other.

As it was, I joined a brigade of boys, an underground movement, who took orders from Ukrainian nationalist groups, opposed equally to the Russian regime and to that of Nazi Germany. One of our duties was to change the flags on the Monument to the Unknown Soldier in Antoniwka. At around four in the morning we would creep out and replace the Russian flag with the blue and gold colours of Ukraine. We were told to say, if we were caught, that we had changed them because we only recognized the flag of Ukraine, a statement that was frankly subversive. Luckily we escaped detection.

The Russian teachers in our schools were taking over the minds of the younger children. It was drummed into us that the hammer and sickle with the red star above it symbolized communism, which would conquer the globe. If we, as sons and daughters of Russia, worked towards that goal, we might be rewarded with the Order of Lenin and Stalin and on some miraculous day, receive it from Father Stalin himself. Many children were impressed. Others, like me, were scornful and declared that the medals, melted down, wouldn't be worth as much as a tooth in our heads.

One day at school, when we were playing football, I kicked one of the Russian teachers and broke his leg. Another time, I missed punching the volleyball and caught our teacher on the nose. Both were genuine accidents but I felt delighted that for once, impotent as I was, I was getting my own back. Those of us who had declined to join the Young Pioneers suffered constant taunts from those who had. They called us *kulaks*, while we dubbed them red herrings, a reference to the salted fish the Russians sent us to supplement our meagre diet.

Rumours of a German invasion were rife. More and more Russian troops threatened our crops with their manoeuvres. People said wryly that first-grade crops were reserved for next year's sowing, second-grade crops for feeding the army, and only third-grade crops for the consumption of the people who produced them.

We were short of almost everything we needed. Matches were split into four with a needle to make them go further. I remember going by train to a place called Nadwirna, up in the Carpathian Mountains, to get salt. The district had numerous salt lakes, producing salt of inferior quality but, for people who had none, this salt had become an absolute necessity. Mother made it her habit to bake four loaves of bread once a fortnight, one for each of us. It was up to us whether we ate it all at once or one slice each day for two weeks. Such was the shortage of flour in the bread basket of Europe!

Many of us lads, with our sisters and some of our mothers, were sent to dig defensive trenches in the hills. We had to take our own axes, picks and shovels and make our way to a point on the far bank of the River Dniester, about four kilometres from home, where we were told we gave our sweat and toil in support of Father Stalin. Our men folk, meanwhile, worked on other projects needed for military purposes. We wondered whether the trenches we dug were really meant to save us from attack or were to prevent our escape. I looked up at the mountains and prayed for a time when I could cross them and discover a new kind of life.

Chapter 5

1941-1942
New Masters

O ur own people were becoming brutalized. People were killed by their friends and neighbours. Cousin Ivan, in the next village, was murdered by another man who had sold out to the Russians. Uncle Makola managed to run from his house and hide in a stable but they got him, and his body had fifty or sixty bullets in it when it was found. The NKVD continued to persecute ordinary citizens. In another village, my cousin Josef and a schoolfriend, Danylo, were shot in their own home for possessing Ukrainian books.

A Jewish family named Kleter were good friends of my parents. Mr Kleter was the son of a shoemaker and a director of the brickworks where my father was once again an official. Mr Kleter's younger brother, in spite of his family's opposition, joined the Russian army as soon as he was old enough for military service and became an enthusiastic supporter of Stalinism. Though the Russians treated some Jews with hatred and contempt, young Kleter rose swiftly through the ranks to become an officer, a skilled propagandist who toed the Party line. We were extremely wary of what we said in front of him.

The spring of 1941 was full of fears and foreboding as we braced ourselves for yet another invasion. My mother had always been a pillar of strength – the best mother in the world; lovely to look at, kind, cheerful, and full of practical common sense. I adored her. Now, underfed and unable to see any glimmer of hope for the future, she declined visibly in health. No longer did she lift our spirits by declaring, 'Nothing is forever'. Instead, she voiced her dark premonition that we were doomed as a family and perhaps as a people.

In June, Germany invaded Russia and we were on the front line. Now it was the Russian cavalry, tanks and convoys retreating, and their soldiers deserting in droves. Within days, planes displaying the swastika were flying freely overhead. Deserters returned to Antoniwka with appalling stories of the death and destruction wrought by their fellow soldiers as they withdrew, robbing Ukrainian villagers and shooting them if they resisted. Uncle Ivan, who had been called up against his will, first by the Poles and then by the Russians – and had deserted from both, was one of those who returned. No one who has never lived under a totalitarian regime could credit such barbarism as he described.

One Sunday morning I was approaching our crossing on the River Dniester, returning home from visiting friends, when I heard planes coming towards me from the west. Looking up, I saw they were German bombers, probably aiming to destroy our bridges and dislocate the Russian retreat. Immediately, Russian fighter planes rushed to attack them and, from concealed positions in the hills, anti-aircraft guns began to stutter and bark. The sky filled with gunfire and smoke. Scared out of my wits, I took shelter under a big tree, clinging tightly to the trunk. At any moment I expected a plane, or part of it, to fall on the tree and demolish us both. Because I was all alone, it was the most frightening experience of my life.

The air battle was plainly visible in the clear blue sky. I was astounded to see the German bombers get away from the Russian fighter planes and ground batteries unscathed. They wheeled around and fled, but not one was shot down.

I was shaking from head to foot, but soon regained control of myself. I crossed the river in the little boat we kept there, and ran like the wind for home. One look at my face told my parents and sister the whole story - which was just as well, since I was speechless with shock! Mother gathered me in her arms and father and Lywosi wrapped their arms around us both. I shall never forget it. At that moment, the four of us were as close in body and soul as we had ever been, and I felt overwhelmed by love for my family, full of an aching desire to protect them always.

Later that day a long column of soldiers came through the village, some on horseback, some on bicycles and some driving horses and carts. A crowd of them gathered outside Uncle Dmytro's house. They were not in German uniform and I asked him who they were. 'Hungarians,' said my uncle in fatalistic tones, shrugging his shoulders. 'They are commandeering part of the house as a billet for their officers. There is not enough room for them, but they are an invading army and can do as they please. Fortunately, your house is too far from the centre of the village for you to be bothered by them.'

Hearing that they were Hungarians terrified me. My grandfather had often described the atrocities the Hungarian army perpetrated in Ukraine during the First World War. People had ears and arms cut off and had been hanged from telegraph poles. Girls had been raped and villages razed to the ground. Uncle Dmytro assured me that these were men of a different, more civilized, generation. I hoped he was right.

Once we got to know them, we realized that the Hungarians were little happier with what was going on than we were. They suspected they were being used as cannon fodder, sent ahead to clear the way and make it safer for Hitler and the Germans.

We had no fire brigade in Antoniwka. When a fire broke out in the village, the alarm was given by ringing the bells in the church tower. Volunteers with horses would drag the fire engine to the scene, while all able-bodied villagers formed a bucket line to pass water up from the river. With their timber frames and thatched roofs, our houses were very vulnerable to fire and often burnt down in no time. However, when fire broke out in a farmhouse soon after the Hungarians arrived, the soldiers billeted in the village, strong young men all, rushed to our assistance and got the fire out, so that little damage was done. We were better disposed towards them after that.

They were not with us long, however. Their places were soon taken by Germans, some of whom wore the dreaded uniform of the Gestapo and gave notice at once that they were under orders to kill or imprison anyone who stood in their way. We had no village chairman now. Petro Romaniuk had taken possession of a farmer's horse and cart and fled with the retreating Russian Red Army.

Photographs of Hitler replaced those of Lenin and Stalin in public places, and a swastika hung in our school classrooms. During this time I understood that it is in our human nature to hope against hope, for many of us believed that tyranny and oppression would diminish once the hammer and sickle was gone. We were allowed to re-open our churches and community halls, which was surely a good sign, and the Germans looked more educated.

We were swiftly disillusioned. Most of our goods and farm produce continued to be confiscated as before. In return, we received promissory notes, not worth the paper they were written on. In place of the Russians' forced labour system for all age groups, the Germans introduced the *Arbeitsdienst*. Young men were required to work long hours without proper food or accommodation, and were beaten with clubs if they did not work hard enough. All of them grew thin and haggard and few would talk about their experiences for fear of reprisals.

However, with boyish resilience, I ignored everything around me and concentrated on my studies. My father had promised me a bicycle if I passed my examinations in every subject and I did not intend to fail.

Making such a promise was a measure of the importance that Father attached to his son's education, because keeping it would entail sacrifices for the entire family. None of that concerned me at the time, however. I buried myself in my schoolwork until I had mastered every subject to the very best of my ability, and I did well in the exams. No concern about financial whys and wherefores dimmed my joy and pride as I showed my father the results. I think I believed that the bicycle itself could be conjured up in some miraculous way, for the prospect was like something in a dream. Not one boy in my school owned a bike, nor did any of the teachers. On the day when he presented me with it, it was as if I had been given a pair of silver wings.

Looking back, I marvel that my father felt obliged to honour his side of the bargain in such difficult times. We were not the most prosperous family in the village; there were others much better off and I can only conclude that he cared more deeply, was more determined, to see me well-educated, than most of the other fathers. I was his only son, and he was anxious that I should not be distracted from educational goals by the political and social turmoil. It was, moreover, unthinkable to him to renege on a promise. He was a remarkable man, always ready to forego short-term benefits for long-term goals.

The friends from Antoniwka with whom I walked to school, Fedir, Taras, Dmytro, Petro, and Maria were, of course, deeply envious of me with my bicycle. However, they took turns riding on the crossbar, which helped preserve our friendship. I didn't dare leave the bike in the schoolyard, however; it would certainly have been stolen. Mr Kleter, the shoemaker, let me leave it at his house, half a kilometre from school, in the morning. Even then I left it locked, with the tyres deflated and valves removed. On my return, in the afternoon. Mrs Kleter used to give me a cup of coffee and a bun. Then I would unlock the bike, replace the valves, pump up the tyres and ride home. I felt a very privileged boy at that time.

The bike was the one bright spot in dark days. Our hatred of the German occupation soon equalled our hatred of the Russian. One incident summed up the Nazi doctrine for me: the sight of a German soldier hitting a Jew named Schwartz. The soldier was so short that he had to stand on a stool so he could punch Mr Schwartz squarely in the face. The rest of the family were compelled to watch. I wanted to kill the *Schweinhund* with my bare hands! Mr Schwarz's son was a friend of mine, and I knew what rage he must be feeling.

It was after that incident that my father sent me to a priest in Oleshiw to obtain a false baptismal certificate for Mr Kleter. The priest readily supplied it, advising Mr Kleter to learn some prayers from the Bible in the Ukrainian language so that he could convince the Germans that he was a

Christian. In spite of this, however, it was only a matter of months before Mr Kleter disappeared without trace. None of us ever heard what became of him.

One day I was with friends near a bridge over the River Dniester when we saw a group of Jewish people carrying bundles of firewood across the bridge. To our horror, German soldiers on the bridge picked them up one by one and tossed them over the parapet into the river, where they drowned. They hadn't the faintest chance. Even if they had survived the long drop to the water, the fast-running current of the Dniester would have prevented them swimming to safety. It was a sickening and terrifying sight. We dared not even cry out in protest, for fear we might go next.

These experiences made me decide to join the Ukrainian Underground, smuggling arms, disseminating propaganda, and carrying out acts of sabotage – anything to oppose the Germans. I was a strong lad, fast on my feet, and might have been useful to them but, before I could do anything about it, events took a new and drastic turn.

A German officer inspected the register at my school and drew up a list of a dozen or so names. He told a teacher that the children named would be required to report to an assembly point in Stanislawiw in three days' time, and should be ready to be sent to Germany or Austria as forced labourers. My name was on that dreadful list.

'Never trust either the Russians or the Germans, no matter what they promise you,' my father warned me.

In the last days before my departure he kept trying to prepare me for the worst. He had learnt the hard way to distrust them both, and feared that it was his chairmanship of the village under the Russians that had got my name on the list of deportees. At fourteen, I was young to be selected, and might have been singled out in order to punish him. Two cousins, Maria and Hannah, aged seventeen and eighteen, were also on the list.

Every word Father spoke to me at that time, together with the things my Mother and Lywosi had taught me, remain engraved on my heart. The depth of our love for one another strengthened me then, and has sustained me ever since. Hard as life was, and haunted by fear, we had survived. So much was requisitioned by the government, we lived mostly on dry bread, soup, and milk, which we drank warm, straight from the cow, before it could be pilfered by passing soldiers. We drank ersatz coffee, made by my mother from roasted barley kernels. Yet even in this last year we had enjoyed happy times together, especially at Christmas and Easter, which we had celebrated in our own church in something approaching the traditional fashion.

These precious memories made up the bulk of my luggage as I prepared to leave home for the first and last time. I had no clothes but the ones I stood up in; clothing had become virtually unobtainable. Everything else I owned went into a strong little wooden case, about the size and shape of a square hatbox: family photos, books (a few works of fiction, and the satirical magazine *Khomar* – full of jokes and cartoons), also writing paper and envelopes, sharpened pencils, my washing things and a supply of food for the journey. With a very big lump in my throat, I offered my bicycle to my father as a parting gift. With tears in his eyes he accepted it – and the tears convinced me of something else. The bicycle was like a deposit: it was my father's guarantee that I would, eventually at great length perhaps, come home.

'*Mij lyubyj synku Stefku*, my loving son Stefan, your bicycle will be a great help to me, saving my tired legs at the end of a working day, but I would gladly walk on my own two feet to the ends of the earth if it would only keep you here at home with us!'

I felt heartbroken as I said goodbye to everyone, but I was determined to show that I was my brave father's son. To friends of my own age who poured into our house with forlorn faces and frightened eyes I quoted inspiring words from our great Ukrainian poet, Taras Shevchenko: 'Love each other, brothers and sisters. Learn about what is foreign but never forget your own.' I reminded the adults and all my weeping relatives of the words: 'God does not forget you. Struggle on and be triumphant. God himself will aid you. At your side fight Truth and Glory. Right and Holy Freedom.' My father and I had recited many of Shevchenko's poems at the concerts and plays put on by Uncle Dmytro in the village hall.

A Ukrainian portrayal of the deportation of slave labourers. The poet Taras Shevchenko urges them to keep their love of Ukraine in harsh times.

The last words my father said to me were:

'My son, wherever you are, remember who you are. You were born into slavery, but I hope from the bottom of my heart that you will die in freedom. I trust that one day you will know the meaning and experience (and how that experience stings!) of living free, and be able to fly, like the birds of the forest, whenever and wherever you wish.'

A solemn moment, and I replied with equal solemnity:

'My dearest father, I swear to you and to God that I will not live as you have had to live, in slavery and oppression. I will not be gagged or go hungry. Nor be denied free speech. I will tell the world about our life and the persecution we have suffered. I'll fight for freedom and make sure that the name of Terleckyj lives on, part of our Ukrainian history, and is remembered for that fight.'

Before dawn on a morning late in May 1942, six young people set off along the path beside the railway line for Nyzhniw station. We were accompanied by a large crowd of young friends, weeping and singing patriotic songs. Our parents would be waiting in Antoniwka to wave their last farewells as the train passed through the village.

At the station, dozens more children stood in miserable clusters along with their grieving families. The parents were telling them to be sure to write letters home. I promised Lywosi I would write every day if I could, not only for myself but for those who had never learned how to write. Since education was not compulsory, many young people lacked even the ability to keep in touch with their families by letter. We reminded each other of the simple codes with which we innocently imagined we might outwit the censors. I burst into tears and sobs as I hugged and kissed my darling sister for the last time. Though I scarcely dared admit it even to myself, I knew I might never see her or my parents ever again. None of us had any idea what would become of us.

Other passengers in the little train moved over to give us the window seats, so we could lean out and shout and wave for as long as we were in sight. Blinding grit and cinders blew in through the open windows, bringing even more tears to our eyes. I had brought along masses of poems I had written in recent years, and planned to toss them out to my parents as the train passed through Antoniwka. I hoped the poems, full of lofty sentiments in the style of Shevchenko, might ease the shock of separation. They did not. I was leaving them, like the messages I had picked up from other trains over the years, to be cherished in loving hands. I went out on the platform between carriages, and down onto the steps, so they would see me fling them to the wind. My father ran alongside the train and reached out to me. By hanging on with one hand, I was able to grasp his hand one last time. Both parents waved bravely as the train gathered speed. My last impression was of them standing close together with their heads in their hands, an image that often rose before my eyes in years to come.

At each stop along the line, our ranks were swollen by more and more youngsters, who joined the train amid heartrending scenes of farewell. By the time we reached Stanislawiw station, there were many hundreds of us. We were met by young men in makeshift uniform, with swastikas on the armbands of their black shirts. They appeared to be Ukrainians and Polish ethnic Germans, and made very free with the truncheons they carried. Either they were halfwits who did not realize what they were doing, or Nazi sympathizers prepared to sell even children into slavery to curry favour with their masters. No power on earth could have made me join their ranks.

They marched us four abreast through the centre of the town. It was a perfect summer day and the streets were full. Many of the people there stared with horror and indignation at the parade of bedraggled young peasants being driven by force; they gave us sad, sympathetic smiles as we passed, obviously appalled by our plight.

Our first stop was a huge building a few kilometres outside Stanislawiw. Here the boys were separated from the girls as we were herded into our sleeping quarters, twenty or thirty to a room. There were no beds or mattresses – nowhere to sleep but on the bare floor. I set down my case in a corner, to reserve a small space for myself, and went to find the toilet. There proved to be just one big wash hut for the use of all.

Back in the room assigned, we sat and gazed at one another like souls on the borders of Hell. The drama and excitement that had surrounded our departure, together with the stimulating sense of danger that accompanies any journey into the unknown, had buoyed us up and kept us going throughout the day. Now night was approaching, we could no longer escape the knowledge that we were hostages of blind fate, on our own and helpless, cut off from the support of everyone who had raised and nurtured us throughout our lives. And furthermore, we were worn out and very, very hungry.

We asked for something to eat. Most of us had bread and fruit, even cold chicken or *solonyna*, precious bits of food which our mothers had packed in our cases for the journey, but we wanted to make it last as long as we could. Eventually we were each given a half litre of ersatz coffee and a slice of black bread.

One of the guards asked who could read or write. Quite a few of us raised our hands, which struck terror into the hearts of the remainder, since, if we became separated, they would lose their last hope of communicating with their families. Nothing further happened just then, however.

None of us slept much that night. As soon as I lay down on the floor, my resolve to endure whatever happened in a manly fashion disintegrated and I gave way to childish tears of loneliness and desperation, no more able to stifle my sobs than any of those around me. As I lay there, everything I had ever heard about the fate of deportees passed through my mind. I had nightmare visions of slave labour camps, of filthy, icy cold barracks, sadistic guards, casual humiliation and torture and slow starvation.

The two or three days we spent in that camp gave us plenty of time for such fevered imaginings, which no one could dismiss as mere fantasy. We all knew people to whom it had happened. Every day more young people arrived to join the exodus, until we numbered what looked like thousands. Some were there because their families had been reported for sheltering local Jews, which had become a serious crime; others because their village had refused to join the German army's work force. In such cases, the whole population had been rounded up and all their young people taken away. Camp officials told us that the authorities were under orders from Berlin to produce 250,000 workers for transportation to Germany and Austria before the beginning of August. Youngsters were taken to avoid, if possible, prejudicing the harvest of food crops in Ukraine.

One day early in June, our guards, the fellows in the black shirts known to us as 'the Black Brutes', rounded us up like cattle for the slaughterhouse and, wielding their truncheons freely as before, herded us before them back to Stanislawiw station. Our journey so far had been in a passenger train, which is what we looked for as we approached the platform, but this time a cattle train was standing on a siding with the doors of its wagons open wide. As the guards started shoving us into the wagons, sixty or seventy people with their belongings into each one, the young man in front of me went behind the wagon to urinate. Immediately one of the Black Brutes rushed over and pounded him about the head and shoulders until he collapsed onto the ground. Seeing that it was a Ukrainian guard treating a fellow Ukrainian in this way, I was so shocked that, with youthful impetuosity, I dashed between them, shouting, 'Don't you have any *shame*? Don't you realize you've nearly murdered your brother?' And with a considerable element of surprise on my side, I was able to continue, with concomitant aggression: 'Where's your *heart*? Where's your belief in God? Look what you've *done* to him!' Having said which, I burst into tears – probably a wise move even if wisdom seemed to have deserted me for the time being.

The young man on the ground had not uttered a sound – and the guard stared at me uncomprehendingly and walked away, perplexed perhaps by this difficult switch of emotions. (In fact this particular Ukrainian Black Brute happened to be an ethnic German.) I was lucky –

I know that now, and I think I would have known the same at the time. Murmuring words of comfort, I pulled the injured man to his feet and half-dragged, half-carried him into the wagon. He was a simple fellow, unable to read or write, and I promised to stick by him and help him for as long as I could.

The Black Brutes crammed more and more of us into the wagons until they were filled to capacity. We were packed so tight there was hardly room to stand, much less sit. German soldiers now took charge of us and handed out a meal of potato soup and black bread. They told us our destination was Lwiw, capital city of western Ukraine, a distance of only about 140 kilometres. Our journey, however, seemed interminable. At one point, the train stopped in the middle of nowhere so that we could get out, stretch, and relieve ourselves, but we saw there was no chance of escape. There was nowhere to go.

We spent three or four weeks in Lwiw while further contingents of young people joined us. We were housed in squalid conditions in a military barracks, sleeping forty or fifty to a room in tiered bunks which were no more than wooden planks. Our clothes became infested with lice and fleas. Our rations were potato soup, sometimes with a few peas floating in it, and a slice of black bread. Boredom and uncertainty added to our misery, but I was kept busy writing letters for those unable to do so, while others took turns sharpening my pencils. At first I wrote down whatever they asked me to, however long and repetitious it became. Then I decided to limit letters to a single page, saying where we were and how we were getting on. What was the point of adding to our families' misery by telling the whole truth?

The strain of not knowing what would happen next began to tell on some of us, who lost weight very fast or became rambling in their speech. Young girls suffered especially from the pains and embarrassment of their menstrual periods, which they were ill equipped to manage, lacking any real privacy. Occasionally, out of the blue, a Polish or Ukrainian guard would show compassion, fetching medical supplies for someone who was ill, or a little extra food from the kitchens. For this we were extravagantly grateful.

One by one we were photographed from all sides, fingerprinted, and issued with a sort of passport. This crude document, on which even those of us who could write were not allowed to sign our own names, was to be our only identification for years to come. It was at this point that my Ukrainian name Terleckyj was changed to the Polish-sounding Terlezki, a change over which I had no control, and that spelling has remained with me ever since.

Then, early one morning, we were once again shunted, unfed, into cattle trucks to continue our journey. This time we travelled a very long way. My little wooden case proved a blessing, since it made a small seat on which I could even sleep, sitting up, if the wagons were not too desperately crowded. The train stopped briefly at Bratislava, in Slovakia, where we were given a drink of warm water but not allowed to get out. From then on conditions in the wagons became unspeakable. The filth and stench left us gasping for air, yet it was not until the next day, when we reached Spittal-an-der-Drau, high in the Austrian Alps, that we were finally released from our insanitary confinement.

Surprisingly we had all survived. We had endured a nightmarish journey believing that the time was in sight when we would return to the world and be dispersed to farms and factories to start work, so it was with real horror that we found ourselves delivered to Stalager 8, next to a military prisoner of war camp which housed hundreds of Russian prisoners. Many of us thought we were being imprisoned for good, or had perhaps been conscripted into the German army.

Conditions were worse than any we had so far experienced. Although Spittal can be a place of heavenly beauty and spectacular mountain views, everything was drenched in heavy clouds and mists. The camp was ringed with barbed wire and had watchtowers at each corner manned by soldiers with machine guns. Searchlights played over the prison camp at night. We were told that any attempt to escape or to contact the Russian prisoners of war would be punishable by death. Nevertheless, it was not long before pebbles wrapped round with bits of paper fell into our side of the camp, and messages began to be exchanged with the Russians. They wanted to know where they were, how far from the border, and other such information. A few of them, together with two of our own young men, actually broke out of the camp while we were there, in an attempt to escape. We never heard what became of them.

The food in this camp was abominable, barely enough to sustain life. Our thin mattresses and one thin blanket were crawling with lice and bedbugs and did not protect us from the cold at night. There was no soap. We cleaned ourselves by standing outside when it rained and running around to get dry afterwards, but even the grass around the camp was hopping with lice and fleas. Day by day we could see the eyes of our friends growing larger, their faces thinner. I didn't understand then, and don't now, why the authorities should have wanted to starve and degrade their potential Slav workforce – mostly sturdy young country folk – causing them to arrive at their workplace in a thoroughly unhealthy condition. We doubted whether we were intended to survive at all, and many of us lost interest in our own preservation.

We did pray, however, in spite of a feeling that God must have forgotten us. As the Ukrainian proverb says, 'Those who are in trouble pray to God, while those who are not forget God.' Our sole prayer was to get out of that appalling camp alive. It is a miracle none of us died there.

One night we were told we would be leaving the camp the next day. When the Russians heard, a message came – wrapped again around a stone – saying, 'You are lucky. Not many of your predecessors lived to tell the tale.' Next morning we were marched out through the gates on the road to another camp, not far away. We went on foot through hilly, cultivated countryside and forest, heavily guarded but not so heavily that we were unable to pick fruit from wayside trees to fill our empty stomachs. It was high summer and the apples were still green, so that bellyache, sickness and diarrhoea soon added to our difficulties, but even these were less awful than starvation. And at least the Spittal camp was behind us.

The administrators at the camp we arrived at showed, for the first time, some interest in our welfare. It started with our disinfection and delousing. There was an ominous smell of burning as we lined up for this process. We were sent to undress, then into showers, boys and girls, and then had every vestige of hair shaved off. Before being returned to the showers a second time, we were smeared with a disinfectant that smelt revolting and was difficult to remove without soap, and our clothes were sprayed with some sort of stinging powder. Although we were mercifully unaware at that time of the ovens of Auschwitz, I think it is true to say that it was only when we finally emerged from that shower that we felt fully confident that it was only the lice they had meant to exterminate and not us ourselves. We were at long last free of vermin and scrupulously clean. The ovens we had smelt had, meanwhile, been used to delouse our possessions. Our clothes had simply been burnt.

You can imagine the shock, however, for young people, most of whom were Ukrainian Catholics, brought up in extreme, even excessive, modesty, when we came out of the bath huts, boys and girls alike, to discover that every single item of clothing we had arrived with had been destroyed. There was not so much as a shred of towel with which to cover ourselves. We ran around naked, screeching and screaming, trying to hide ourselves amidst groups of friends, but even that was not easy. With our shaven heads and skeletal bodies, flea-bitten and scratched, we could hardly recognize friends from strangers. There was total panic and confusion.

'Calm yourselves,' bellowed the guards, who had seen it all before. 'That's enough noise. We are trying to get you some clothes. They're on the way. We've sent for them from a store somewhere.'

'But when?' we cried.

'Before long.'

A few hours later a lorry turned up with clothes, which were distributed at random, without regard for size. We grabbed shirts, trousers, skirts and blouses gratefully and hurriedly put them on. Only then did we look around and see how comical we all looked, every one of us bald-headed and wearing nothing that fitted. A circus troupe could not have got itself up to look more ridiculous. Our painful embarrassment and shame found an outlet in almost hysterical laughter as we teased and poked fun at one another. We were all in the same boat, so there was no malice in our laughter, only relief and youthful merriment. Some of the degradation and humiliation we had felt at being dirty, lousy, half-starved, and in fear of imminent death, washed away in a great flood of giggles and guffaws. The girls were half-crying as well, mourning their long, thick plaits. The guards looked on tolerantly, amused and not untouched by our situation.

It soon became plain that in this camp we were to be made presentable to the outside world. It still looked like a prison camp, with its barbed wire, watchtowers and machine guns, but it was clean and well-regulated. Our food improved in quantity if not quality – for the first time, we were allowed to ask for second helpings of bread and soup – and we were soon issued with appropriate clothing of the correct size. The only thing we craved was up-to-date information. No one would tell us where we were going next, what we would be doing, or when we would be leaving.

One day, however, we were told to get ready to go to centres from which we would be dispersed to the various jobs that awaited us. What a cheer went up! By this time, the prospect of taking up work as slave labourers, instead of distressing us, was positively welcome. It took no time to pack my things. The papers and photos that had survived the delousing process went into my wooden case along with such clothes as I had been given. At the station we were shown into passenger carriages bound for Graz, the second largest city in Austria, and felt almost human again, sitting in proper seats and able to look out of the windows! We studied the landscape we were passing through with eager interest.

We reached Graz by lunchtime, but our hearts sank when we found ourselves transported to yet another camp. A certain number of us, however, stayed there only long enough to eat lunch before returning to the station. We said sad farewells to those we were leaving behind, who would shortly be going elsewhere. Our destination this time was the town of Voitsberg, a short journey away through beautiful mountain scenery. It felt like the beginning of a totally new life. What on earth would be expected of us? All we asked was to be treated like ordinary people and be given enough to eat. None of us was in very good shape physically, but we were prepared to work hard for anyone who would treat us decently. Skin-and-bones as we were, we tended to forget that with shaven heads, we looked anything but normal, and not unlike escaped convicts.

There must have been close to a thousand of us when we arrived at

Voitsberg station. We were formed into columns and marched through the town, with contingents hived off in different directions as we went. Eventually several hundred of us found ourselves in a compound surrounded by a wire mesh fence, penned in like cattle up for sale on market day. No one told us that we were actually for sale there, on display with our pathetic little rucksacks and boxes.

Then people began to arrive and stare at us, speaking to one another in an incomprehensible dialect. There appeared to be couples looking for someone, perhaps a shop worker or housemaid, and men selecting farmhands and factory workers. There was a palpable sense of embarrassment on both sides, but before long it was clear that some of them had picked out a boy or girl whom they wanted to examine more closely. That's how it was with me.

A young man eight or ten years older than myself and about my size, wearing the uniform of the German navy, caught my eye and we exchanged glances. He pointed a finger at me and beckoned me closer to the fence. Eager to be chosen by somebody – anybody – so as to escape from that cattle pen, I went forward and stood in front of him. The German uniform frightened me, but he gave me a sort of half smile. Trying to look agreeable, I responded nervously, then looked away and waited. He looked me over, obviously trying to assess my physical condition, my capacity for hard work, and my general trustworthiness. At the same time other people were also inspecting me and I glanced back at the sea of weathered foreign faces, trying to judge which of them might prove the kindest master. Should I try to appeal more to one than to another? The sailor kept an eye on me. Suddenly, he jerked his head in the direction of the gates, a sign that I should go and meet him there.

A number of officials, and an interpreter, sat by the gates, at tables piled high with documents. I was asked my name and soon saw a sheet of paper with my name and photograph on it shuffled to the top of the pile. Without further ado, or any attempt to obtain my consent, I was asked to sign it, not in a dignified way with my written signature but by stamping it with my thumbprint. An exchange of words followed between the sailor and one of the officials, after which my new master took out his wallet and handed over a number of Reichsmark – I have always wondered how many. Then he too signed a document and that was that: officially sold to the Austrian sailor. I was not asked any questions about myself or my capabilities, nor told where I was going, what work I was going to do, or the name of my purchaser. I changed hands like any low-priced commodity disposed of with indecent haste. The sailor tucked the bill of sale into his pocket.

With another jerk of his head, my new master indicated that I was to follow him, so I picked up my case and fell into step behind him, feeling numb and dazed and totally disorientated. I was too weak and undernourished for the notion of escape to cross my mind. What tore me apart was the realization that I had not said goodbye to any of my friends, whom I might never see again, and that I was now parted from everyone I had ever known in my whole life. That overwhelming sense of isolation was made worse by the fact that my captor and I did not appear to speak any common language. The Austrian dialect sounded nothing like the German I had learned in school, so that I could not ask him the simplest question, and had to remain mute, like an idiot; a clod of earth. Feeling desperately sorry for myself and sobbing deep inside, I walked behind him, doing my best to maintain an impassive face.

For the next three-quarters of an hour, I concentrated on keeping pace with the sailor, whose name, I later discovered, was Hansel. Even in the Navy, men evidently did plenty of marching! I had to take two steps to his every stride. Our route took us back through Voitsberg and out to the south-west of the town, through a stretch of forest, climbing uphill most of the way. The day was boiling hot, and I trotted along, half walking, half running, breathless and sick at heart, wondering if our journey would ever end. I longed for a friendly word, but Hansel did not speak to me. When I asked how far we still had to go, with signs to make my meaning clear, he pointed straight ahead and snapped out an order that sounded like, 'Just keep walking!' in such a disagreeable voice that it reduced me to total silence.

Then, at last, we emerged from the forest into an open space high above Voitsberg, with a view far into the distance. The hills and mountains were dotted with farms and orchards, interspersed with woodland. Hansel stretched out his arm and pointed to some buildings still higher up. I raised my eyebrows, enquiring whether this was the farm, but he shook his head. However, once we had reached the barns, we walked through the farmyard and Hansel, to my relief, jerked his head towards a farm immediately beyond it with a sort of half smile. As we negotiated the last few hundred metres of rough mud track, I got my first impression of the place. There was a large old stone-built house, with outbuildings, orchards, and fields that stretched steeply upwards to the sky. Close by was a third farm.

The outbuildings consisted of a barn, stables, pigsty, cow-shed and sheds which I later learned were used for schnapps and cider-making. On the left of the house was a kitchen garden surrounded by a wooden fence. The farmhouse itself was somewhat run-down, but not unlike farms I had known in Ukraine, surrounded by trees and flowers and very pleasant to the eye after the weeks in transit camps. Wooden steps led up to a large square verandah, from which one could see miles across the countryside.

Perspiration and apprehension made me damp and sick respectively. Setting my case down outside the door, I followed Hansel into the kitchen, where a family of about six to eight people were just sitting down to lunch. They moved over to make space for us at the table, not even offering us an opportunity to wash. Though I was certainly hungry, my head was throbbing so violently and my throat was so constricted I could hardly swallow. In my nervousness, I imagined they were all staring at me and commenting on me to one another, and I felt more stupid than I had ever felt in my life. They were all talking at once and I suspected they were jeering at Hansel for having made a bad bargain. I had no idea what they were saying, but, to my acutely self-conscious ears, it didn't sound flattering.

They were all women and children except for Hansel and a younger fellow, not much older than myself, whom they called Toni. Of the women, one stood out as the head of the house and owner of the farm – a huge, dominant figure, tall as well as stout, with a round face and fair hair pulled back tight into a bun at the back of her head, whom everyone called 'Mutti'. I was soon to learn that her word was law. She scrutinized me unsmilingly, inch by inch. Then she pointed at my plate, indicating that I should eat something, but my throat was so dry I made signs to ask if I could have something to drink. I expected to be given a cup of water or milk, but a jug was thrust into my hand.

I had noticed them all drinking from this jug, which seemed to me very strange and unhygienic. There were no mugs to pour the liquid into; everyone, including the small children, just picked up the jug and drank from it. I knew enough about hygiene to wonder at this. What's more, the contents of the jug looked cloudy, not clean like water. However, it had been pushed at me peremptorily – clearly I was under orders to drink – so I did as I was told. The taste was nauseating; not just sour but bitter! Seeing from my expression that I did not know or much like what I was drinking, they all shouted its name at me: *must, must,* as if I were deaf as well as ignorant. This *must* is a kind of fruit cider very popular in the farming communities in Austria. In time, I came to like it as much as they did.

The clatter of cutlery on plates took the place of conversation for a time, and I could hear a radio playing in the corner of the kitchen, which was the main room of the house. I had never heard anything but news reports on the radio and the idea of a radio just playing on, providing background music, enchanted me. The sound of music was such a novelty that I felt briefly transported from the bewilderment and loneliness I felt in the midst of this stupid crowd of people. Their response to me seemed without any normal human feeling, after all even the pigs were invited to eat and drink.

I felt certain that I would never be able to settle down on this farm. It was totally alien, not at all as I had expected it to be. There had been none of the welcome into the family which any stranger, however humble, was entitled to in Ukraine, but somehow the music made me imagine it might be possible to escape to the mountains and forests, or even make my way home. Such is the power of the music!

After lunch, everyone moved out into the fields. No one had asked my name. They simply ordered me around by saying '*Du! Du!*', 'You!, You!' to attract my attention, and then pointed at what they wanted me to do, or pulled me where they wanted me to go. I wondered if anyone would ever call me Stefan again. Meanwhile I watched the others closely and carried out instructions as best I could.

Immediately behind the farmhouse and stables there was a big acreage of ripe corn, wheat and barley which they had begun to reap. Hansel handed me a scythe ninety centimetres long and told me to start cutting the corn. At home we had used a sickle for this job, so I had never handled such an awkward, unwieldy implement. I did not even know how to grasp it. With some impatience, Hansel gave me a demonstration and left me to do my best.

It was not as easy as it looked when he did it. A scythe is quite difficult to manage. At home, only the men used scythes and that was for cutting the hay. One moment I was stabbing the earth with it and the next moment cutting the stalks off far too high. It was horribly frustrating. I felt particularly stupid when one of the girls noticed my clumsiness and started to giggle. No one showed any consideration for my plight. Hansel eyed me with contempt and tossed his head at the end of the row, as if to say, 'Just keep on cutting till you learn how!'

The strangeness of my situation made it hard for me to concentrate. How were things at home? Were they harvesting corn in Antoniwka? Who was helping my mother and sister with the animals? I could not stop thinking about my friends, all scattered. Were those who had started out with me that morning already at work as I was that afternoon, on farms not far away? Or were they working in factories, or breaking stone in quarries? Some of them were probably still confined to the camps. Then my thoughts strayed to others, like Uncle Roman and Wasyl, doing hard labour in Siberia. How were they occupied at that moment, supposing they were still alive? Did they feel drowned in despair as I did? I felt ashamed when I thought of them. At least the NKVD were not watching me. I kept wondering whether I should just throw the scythe down and start running for the hills. What would happen? Would they shoot? My only alternative was to try to adapt myself to this lonely life.

Even while such thoughts chased themselves around in my head, I persevered with my work and became a little more skilful with the scythe. At about six in the evening, I reached the end of the row at last and, sweating profusely, paused for a moment's rest. Looking round, I saw that two girls, somewhat younger than myself – one the youngest daughter, the other a granddaughter of the farmer – were eyeing me with amusement, almost flirtatiously, and not without some sympathy for my plight. I felt heartened. Perhaps I could be friends with them at least. I did eventually get on friendly terms with the granddaughter, whose name was Hilde, but that day was a long way off.

'It's only the first day,' I told myself. 'Put it down to inexperience. I may not be so totally hopeless at the job tomorrow.'

That farm, whether I liked it or not, was to be my new home.

Chapter 6

1942-1943
Prison Without Walls

At bedtime I was taken up the back stairs to a small room in the attic, empty except for a bed. The room was also dim; although the house had electricity, there was no light up there. The only light and air came through a small window above the bed – above *my* bed. The remaining panes were cracked and broken, but most of the glass was missing. The floorboards were old and rotten and creaked at every step. Looking out, I could see the stables of the farm next door, only ten or fifteen metres away, and beyond them orchards, farmland and forest.

In bed that night, I dissolved in tears, overwhelmed with loneliness in a situation where I could not understand anything that was said to me. Furthermore, I experienced the feeling that I was being prepared for something: buttered-up, toughened up. Even in the worst of the transit camps, I had had as good a notion of what was going on as anyone else. Here I did not know what my duties on the farm were to be and could not ask for information or follow instructions. I could only guess what members of the family were saying about me when they laughed among themselves. It was demeaning. I felt, as I had never felt before, an utter dolt among people who were in no way better or more intelligent than myself. I was completely at their mercy, with no one to share my servitude, a prisoner in a prison without walls. I prayed to God for strength and guidance.

In spite of the language difficulties, no time was wasted in making certain things clear to me. My working day began at five o'clock in the morning and lasted until nine or ten at night. The harvest had still to be gathered in. From the start, I did exactly as I was told, performing any job given me to the best of my ability. I knew I had nothing to gain by annoying my new masters and might possibly win some favour or kindness by pleasing them.

At least I got three meals a day, with two breaks in between. Breakfast consisted of maize porridge, without milk but with a limited amount of poor quality sugar, and black ersatz coffee. On good days there were boiled jacket potatoes with home-made butter. At mid morning there would be bread, fruit and *must*. At lunch we had vegetable soup, with bread, and boiled *speck* (ham), pork brawn, or chicken when available, and excellent salads dressed with oil and home-made vinegar. I was allowed to have a second helping of soup. At our afternoon break we had bread and cider, and sometimes a little cold *speck*. For supper it was soup, bread and fruit.

It was good farm food, better than we could afford at home through the war years, but there was never quite enough of it. As a growing lad doing very heavy work, I was permanently hungry, and had no scruples about filching bread, or any other kind of food, if it was left about when no one was looking.

I could never get really clean. There was no such thing as a bathroom and no one offered me a bath or a change of clothes. We washed in a basin of cold water, using a kind of grey-black soap. From the day I left home until well after the war ended, I never had an opportunity to wash in hot water.

Having no change of clothes, I lived in those I had arrived in, working out in the fields and in the stables with the animals, as unable as the animals themselves to put on fresh garments. It amazed me that Mutti, the widowed owner of the farm, who was mother or grandmother to them all, never seemed to mind that I sat down at the table dirty. She certainly never offered to add my underwear, shirt, or trousers to the family wash. If my clothes became so filthy, torn, or rotten that they fell off me altogether and had to be discarded, someone would find me some cast-offs to take their place, and for that I learned to be humbly grateful.

Little by little, by listening closely and repeating words said to me, I began to make sense of the Austrian dialect and relate it to the German I had learnt at school. As my understanding increased, I began to sort out the conditions and prohibitions governing my new life and that of everyone in the foreign labour force. A Polish worker named Marian, on the farm next door, explained many of them to me. According to the regulations laid down by the Gestapo, we were not allowed to travel more than fifteen kilometres within the area where we were based. Even for that we had to have passports, permission from our employers and, if we wished to go further, from the local Burgermeister as well. Slave labourers were not permitted to ride a bike, go to the cinema, nor attend local dance halls. We were never under any circumstances to wear the typical Tyrolean outfit of leather trousers, jacket with green oak leaves embroidered on the lapels, and hat with a feather in it. That might cause us to be mistaken for Austrians. We were required to wear a label designating our origins at all times: P for the Poles, OST for all those like me who were classed as *Ostarbeiter*, or eastern worker.

The penalty for being caught breaking any of these rules was twenty-five (single) or fifty (double) lashes administered by members of the Gestapo. Marian, who became a close friend and ally, told me exactly how it would be done. The Gestapo would either take the offender to their headquarters in Voitsberg or punish him there on the farm. He would be tied to a plank, head down, by his ankles and shoulders, and one of the Gestapo would beat him on the buttocks with a truncheon with as much force as his strength allowed. If the punishment was double lashes, it would be fifty strokes laid on alternately by two Gestapo officers, one on either side. Marian said he couldn't sit or walk properly for six months afterwards, and he warned me, time and again, 'Don't break any of the rules, however pointless or inhuman they may seem to you. If you are told to wear a label, wear it. If you are told not to ride a bike, don't ride one.' His crime had been to be caught out without the letter P on his shirt. I made sure that OST was prominently displayed on my clothing at all times.

Once I could understand her, the farmer, whom I was soon calling Mutti since everyone else did, told me that I would receive twenty marks a month wages, and some clothing coupons. There would be sufficient coupons to buy one suit, made of a synthetic fabric derived from wood, as well as an overcoat (expected to last two or three years), and one shirt, a pair of trousers, a set of underwear and a pair of shoes per year. First, of course, I had to earn the money to buy them, and then I had to find them in the shops. Wooden clogs were cheap, not rationed, and were not in short supply like shoes. So I wore those most of the time.

With wages of twenty marks a month (which I did not always receive) it took some time before I could buy a suit, at seventy-five marks, or any of the other things. Luckily, whenever Toni discarded old clothes, he passed them on to me. Toni and I were nearly the same age and worked together much of the time, so that he, at least, regarded me as human. He noticed that my only pair of shoes was wearing out and that I had none fit to go to church in, and found me a more presentable pair.

I kept the shoes he gave me for Sundays and I still wore clogs for work, summer and winter. The one bright spot in my life was the chance to meet *Ausländers* like myself at church on a Sunday, when I had half the day off. At other times it did not matter what I looked like, but gradually I acquired a few decent garments, which I looked after with the greatest care, content to work on the farm in rags.

Only the most minimal obligations towards us *Ausländers* were imposed on those who had bought our services. Self-interest dictated, as with livestock, that we should be adequately fed, clothed, and sheltered, so we did not perish. Yet, when winter came, I had been moved out of the attic room because all the grain was stored there; I had to sleep in the open attic where there were mice crawling all over me. The attic became frozen and bitterly cold and very draughty. I then took my blanket with me and went to sleep in the stables with the cows and horses until the spring. This was a big improvement, and much warmer, but the aroma was sometimes unbearable, as was the noise when the cows and horses started telling each other jokes in their own way.

The Gestapo made frequent checks on foreign labourers to make sure we were complying with the rules, and doing whatever work the farmer required without complaint. Two Gestapo officers arrived one day when I was in the yard with some of the farm women preparing to kill a pig. I had in my hand the spring-activated bolt-gun that we used to stun the pig into unconsciousness. The Gestapo officers took the women aside to make enquiries about me, asking whether I was behaving myself or had broken any of the rules. When they returned, Mutti smiled reassuringly at me, as if to say, 'I've given you a good report,' but the two men, obviously not satisfied, took me up to the attic. They made no comment on my bed or the broken window, or on my meagre possessions, but searched an adjacent room where they found an old bicycle of Toni's, all in pieces, and asked me if I had dismantled it. I hadn't, of course, because I knew the rules, but one of the Gestapo men took his gun out of its holster and ignoring the bolt-gun still in my hand, pressed it to my chest, barking, 'Have you ever ridden that bike?'

'No!' I declared vehemently.

'Could you put it together?' he asked.

'I could try,' I said.

'Why would you do that?' he demanded.

'I would only do it if ordered to, not otherwise.'

'Make sure you remember that!' he growled, screwing the muzzle of his revolver into my chest menacingly. 'If I ever hear you have been riding it, or doing anything else you are forbidden to do, I will not hesitate to press this trigger.'

The other man gave me a sardonic look and asked how I liked sleeping in the attic with all that fresh air. It must have been obvious that I would freeze in winter.

'I don't mind the air,' I told him. 'If it gets too cold, I take my two blankets and sleep in the cowshed, where the air is not so fresh, but much warmer. What I don't like is mice running over me at night, keeping me awake.' They laughed.

Further questions concerned the radio. They were keen to know if I, or anyone on the farm, listened to foreign broadcasts, Of course, people sometimes did, particularly to Swiss radio or the BBC, where the news reporting was comparatively truthful: it was the only way we could find out how the war was going. However, I feigned a total lack of interest in the news, and said how much I liked music, though I knew that was not the point of their questions. The Gestapo also wanted to know what contacts I had with a prisoner of war camp nearby – I had none at that time – and whether I ever wore Austrian traditional dress. He pointed at the hat I was wearing, an ancient black thing riddled with holes, admittedly of Austrian provenance but certainly bereft of any feather. I assured him I knew I was not allowed to do so. They seemed determined to probe my attitudes in every way, hoping, perhaps, for an excuse to administer twenty-five lashes on the spot, but they went away in the end, thank God!

I was glad to get back to slaughtering the pig, although it was not usually a favourite chore. Meanwhile Mutti dutifully repeated the warnings and admonitions the Gestapo had tried to impress on me. She said I must obey her absolutely and work very hard if I wanted to stay out of trouble. But I knew that already!

On the farm itself, things improved once I had learned enough of the Austrian dialect to communicate with the others and understand what they were saying. Being young, I enjoyed good moments, playing cards late at night with Toni and some of the younger women, with Marian sometimes joining us from next door. Or Marian and I might sit and talk about our homes, exchanging whatever news we received from our families. My father wrote regularly. I had spoken the truth when I told the Gestapo I was fond of the music of Strauss, Schubert and Wagner, and that I enjoyed the Austrian folk music, which was constantly on the air; but everybody was grateful for the radio, not just me. I was desperately envious when people from the farm went off to the cinema in Voitsberg. When they came home, they regaled the rest of us with every detail of the films they had seen, rehearsing the stories and dances, and humming the airs of the songs for days afterwards.

The farm boasted few luxuries. The toilet was no more than a large bucket under the steps of an outside verandah, and naturally, it fell to me to see to the slopping out whenever it was full, emptying it onto the manure heap outside the cowshed. It was difficult to avoid getting ordure on my hands or clothes. In winter, when snow covered the manure heap, the smell as I emptied it was not too bad, but in summer it turned my stomach and attracted swarms of flies. It was on the verandah that we used to play cards in summer, so, unless the bucket was emptied frequently, the stench from below was more than we could bear.

The farm had no water supply, not even a well. Once or twice a day I had to take the cart with a big barrel on it, harness it to a cow or horse and take it half a kilometre downhill through the forest to a spring to draw water. This was a back-breaking job at the best of times, but cruelly hard in winter, when the track was snowed up and the water frozen. All the most unpleasant jobs fell to Stefan, but I never dared to complain.

The work never ended. Crops of corn, barley, potatoes, and every kind of vegetable were grown. There was hay-making to be done, wheat to be threshed, orchards to be tended, and *must* to be made. There was always livestock to be tended – a horse, four cows, five or six pigs, four or five sheep, numerous chickens, geese and ducks. As well as growing enough food for the family, and sufficient produce to sell, there were government quotas to be met. With Hansel away on submarine duty most of the time, the only young men to do the work were Toni, who was about seventeen, and myself. Of the half dozen women, some were too old or too young for heavy work. There was no other labour on the farm.

My first job, at five in the morning, was to go to the stables and feed the horse, cows, pigs and poultry, then clean the stables and groom the horses. The latter task constituted no great hardship: I liked making sure the horse was spick and span. After an hour or so in the stables, it was up the steps into the kitchen for breakfast. Everyone around the table, including the children, helped themselves from one large bowl. Except for our meal breaks, it was back to work all day in the fields and orchards. In summer we were at work until late at night but in winter, there was the blackout. Then, after supper, we sat in the kitchen listening to the radio, playing cards, and drinking *must*. There was always the fear that the Gestapo, checking on the blackout, might overhear what we were listening to, so we usually restricted ourselves to Austrian programmes, but once in a while someone would take a chance and tune in to a foreign station for news.

In winter, we worked in the woods, cutting trees for firewood, since coal for domestic use was strictly rationed. It was dangerous work for a lad, as many of the trees were very tall, and snow and ice made the hillsides slippery. I was fortunate not to suffer injuries other than cuts and bruises, and the inevitable splinters. The worst thing was the extreme cold. I used to pad out my clogs with rags and brown paper, drying them out later before the kitchen fire, but even rags were very scarce and they did not prevent frostbite. My head used to ache all winter long, for months on end. Since no one offered any remedy, I simply had to bear the pain.

My only respite from labour came on Sundays, when, after doing the usual essential chores, I was allowed to go to church in the morning, and had several hours free in the afternoon. Sunday lunch was also something to look forward to, for there were dumplings in the soup, and a meat course with vegetables and salads, and doughnuts, pies or pancakes, for dessert. On Sundays we could have second helpings, too. I looked forward to it all week.

Once I had acquired a few respectable clothes, my Sundays became truly happy. Well washed and dressed in my best, wearing the leather shoes Toni had given me, brightly polished, I would walk down the hill through the forest to Voitsberg and the Roman Catholic Church, where everyone was kindly received. I could count on finding friends there among the workers of all nationalities, who came whenever they could. The singing was magnificent. I would pray for strength and courage for myself and for the health and well-being of my family, especially my mother, whose health grew steadily worse.

The service lasted nearly two hours. When it ended, we often found a Nazi officer outside, standing on a stool and taking the opportunity to deliver a propaganda speech glorifying the Führer and urging us to strive ever harder to defend the Fatherland. Every so often he would raise his arm in the air and shout, 'Heil Hitler!' to which we had to respond in like manner. If we didn't, one of the local Gestapo attending in civilian dress, would notice, and there would be a tap on the shoulder, followed by a demand to know your name, nationality and address. One day I was talking with friends and failed to hear the 'Heil Hitler!' for which I received a severe warning. Eventually we learned to sneak away quickly, before the peroration began.

On Sunday afternoons, most of the foreign workers in the district met together in the depths of the forest. There were dozens of nationalities – Ukrainians, Poles, Czechs, Hungarians, Byelorussians, Russians, Caucasians, Mongolians, Tartars, Georgians, and some from the Baltic countries. My childhood friend Fedir, from Antoniwka, turned up there; he was working on a farm not far from mine. Someone would produce a mouth organ or accordion borrowed from an Austrian farmer, and we would sing and dance and exchange news from home. Most of us got letters, which with our simple codes, told us more than was actually written. We had to be discreet in our conversations, however, to make sure such items of news did not reach the ears of the authorities.

Many people were working in factories, on the railways and in coalmines. A lot of the miners were British, French and Italian prisoners of war from the camp near my farm. They were very badly treated and never got enough to eat. I felt sorry for the girls who worked in brick factories and other heavy industries. They had impossible quotas to fulfil and their hands were often raw and bleeding. Underfed, they were often bullied by their masters. A Russian girl named Olga, from the Urals, showed great spirit in standing up for her friends in the factory where she worked. I admired her courage, and we became good friends for a time, but drifted apart when I realized she wanted a more permanent relationship. I was not ready for a long-term commitment and preferred meeting as friends. Sometimes I wrote letters home for girls who could not write, so that their parents would at least know where they were, and that there were people at hand ready to help them. Those Sunday meetings were our lifeline.

By the end of my first year, I had acquired most of the skills needed to run the farm. It was important that I should, since Toni expected to be conscripted into the armed services at eighteen, and then there would be no man on the farm but me. I learned to plough the fields, steering the horse up and down the steep hillsides, making sure the plough cut into the earth to exactly the right depth. On good days I exulted in this activity, whistling and singing as I went along, striding freely and surveying the town of Voitsberg far below. I learnt to sow from a sack of seed slung over my head and left shoulder, casting the wheat, corn, or barley in a wide arc evenly over the land. I raked and hoed the fields, mixing seeds and soil, making sure that the winter wheat, especially, was well enough covered to protect it from frost. I learnt how to kill a pig and remove its bristles. Then, twice a year, I took the horse to the blacksmith to be shod with their winter or summer shoes. It required considerable brute strength and skill to control the horse and not get kicked or bitten, and to avoid the sparks from the anvil, so it was quite an ordeal. The blacksmith was a powerful, beetle-browed man, forever swearing at me for incompetence.

With the help of the women I did the hay-making and brought in the harvest, did the threshing and bundled up the straw. After the fruit was picked and sent to market, I helped with the cider-making. It was all new to me since we had never made cider at home. I even acquired the art of making schnapps, the highly potent spirit made from cider apples, potatoes or barley. Schnapps-making was strictly controlled by the Ministry of Food, under whose orders the equipment used to make it was sealed from one year to the next. Each family was rationed to one or two litres per person per year of the schnapps they produced.

One winter's day, two officials from the Ministry of Food arrived to break the seal. They gave us just twenty-four hours in which to make the schnapps. I felt excited to be taking part in a process I had only watched in the past. Special logs had to be ready for making the fire and all the containers had to be clean and ready for use. The cider sediment, collected from countless barrels of cider, had to be on hand, and the heat of the fire had to be controlled throughout the distilling process. It wasn't easy, and I looked forward mightily to a taste of the resultant spirit. It was a point of pride for farmers to produce a good few litres over the limit without the officials' knowledge, so I knew I would get my reward.

I also became proficient at cider-making. We had our own crude but efficient cider press, run off an electric motor, which produced thousands of litres of cider every autumn: enough to keep us going for the year. *Must* was drunk with all our meals, because the local water was not fit to drink. It was said to produce goitre in the throat, which was no doubt true, since men and women with goitres were a common sight. Therefore a jug of *must* was on the table at every meal, and in between times, too. What never ceased to astonish me was seeing everyone drink from the one jug, even when guests came from Voitsberg, as they sometimes did.

Life was grievously hard for a slave labourer on a farm, working summer and winter without rest, but it was better than in the factories and mines. It felt good to live close to the land and be part of the seasonal round, and the longer I worked there the more I accepted that certain routine jobs, especially caring for the animals, had to be done.

Letters from home were my greatest joy, but they were tinged with pain. My father's were carefully worded so as not to upset me unduly, but I knew from what other relatives and friends wrote that my mother, broken hearted at the loss of her only son, was seriously ill. I tried to keep her alive with hope of a reunion. Every letter and postcard I sent to anyone in Antoniwka ended with the words, 'Please help my darling mother to get well, so she will be there when I return.'

Then, six months or thereabouts after I left home, my father warned me she might not recover. I failed to disguise the pain and frustration I felt at being unable to rush home and be at her side. Even the dullest-witted members of the household were aware of my grief. The normally impassive Mutti, mother of three sons – the third, Pepi, was working in the coalmines in Germany – appeared touched and said she would ask permission for me to return home briefly to see my mother before she died. She knew the Director at the Ministry of Labour in Voitsberg – a one-legged man whose 'social' calls always ended with him carrying away a gift of ham or chicken, so there was a reasonable chance she might get a favourable answer.

This unexpected kindness roused mixed feelings. Wanting nothing more than to see my beloved mother, I nevertheless could not forget the horrors of my original journey from Ukraine. Was all that to be endured again? However, I didn't have to worry long. The authorities curtly refused to consider the matter. For the next weeks I lived only for letters from home.

Then, one winter Sunday, Fedir called early at the farm. With tears in his eyes, for he had known her too, he imparted the news of my mother's death. Father had written to Fedir, saying he would rather I was given the news by someone I knew than have the shock of reading it in a letter. She had, he said, died of a broken heart. My Uncle Dmytro had given him a postcard from me, which he read out to my mother just before she died, so she knew in her last moments how dearly her son Stefan loved her. She was only forty-two.

For a time I wanted to die myself. If she had been heartbroken, so was I. Fedir walked with me that day in the woods and was very kind, but I felt that my life had ended. Everything good – everything kind and beautiful, which gave comfort in times of trouble, had been embodied for me in my mother. In the days that followed, my only comfort was in singing to myself the melancholy German song, full of nostalgia for times past, that perfectly expressed my grief: *Verlassen, verlassen, verlassen...*

In English, it runs:

Forlorn, forlorn, forlorn am I, like a stone on the road.
Forlorn am I.
To my father I cannot go,
My mother I will never see again,
And die I cannot, being so young.
When I die,
Carry me to the graveyard please,
Cover me with earth tight,
Only then shall I have peace.

Long letters I wrote to my father and Lywosi, begging them for every detail of my mother's final days – how she looked and what she said – and of her death and funeral. Beyond that, I found solace in the unremitting labour of the farm.

Out of the rest of that first year on the farm, one event stands out. One day in spring, when I had become sufficiently fluent in the Austrian dialect to imagine that I might pass myself off as a native, I decided I had to take the risk of going to the cinema. Because what did it matter if I were killed? I did not care what happened to me so long as I could spend an afternoon in dreamland!

For months I had been hatching a plan. If asked who I was and where I came from, I could identify myself as Toni, and give the address of the farm. By then I felt sure that Toni, if questioned, would support my story and swear he had gone to the cinema in Voitsberg on the day in question. We were similar enough in age and appearance to pass one for the other. As we worked together in the fields, I broached the subject.

'Toni, I want to go to the cinema so badly, more than anything else on earth! I've heard you talking about films you've seen, but I've never even been inside a cinema. Do you think you could possibly lend me some of your old clothes so I could go – just once – looking like a typical Austrian, and see what it's like?'

Toni laughed. 'You don't mean that, do you?' He looked at me with amazement, but not without a certain admiration. We both knew the risk I would be taking. After considering my proposition for a few moments, smiling to himself, he said, 'Okay. I'll lend you some clothes, but not my old clothes. If you're going to the cinema you'd better go in Sunday best. That way the Gestapo would be less likely to stop you. Let me think about it. I'll work it out so that you can go to the cinema without getting into any trouble. Leave it to me.'

Toni must have spoken to his mother and the rest of the household, because suddenly there was an air of excitement around the farm. A conspiracy was afoot. The realization that Stefan, at fifteen years of age, had never seen a film, was like a challenge. They had decided to play fairy godmother... and make Cinderella ready for the ball – but sensing this made me nervous. Were they fascinated by the novelty of sharing in my experience of what was to them a commonplace occurrence, as curious to hear my reaction as if I were a native of the jungle confronted with modern civilization for the first time? Or were they taking advantage of my ignorance to set me up for a well-deserved beating by the Gestapo: to teach me a lesson as to who was the master race? I did not know them well enough to be sure.

A plan was formulated to which everyone agreed. I was to go to church on the following Sunday morning as usual. Then, in the afternoon, when ordinarily I should have been seeing to the pigs, cows, and horses, before going off to meet my friends, they would dress me up to look like a typical Austrian boy in his Sunday best and send me to the cinema. The routine of the *Ausländers* was well known to the Gestapo, so they would not be looking for any of us among the cinema audience.

The day came and off I went! I did not know what film I was going to see, nor did I know my way round the town. My worst fear was that someone I knew from our Sunday meetings in the forest, a factory worker perhaps, might be walking down the street in Voitsberg and hail me by name, recognizing me in spite of the handsome Austrian apparel. Yet not for one moment did I think of abandoning the project.

As always, the Gestapo were marching up and down the main street of the town, but I soon felt confident that there was no one else who could ever have known me before. I had been given clear directions and recognized the cinema at once. Nevertheless, I approached the doors anxiously, keeping my eyes peeled for any threat. The cinema manager sold me my ticket and a pretty girl in a full skirt and embroidered blouse led me to a seat in the second row of the stalls. The lights were still on and music was playing.

Before I could adjust to my surroundings, however, the hall was abruptly plunged into darkness and I heard the thunder of guns and cannons. Looking up, I saw military tanks, guns ablaze, rolling straight at me and I nearly screamed aloud. Then I heard the commentator's voice and realized this was the Newsreel – I had, of course, heard of such things – showing incredibly vivid scenes of the fighting on what I took to be the Eastern Front. There were scenes of street battles and burning villages, of aircraft leaving hideous trails of destruction. Casualties, wounded and dead, littered the streets, bleeding bundles of rags. Columns of prisoners and refugees dragged themselves painfully along roads banked with dirty snow. It was one of the most terrifying moments of my life, for these tragic events were taking place in front of my eyes, a few metres from where I was sitting. I wanted to shriek as tanks tumbled towards me, full of deadly menace, for, whatever I knew in my head, deep in my bones I did not doubt that I would shortly be mashed dead, like the rest of those flattened corpses. Fortunately I kept my mouth shut and my wits about me.

All that prevented me from running for my life was the knowledge that, if I made a commotion, I would surely be interrogated by the cinema manager or the Gestapo. I hung onto my seat with both hands, reminding myself of the twenty-five or fifty lash punishment I would certainly incur, and made myself endure the noise and pandemonium for as long as it lasted. In particular I banished all thoughts of my own family and what they might now be suffering; if the Russians were driving the Germans back towards the west, what I had seen could have been in Ukraine – the battered towns Lwiw or Stanislawiw, or the burning villages Antoniwka or Oleshiw.

Then, suddenly, it was over and, before I could fully adjust to the change, a love story filled the screen. Gradually, I relaxed and let the enchantment take me over. There, before my very eyes, were people in charming costumes, singing and dancing, while Viennese waltzes and country folk tunes delighted my ears. For the first time, I was part of a world unlike any I had ever known, in which people seemed occupied with smiling and laughing and enjoying themselves.

What beautiful manners they had! How delicately they ate and drank! How graciously they spoke! How gracefully they moved through luxuriously appointed rooms and gardens in which nothing grew but flowers! Were they never hungry, angry or afraid? (The pettishness of the lovely heroine scarcely counted as anger.) Was it possible that people anywhere on our planet lived such a life as the characters on the screen, rustling through their days in silks and satins, dancing to sweet music in a landscape where the sun or moon always shone bright?

I was not so simple that I did not know it was make-believe, yet such convincing make-believe, acted out by flesh-and-blood people with shining hair and sparkling eyes, that I felt transported to a better world. There were even young men dressed as I was that day, in leather trousers and embroidered jacket, and hat with a jaunty feather in it. It told me that life was not just a matter of scraping a living, a matter of armies and the Gestapo trampling over helpless citizens, flogging and imprisoning them and depriving them of all rights. If I could only hold on, as I had held onto my seat in the darkness through the Newsreel, I might find myself inhabiting such scenes as I had been shown: dancing with pretty girls, mingling with aristocrats, wise in the ways of the world and fearless in my encounters with people high and low. I must simply hang on to my aspirations, which could not be denied forever.

As I emerged from the cinema into the light of day, the sun was shining, too. The citizens of Voitsberg were strolling in the streets, minding their own business, in a peaceful Sunday frame of mind. German soldiers were on patrol but even they seemed hardly in a mood to take people into custody.

On air I walked home, feeling infinitely older, wiser and cleaner, as though I had just completed my first day in the University of Life. I had experienced the widest gamut of emotions, the atrocities of war and the paradise of peace and prosperity, the awful reality of man's inhumanity to man, and the bliss of impossible dreams. I was not the same boy as the one who had hesitantly asked to borrow clothes for an afternoon at the cinema. I had been transformed into a world-beater, on my way to the stars.

When I arrived back at the farm I found myself, for the second time, the centre of attention. This time I was able to enjoy it, since I was certainly looking my best. Everyone crowded round me, wanting to know how I had got on and I was flattered and astounded by their curiosity. Mutti quickly hushed them up and hustled us all indoors. 'Get into the kitchen,' she ordered. 'Do you want to advertise Stefan's adventure to every stranger who might be passing?' It was no secret that some of the farmers who lived close by were in the pay of the Nazis and could make trouble for us.

We gathered around the kitchen table with a jug of *must*, as if for some sort of celebration. The farm work was forgotten. Even the small children were infected by the desire to know every detail of what had happened to Stefan that afternoon. With every pair of eyes fixed on me, I began to feel like a film star in my own right, so I satisfied their curiosity as best I could. They laughed uproariously when they heard of my terror as the Newsreel began, and told me I should have paid a little more for my ticket and sat farther back. They seemed surprised and impressed by the strength of my feelings on seeing newsreels of the war now raging in the east. It had never occurred to them that the farmlands, villages and towns being laid waste by opposing armies could have been my home. Until I saw it, I too had been unable to visualize the scenes of devastation wrought by war.

However, the people around the table surprised me with the understanding they showed. I considered them stupid and ignorant of the outside world, yet they seemed ready to agree with me, an enemy alien, about the pointlessness of war... For the first time I realized that they, too, were under strain. Mutti's sons were serving in the German Navy and down in the German mines, while her eldest daughter Frieda's husband was attached to a cavalry division in France. (France has ever since been associated, for me, with the taste of the sardines he brought home with him when he came on leave, which I was allowed to sample.) The things we said among ourselves at that moment, however, were not to be said outside, and I cannot recall that we ever reverted to them again. If we had been reported to the Gestapo, swift retribution would have followed.

'What did you think of the main film, Stefan?' they asked.

I waxed lyrical, recalling every detail of the wonderful, romantic story. I told them in all seriousness that I had learnt a great deal about how people dressed and behaved towards one another in polite society, adding that I hoped to live among such people one day. They did not laugh or take offence, but perhaps they considered for a moment how far their own manners and behaviour fell short of my ideal. By this time we had drunk six or eight jugs full of cider and were getting red in the face. Time to come down to earth.

Mutti expressed satisfaction that I had enjoyed myself so much on my first visit to the cinema and her relief that it had not led to a confrontation with the Gestapo. Her sentiments were echoed in a friendly way by the others. 'However,' she said, 'life must go on.' The entertainment was over, mine and theirs.

That was the signal for me to doff the magnificent clothes and return to my rags. However much I might feel that nothing would ever be the same again, my situation had not altered. It was back into working clothes and off to the stables to feed the horse, cows and pigs. Cinderella was back among the cinders. The future I dreamed of was still a long way off.

Chapter 7

1943-1944
Guest of the Gestapo

One magnificent autumn day, I was ploughing the field with a horse and cow, keeping an eye on the furrow in front of me, when, all of a sudden, I heard a noise and looked up to see four aircraft flying very low overhead. A second later there was the horrendous sound of explosions, as bombs fell on Voitsberg, below me, only a few kilometres away. I expected the animals to bolt, to overturn the plough and cause all kinds of damage, but luckily they just flicked their ears and marched on patiently, dragging the plough, apparently unperturbed and certainly less frightened than I was! We heard afterwards that the bombs, meant for the local power station, had missed their target and fallen harmlessly in nearby fields. No air-raid sirens had sounded; there had been no warning at all.

In the year that followed, we got used to the threat of air-raids. Usually the planes were heading for Graz, some twenty-five kilometres from Voitsberg, and though there might be hundreds of them, they were flying extremely high, leaving a trail of smoke behind them. We would hear the rattle of anti-aircraft guns but they rarely seemed to find their mark. No aircraft that I heard of was shot down near us. There were Austrians who were less than enthusiastic in their support for Hitler. Even the submariner Hansel, when he came home on leave, used to get blinding drunk in Voitsberg and walk home cursing the Führer and the whole German nation, until Toni and I got out of bed, fetched him indoors and hushed him up, lest the neighbours hear him.

Late in the summer of 1943, Mutti died. She fell down the steps one day and broke her hip, and being a very heavy woman, she went down hard. She was taken to hospital to have the hip repaired, but both her age and her size were against her and she never recovered from the operation. I was very sorry. She was a stern, hard woman, but just, and she had occasionally shown me real kindness. Her daughter Frieda, who now took charge, was selfish, vain and very demanding, just when the farm was shorter of workers than ever before.

Though I was quite used to horses, and to riding bareback, one of the most nerve-racking jobs I had to undertake was breaking in a young stallion to fit him for farm work. If I had been brought up on films of the Wild West, like boys my age in many other countries, I might have taken to it more easily, for the method was much the same. I had to gallop the young creature round and round on a long lead, within a fenced enclosure, until he was tired enough so that I could attempt to put a blanket on his back. When he began to kick and buck and rear up in the air, I had to retreat swiftly and leap over the fence before I could be kicked in the face or back and seriously injured. The process had to be repeated until the horse would accept not only a blanket but the harness for the cart or plough. After Toni was called up, in the autumn of 1943, I did this job virtually alone, as I did all the heaviest farm work. In the time I spent on that farm, I broke in three horses.

In the middle of that winter an order came from the Ministry of Labour telling Frieda that, as a patriot ready to make sacrifices for the German Reich, she must send someone to go to work in *Arbeitsdienst*, a 'volunteer' labour force working for the government. By that time Toni was in the army so the 'volunteer' clearly had to be me. *Arbeitsdienst* involved digging trenches and keeping communications open in and around the town of Radkersburg, on the border with Yugoslavia. German forces retreating from the Eastern front, together with a tattered crowd of Russians from the army of General Vlasov, who had recruited his men from among prisoners of war and defected with them to the Nazis, were digging themselves in there to protect southern Austria from invasion by Marshal Tito's partisans. It was midwinter and Radkersburg was located in the mountains, but we were given no extra clothing, either by the Ministry of Labour or by our own employers, though we would be working in snow a metre deep. My orders were to take a shovel and pickaxe and a few personal necessities and go.

When we arrived in Radkersburg – hundreds, perhaps a thousand, of us – we found that there wasn't a single Austrian national among us. Every other nationality under the Nazi yoke was represented, and I was shocked to see girls as well as men. It was blindingly obvious that the foreign workers were looked upon by their masters as totally expendable. We were marched from the railway station to Adolf Hitler Platz, in the town centre, and billeted in a large municipal building. Our beds were bundles of straw; not even a blanket was provided. Fortunately, I had my two blankets with me.

Work digging trenches and clearing the railway lines of snow went on from seven in the morning to six or seven at night. I was put in charge of 100 foreign workers and told to make a list of their names, addresses and employers. I had to keep track of them at all times. We had a roll call every morning.

Our meals were the usual miserable ersatz coffee, black bread, and thin vegetable soup or stew, and had to be fetched by us from a cookhouse on the edge of town. Anything hot was guaranteed to be barely warm by the time it was dished out into the metal containers we ate from. The only redeeming feature of our situation was that, shivering and hungry as we were, we were all the time in the company of our peers, not isolated, and that kept our spirits high.

In the evenings we contrived entertainment for ourselves. A guitar, mouth organ or accordion would be produced from somewhere and we would dance. We were not paid anything for our work, but most of us had a little money and we could raise enough for a few litres of *must* to make us merry. Some of General Vlasov's Russians usually gatecrashed our parties, to find people who spoke their language, but this made trouble more often than not. We had been told to treat them politely, since they were fighting for the German Reich, but few of us respected either the Russians or the Germans. They chatted up our girls, forcing them to dance with them, and that led to fights. One night a Russian soldier drew his knife and went to stab me with it, but I managed to grab his arm and twist it, forcing him to drop the knife and very nearly breaking his arm. We *Ausländers* had practiced self-defence at our meetings in the forest on Sundays.

Other Russian soldiers joined in the fight and, finding myself outnumbered, I slipped away in the mêlée and escaped by jumping out of a window into the deep snow. My right hand was cut and I still have the scar, but it was nothing compared with the damage that might have been done had the Russian got his knife into me!

Next day I was warned that the Russians were out to kill me for having made one of their number look ridiculous. I refused to worry, feeling sure I could take care of myself so long as not too many of them attacked me at once, but it felt like the last straw. The situation in Radkersburg was intolerable. Life on the farm was miserable enough, but I had at least the satisfaction of doing productive work, far preferable to this. After four or five weeks' service, I saw no reason why I should clear railways and dig trenches in defence of Austria any longer. It was tempting to think of escape into another country, but that would almost surely end in death, so all I could do was return to the farm. I packed my belongings, told a few of my friends that I was going, and left. My identification as one of the workers on *Arbeitsdienst* was sufficient to get me onto a train.

Frieda looked surprised when I turned up, even though she had been warned to expect me, and she pestered me with a lot of questions about my time in Radkersburg. I told her what it was like, trying at the same time to give the impression that my return was perfectly in order. I said I had completed my service and hurried back because I knew how much work there was to be done on the farm, now that there was no other man to do it. She and the other women were so relieved to have me back that they accepted my version of events at face value. I resumed work as before and nothing more was said.

Friends in the area gave me a warm welcome and all the latest news. Our travel restrictions had been eased, so that we could now go thirty kilometres without having to get permission from the Gestapo or Bürgermeister. This meant that the camps set up for foreign workers employed in factories were no longer out of bounds; we could visit them whenever we had a few hours off. We could also visit the prisoner of war camps under certain conditions and, on the few occasions when we did so, we were admitted without fuss. We enjoyed talking to these older men from England, France and Italy, who shared our misery and daily humiliations but who had skills and experience, and regaled us with stories of places far beyond our ken. They were envious of us working on farms, since most of them were employed in the coal mines and were perpetually famished. Their rations were the same as those for foreigners doing light work in the open air, whereas they spent extremely long, punishing hours deep underground.

We began to consider whether we could do anything for these prisoners, since few of them spoke fluent German and there was no one to speak for them. We farm workers had grown up under regimes, which though oppressive, were nevertheless made up of men who would sometimes listen to a reasonable case, if it were put to them politely. Surely it would do no harm to enquire whether these prisoners might not be entitled to the food coupons issued to people doing heavy, not light, work. How often I had heard my father discussing the best, most tactful, approach to the authorities in a like situation! And he had had notable successes among his many disappointments.

Inevitably, I was elected spokesman. We agreed that I should go to the offices of the Ministry of Labour and say that the prisoners of war accepted the conditions in their camp except for the fact that they did not get enough to eat. Not enough, that is, considering the heavy work they performed in the coalmines. What could be more reasonable?

I had nothing to lose. By early spring of 1944 it seemed as though the war would never end and I was exceedingly restless. I carried out all the heavy work of the farm, and much of the light work, too. When the farmer, at my urging, had scraped together enough money to dig for her own water, it was I who laboured, digging down to a depth of fifteen or twenty metres, until a trickle of water appeared. It was I who installed the concrete casing and pipes, comforting myself with the knowledge that it would save those daily trips into the forest with the water barrel. I was the only one who could do such things. What gave me a deep sense of grievance, however, was the fact that the women imposed work on me that they were perfectly capable of doing themselves, and had previously done. Toni would have refused, but I could not. Yet, when I pointed out that I needed more to eat, being a big fellow and still growing, no notice was taken of my complaints. I still had to resort to stealing what I could. Perhaps it was my anger at the utter indifference of the farm people to me as an individual that made me take the risk of speaking up on behalf of the soldiers in the prisoner of war camp.

I knew my way around Voitsberg quite well by then, having lived in the area for almost two years, and listened to people talking. I knew how best to approach people in authority, and who was considered trustworthy and who not. I suppose, consciously or unconsciously, I was re-enacting my father's persistent, unflagging struggles with officialdom when I set out for the offices of the Ministry of Labour. I asked to see the director, the one-legged man who used to come to the farm to see Mutti, and went away with gifts of fruit, lard, chicken and ham for himself and his family. It was to him she had appealed, though in vain, when my mother was on the point of death.

'What is your business?' his clerk demanded.

'It is a private matter with Herr Direktor,' I replied.

'You will have to wait then.'

'I am quite prepared to do that.'

There were no benches to sit on while waiting, so I stood, or paced up and down, for the hour or more it took till I was called in to see the director.

'I was going to send for you, Stefan,' he said, without a smile. 'What have you come to me for?'

Wondering why on earth he should have wanted to see me, whether to offer me a transfer to another farm or to admonish me for some misdemeanour, I explained my business. He barely heard me out before saying curtly, 'Go back to the waiting room and stay there.' He offered no reason, nor did he say what he had previously wanted with me.

I paced up and down as before. Something was looming and I felt apprehensive. Half an hour later, two formidable members of the Gestapo entered the waiting room. They looked hard at me and went through into the director's office, scarcely pausing to knock. Fifteen minutes later they emerged and said, 'Come with us.'

I looked at them and back at the door of the director's office, which was now shut. 'Where?' I asked, assuming that the director must have some say in the matter. They simply took up positions on either side of me and repeated the word 'come' with growing impatience, leaving me no option but to accompany them. I was terrified. If the director had simply wanted to kick me out of his office, he would surely not have had to get two large Gestapo officers to do it.

They marched me straight through Voitsberg to Gestapo Headquarters, the most dreaded building in the town, where I was told I was under arrest and made to sign a form which they then filled in. From there, I was marched to a building I recognized as the prison. There I was ordered to take off my belt, and the string that held up my underpants, remove the laces from my shoes, and hand over any matches I might be carrying. Driven to tears of desperation as I realized the hopelessness of my situation, I begged them to tell me what I had been arrested for.

At first they would not answer. Then one of the Gestapo officers relented and explained,

'Since you must know, you have grossly exceeded your rights! That's why we're holding you. Who do you think you are to intercede for prisoners of war? You are an *Ausländer*, a nobody. You have no business even going to their camp. You should concentrate on doing the job to which you have been assigned and doing it well, so that no complaints are made against you. It's not your place to criticize.'

Then I understood. I never knew whether my defection from the *Arbeitsdienst* had added to the sum of my crimes.

Panic enveloped me as I was led away. Was I in line for the twenty-five or the fifty lashes? Clearly they could do whatever they liked with me. My friends would not know where I was and my farmer, Frieda, would not interfere. She had been suspicious of me ever since I returned from Radkersburg. She would be told, in any case, that nothing could be gained by enquiring into my disappearance.

The panic, which by now had numbed my fingertips and toes, only worsened when I realized that I was about to be imprisoned. Panic left me, and horror moved in; then horror left me as, with a shove from behind, I was introduced to a dark and near-empty cell. Briefly my heart also emptied; I had no idea what to do, what to feel. For the time being, hope had abandoned me. I turned to my tormentors and tried to protest, but all I received in reply was a vicious snarl of a smile. Quickly I closed my mouth.

'Did you see that charred door on your left as we came in?' my gaoler asked. 'And do you smell that burning smell?'

'Yes.' The answer was the same to both questions.

I was warned to be a model prisoner by means of a powerful anecdote. The guard told me about a Polish detainee who had tried to burn down the door of his own cell the night before, but had suffocated in the smoke. The guard even showed me the cell in question, at my request; but I was soon back to where it was assumed I belonged, with my heart dipping slowly. As my heart sank down into my chest, I stopped momentarily, bowed my head and said to myself 'you shall not be forgotten'.

The door was slammed. The defeat felt total. My eyes were prickling, heavy with unshed tears. I turned on the spot, round and round. Did I thump on the door and scream about civil liberties or human rights? I did not; for young as I was, I knew that the situation could be made even worse, possibly by physical punishment followed by long, thoughtful hours in solitude, or possibly by a bullet.

I tried very hard to relax, and to take in my surroundings; the wooden bed chained to the wall (as if I would try to steal it!); the bucket. I sat down on the bed, my head cradled heavily in my hands.

Chapter 8

Spring 1944
In a Nazi Gaol

Each day after that followed the same dreary pattern. I got up and chained my bed to the wall. Then, there being no mattress, only a blanket, I sat on the concrete floor, using the blanket for a coat as well as a cushion. If I wanted to look out, I had to jump up and grab the window bars and hoist myself up by my arms, but there was another black-painted wall a few metres from the window, so there was nothing worth seeing. Breakfast was ersatz coffee and a slice of black bread, lunch a disgusting soup, and dinner some sort of goulash or stew, with a lump or two of meat and a slice of bread. I was not permitted to unchain my bed and lie down again until nine o'clock at night.

The cell was cold; it was still only March. Frantic for some exercise I did push-ups, pull-ups and stretching exercises to keep warm and to pass the time. The bucket was always in the way. It had no lid and got smellier as the day went on. Emptying and washing it in the morning was no great penance. I had been doing that for years on the farm and was used to it; but what I really hated was having no opportunity to wash myself or clean my teeth. On the farm I had no toothbrush, nothing to clean my teeth with but wood-ash rubbed on with my finger, but now I could not wash at all.

The worst thing, however, was not knowing what the penalty for my supposed crimes might be – whether I must expect to be beaten or tortured or shot. How long was my imprisonment likely to last? Was my appeal to the director at the Ministry of Labour the sole grounds for that imprisonment? Had I been quoted making some subversive remark? Or was I being punished for clearing off from my spell of *Arbeitsdienst* without permission? It was most of all the uncertainty that threatened my sanity. I felt so despondent at times that I feared I might attack my gaoler in a fury of frustration and so increase my punishment. My future looked so black that I would have had little compunction about killing anyone in Gestapo uniform, had I possessed a knife.

I spent most of my days reliving the past, going over the events of my childhood in Antoniwka as if re-running a film that was a faithful record of every moment; every conversation with my parents and sister, every exchange with friends and teachers. I walked through the village, reminding myself of each house and garden and the people who lived there. I strolled through the orchards, first in blossom, then hanging with apples, plums, pears and cherries, tasting them all, and combed the hills for wild flowers and mushrooms. I worshipped in our wooden village church, entering it hand-in-hand with Lywosi, both of us in our Sunday best. I recited the lines from a school play called *Rusalka Poltawka,* a Ukrainian fairy tale about a mermaid. I recalled afternoons in the forest with the other deportees, learning to play the mouth organ and accordion, practising self-defence. It seemed inconceivable, surfacing from such dreams, that I could be sitting on the cold, damp concrete floor of a Nazi gaol, with no crime behind me and yet no prospect of release.

For entertainment – to kill the hours – I tried yodelling and I rehearsed my entire repertoire of songs; the cheerful and romantic, patriotic and comic, as well as the sad and the nostalgic. Over and over I sang the mournful song, *Verlassen, verlassen, verlassen...* Humming tunes, I practised the steps of Ukrainian dances.

I remembered the hard-bitten people on the farm, careless of my wellbeing for the most part, yet occasionally capable of kindness. The previous autumn, one of the granddaughters, Anna, aged about fifteen, began to collect discarded bits of woollen fabric or knitwear, and cut them into strips. Her grandmother had asked her to make me some slippers for my Christmas present. I watched her twisting the strips into a sort of yarn which she wove, basket-fashion, into the shape of slippers that would come right up over my ankles. This was a magnificent gift, the slippers were an immense comfort when I came into the kitchen from the snowy fields on frozen feet. I would take off my clogs and the soaked rags or paper with which they were stuffed, slip my feet into those wonderful soft slippers and walk around in their luxurious warmth. I was most grateful to the family, who genuinely couldn't afford to buy me anything, and those slippers were very special. Such happy days seemed very far away.

The attic where the mice had scampered over me, or the cowshed where I slept in winter – even the insufficient meals and unceasing heavy labour – seemed desirable compared with what I was enduring. I would go over, item by item, each dish put on the table for Sunday dinner – the dumplings and puddings and cherry pies and sweet pancakes, the stewed apples, rhubarb, and pears and the splendid torten. Thinking about them would lift my spirits briefly, then plunge me into deeper desolation.

I turned back to memories of home. Even the beatings my father inflicted when I failed to do something he required of me seemed wreathed in an atmosphere of kindness. I thought lovingly of Lywosi, my sister, who had been taken ill a few months back. My father had written to say how worried he had been about her. Strange to relate, it was a German doctor who made her better, an army officer whose unit was withdrawing from the Eastern Front through Ukraine. Under no circumstances was he permitted to treat civilians, yet somehow he had heard about my sister and taken pity on her. He had given her the medicine she required. Thanks to that German, my father could report that there were still three of our little family alive when he had feared there would be only two.

In the last letter I had received, my father described how he had been taken off to be shot. Two German soldiers had picked him up as he was returning from the brickworks to my grandfather's house. They accused him of being a Ukrainian partisan and said they intended to shoot him in the yard of the house. They marched him there and stood him against the wall, preparing to shoot him. But by a miracle, a German officer arrived and asked what was going on. When they told him, he said, 'That is nonsense. This man is no partisan. I've been billeted in this village for six months and I know him. He's a good citizen.' He ordered the soldiers to put away their guns and release my father. He was beaten up by the soldiers, nevertheless – a second choice, as it were – and I worried that they would return later to shoot him anyway, for it turned out that the officer did not know my father at all. He was simply disgusted by the actions of the SS, and was trying to prevent further bloodshed.

It's fair to say that I both longed for and dreaded the arrival of letters. A letter, of course, was a lifeline to the outer world – to the world I feared I had viewed for the last time – but a letter might also bring grave news. Not many missives were received, however: mail from Ukraine had now all but ceased. To get a letter, someone needed to travel into Austria and agree to take the risk of posting letters confided to them. Occasionally, even retreating German soldiers would promise to do so in return for a loaf of bread, but no one knew if the letters found their destination. Day by day I wondered if I would ever hear from my father again.

Constantly I dreamed of escape, of getting out of my prison and running so fast my feet would scarcely touch the ground! I tried to plot my escape route. In Radkersburg we had been close to the Yugoslav border. The partisans there would surely have helped me, or if I could find my way to Switzerland, which was neutral, I would be safe. We had heard that Italy was falling to the Allies. It might be possible to join the British or American forces there but these fantasies were based on little more than rumour. I had no access to hard facts about the war's progress.

Every day I asked my gaoler when I was going to be released, and every day he told me to shut up and do as I was told. I had nothing to write with so, to keep track of the days, I loosened one tiny thread of my blanket each morning, in such a way that I could count the threads. By the second week, I began to wonder whether my crime was greater than I supposed, since it took so long to prepare the case against me. Such thoughts were unnerving, until I reminded myself sternly to put my trust in God. I said prayers three times a day, always in Ukrainian. God was my only hope.

After lunch one day, in the middle of the third week, a new member of the Gestapo came into my cell. He had a revolver in his holster and carried a gun with its bayonet pointed at me. He gave me back the string, shoe laces and belt which I had surrendered and ordered me to put them on quickly, which I did with shaking hands. Whether it was freedom that beckoned, or a beating, or even death, at least I was leaving that loathsome cell.

Ordering me to keep about two metres in front of him, and not to look round nor think of escape, since the gun was loaded, he marched me back to Gestapo Headquarters.

It was heady to breathe some fresh clean air again and to see people going about their ordinary business, talking, riding bicycles and boarding buses. However, this moment of freedom was brief. Soon behind bars again, I was locked in a basement cell, although it was clear that I would not be there long since the cell was stacked full of wood and old furniture and was obviously a temporary lock-up. My fate would surely be to move again soon and I feared flogging or execution, not knowing what to expect. Despite my faith, it had needed only this storage room, with myself reduced to the status of useless timber, for me to fear the worst.

After about half an hour, the door opened and I was handed a pick and shovel and led outside. This time a member of the Gestapo was in step on either side of me, fully armed. Since they refused to tell me where we were going or why, greeting my questions with silence and staring straight ahead, I jumped to the sinister conclusion that I was being taken out of town to dig my own grave before being shot. It was patently obvious. We heard of it happening often. It was the simplest way to deal with inconvenient prisoners, whose loss would be of no consequence. It was difficult to keep walking.

When we reached a secluded place newly planted with young trees, like a recently laid out cemetery, one of the Gestapo officers ordered me to start digging. Staring me hard in the eye, he said, 'Make the hole about one metre in diameter and a metre deep. Do you understand?'

I needed no further urging. His words were the sweetest, most reassuring I could possibly have heard. This was no grave I was digging. It was the hole for another young tree! In spite of being cooped up for two-and-a-half weeks on inadequate rations, I went at my work with the speed and power of a mechanical digger. My prayers had been heeded; God had protected me. I would gladly have dug my way to China! I shifted the earth so energetically that the two Gestapo men looked on with surprise and admiration. Six holes were dug before we returned to Gestapo headquarters.

I was given back the few remaining odds and ends taken from me when I was arrested, and told to return to my farm. Not to stay there, however, but to pack up everything and report back to the Ministry of Labour at 8 o'clock the following morning, when I would be transferred to another farm. Even at the moment of exulting in my release, I found that a cruel blow. I dared not enquire whether Farmer Frieda had asked to have me moved or, if so, why. Although the people on the farm often treated me contemptuously, calling me *Ostarbeiter* or *Schweinhund*, as if I were without human feelings, I could not see how they would manage without me. I had hoped to remain there until the war ended. It was a shock to find that I might have to leave the only home I knew and be parted from the only friends I had.

To this day I cannot get over my anger at the manner of my departure from there. When I turned up after my spell in prison, no one on the farm asked me any questions or offered any explanation. I was not shown the slightest sympathy, though they obviously knew what had happened. Perhaps they had been told not to speak to me. The customary greeting, '*servus*', was given in a tight-lipped way, not looking me in the eye, and when I told them I was to be transferred to another farm, they showed no trace of regret, although I had been with them by now for almost two years. Nor did they attempt to counteract my anxiety at being sent, God knows where, out of reach of my friends. I saw more plainly than ever before that, in spite of all I had done to keep the farm going, they regarded me as they might have a machine; serviceable but perfectly capable of being replaced by another. No one cared what became of me. They did not even provide the usual supper that night and I went up to my attic without a kind word or a bite to eat, all but annihilated by their indifference.

Nevertheless, they woke me at five the following morning to get up and see to the animals. From the stables, I slipped into the cowshed of the farm next door to say goodbye to Marion. He sat on his milking stool looking horrified at the story I had to tell, and very sorry to see me go. 'It'll be lonely without you, Stefan, but it could happen to any of us,' he commented glumly. 'We have no control over our destiny.' He was the only one of my friends to learn what had happened. After that, I packed my little wooden case, parted formally with Frieda and the rest of the household, and left. My only mementos of my time as their slave were a postcard from another *Ostarbeiter* addressed to me at the farm and a photograph of Hansel in his German Navy uniform, which I decided to keep.

When I arrived at the Ministry of Labour in Voitsberg at 8 o'clock, Herr Tiszler, the new farmer to whom I was assigned, was already there. He was a short, thick-set, strong-looking man in his fifties, with a pleasantly straightforward manner. Together we boarded the train to a place called Stallhofen, about ten kilometres to the south-east, nearer Graz. He was not very talkative but by now I spoke the Austrian dialect like a native, so I had none of my earlier difficulty in communicating with him. When we reached the farm, however, I still found it hard to understand some of the older people, who spoke in a distinctive patois of their own. A lot of elderly people were working there, too old to serve in the army but capable of keeping a farm in good working order. The farm itself was on level ground and much larger than my previous farm, with a more prosperous air. The amount of farm equipment made me wary at first, as I had been led to believe that only members of the Nazi party were lucky enough to get up-to-date farm machinery. However, on further acquaintance, I doubted whether these people were fervent Nazis.

I shared a bedroom with four other men – Austrians, who for one reason or another were unfit for military service. One had a limp, one poor eyesight, one was slightly backward mentally and the fourth was too old. We each had a bed of our own and, although the older man snored, he would stop when the others shouted, 'Still!' Our sleeping arrangements were infinitely homelier, friendlier, and more civilized than the attic I had been used to. Better still, I soon found that the workers on that farm got plenty to eat – jacket potatoes with butter every morning for breakfast, along with maize porridge and second helpings on occasion.

Herr Tiszler was fair-minded and God-fearing. At mealtimes, with ten to fifteen people sitting together around a long table, he would stand at one end, remove his hat, which he wore at all other times to make him look taller than he was, and say grace before sitting down. During meals, he and the others asked me countless questions about the farm I had come from. They could hardly believe it when I told them how much work I had carried out single-handed, such as digging the well, killing pigs, ploughing fields and breaking horses. On this farm I had no specific responsibilities, merely being expected to give a helping hand to the older people as required. When they learnt that I was not yet seventeen, and had had to sleep in the cowshed to avoid freezing to death in the winter, they became indignant on my behalf. All the same, they made allowances, knowing it was not easy for women to maintain a farm on their own when the men were away at war. As if to make up for my earlier hardships, they went out of their way to assign me agreeable work, the kind of jobs they might have given to their sons or grandsons; just walking behind the plough or sitting on a tractor collecting up bundles of hay or sacks of fruit. It was like a holiday after the back-breaking drudgery I had been used to. We still worked a six-day week, with a half day on Sunday, but we got up an hour later and the daily routine was never onerous.

Even so, I pined for the company of my friends in the Voitsberg area, and missed the church there. In their kindly way, the farm people noticed this. I had told them about our meetings in the forest and one of the old men offered to lend me his bicycle. 'If you look after it, you can take it and cycle to church on a Sunday in Voitsberg and then go singing and dancing with your friends. I trust you to be careful, and young people should make merry while they can.'

A wonderfully generous gesture – for the Gestapo might have dealt harshly with him, as well as with me, if I were caught and revealed where the bicycle came from. The old man seemed willing to take that risk and certainly I was. The tide of the war was turning against Germany and certain rules had been relaxed. For example, those of us who had been born in western Ukraine while it was occupied by Poland no longer had to wear OST (*Ostarbeiter* – Eastern Worker) labels, being designated, unlike our fellow nationals from eastern Ukraine, as part of the German Reich. Bicycles were still forbidden, however, so I took great care to avoid the Gestapo and any of those Nazi-sympathizers who took pride in the swastikas pinned to their lapels. With suitable precautions I used the bike often, not only on Sundays but when we finished work in the evenings, sometimes as late as eight or nine o'clock. It took me about an hour each way to go to Voitsberg and I could be back at the farm by midnight.

By mid-summer 1944 I felt quite at home on the farm, though I was careful to work hard and behave well. However, my new friends were concerned at my lack of other young company. One Sunday the farmer said to me: 'Stefan, you're a good boy. You do everything we ask you to and you are very capable, but we can't help noticing you're forlorn. I'm going to find out if there are any farmers nearer Voitsberg who are looking for a worker – somewhere where you would see your friends. I could recommend you and assure the Ministry of Labour that I am willing to let you go.'

I accepted this offer gratefully. I was indeed lonely for, in addition to being separated from my *Ausländer* friends, there had been no word at all from home. I did not know whether the Germans had finally shot my father as they retreated, or whether the Russians, who had now occupied the area, were deporting the population to Siberia. On top of all that, bombing raids over Graz and Vienna were increasing all the time, making our nerves jagged, causing all of us to fear for our lives. So many British and American planes came flying over, that they often shut out the sun. When they came at night, bombers dropped flares to guide them to their targets. 'Christmas trees' we called those flares, seeing how they lit up the night sky. The raids were terrifying and did considerable damage to outlying farms.

Of course the raids also gave hope of an Allied victory. I took no pleasure in the death of people, even those who had made me suffer, nor did I enjoy the destruction of towns and cities, but they showed that a German capitulation was certain. At the same time, I never ceased worrying about what I would do when the war was over. What if Antoniwka had been destroyed and my family wiped out? What if no one I knew lived there any more? Would I want to return to Ukraine? I still retained my early scholastic ambition to make something of my life, to pursue my education and become, perhaps, a professor of history or geography. Would the pursuit of learning ever again be possible in Ukraine? One reason I longed to be with my friends was to talk about such things, make plans together and decide how we might rebuild our lives when the war was over.

Then, at the end of October, the farmer told me that a transfer had been arranged. I was going to a farm near Voitsberg.

Chapter 9

Spring 1945
The Russians Again

On the day I left the farm, everyone present shook my hand in a friendly way or embraced me, and wished me well. The last person to say goodbye was Herr Tiszler.
'Good luck, Stefan. If you're unhappy there and feel you'd like to come back to us, let me know. You'd always be welcome to return and I'm sure I could arrange the transfer.'

He gave me a letter of introduction and said: 'Report to the Gestapo here before you board the train, and again when you arrive. This paper should make everything clear. God bless you. I don't think you will have any trouble.'

Nor did I. At the Gestapo Headquarters in Voitsberg a chill went down my spine when I was recognized by one of the men, who gave me a sharp look and said, 'So you're back again, Terlezki! I trust you're not going to stir up more trouble. The gaol is still there, so behave yourself. Do you understand?' Without speaking, I nodded and left, thanking my lucky stars he knew nothing of my bicycle rides. Already I felt happier, back in the familiar surroundings of Voitsberg. It was a pleasant late autumn day, with most of the leaves fallen from the trees. As I walked out to the new farm, I could see it in the distance, one of a number set on a hillside, with orchards and woodland surrounding it, a smallholding like many I had known in Ukraine.

The farmer turned out to be a friendly young woman in her late twenties called Gretel, slightly built with short, straight, blonde hair, blue eyes and a mass of freckles. Her throat was thickened by a goitre, something not uncommon in those parts. Two very small children – one a toddler, one barely able to crawl – clung closely to her. When I knocked on the kitchen door, she gave me a warm welcome, and after drawing me into the house and showing me to a seat at the kitchen table, she offered me *must* to drink while telling me everything I needed to know about the farm. Evidently she was delighted to have someone to talk to. The little boys regarded me with deep suspicion but they were attractive children and looked well cared for. I would make friends with them in time, I was certain.

Their mother eyed me with misgivings. In her direct way she said,

'You don't look very old. I was told I'd be sent a man to take charge of the farm. My husband's away in Germany, in the Wehrmacht, and the hired man, Karl, is a good worker, but not right in the head, so he needs strong supervision. I really need someone to take responsibility for running the farm and making sure that everything is done. You'd have to keep on the right side of Karl, too. He's touchy. You mustn't tease him or provoke him – he's quick to take offence – but if you can avoid quarrelling with him, he's trustworthy and will do whatever he is told.'

I felt pleased to be taken into her confidence like that. I had only just turned seventeen, and had had it easy, being treated like a boy, on the previous farm, but when I described the work I had had to do single-handed on the first farm, Gretel looked satisfied and declared, 'Well, then, I don't expect we shall have any problems.'

The prospect of shouldering more responsibility did not worry me, since now I would have a grown man to work with. While she showed me photographs of her husband who looked nearly twice as old as she was, and chatted on about the farm and her family, I was envisaging the possibility of getting a whole Sunday free now and then, enough time to visit even those friends who lived at a distance. Karl apparently did the milking and looked after the animals, rarely leaving the farm. However, I knew I would have to build a good relationship with him before broaching the subject. My new farmer seemed unlikely to object so long as our work went smoothly.

Karl turned out to be a strange fellow, eyeing me obliquely and saying little. Once we had been introduced, he took me round the farm, showing me where everything was kept and pointing out the most urgent jobs. He seemed glad to know I would make the decisions, which were a worry to him, and we got down to work straight away, getting the last of the harvest in. Then we set to on the maintenance work, which had been sorely neglected over the last year or so. Ploughs, scythes and other bits of equipment had to be cleaned, sharpened and mended. We carried out repairs to the farmhouse and outbuildings, mending roofs, replacing rotting boards, stopping leaks, filling in holes. It was all within my capabilities, given a second pair of hands to assist me, and I did it willingly, happy in the knowledge that there was no one standing over me to tell me I had done it wrong.

The farm was the smallest and least prosperous of the three I had worked on, and the food was not especially good – there was only Gretel to do the cooking – but we had enough to eat, which was what mattered most. I had a properly furnished bedroom all to myself, with two big windows giving a view of distant mountains, and a looking glass and reindeer heads on the wall. I could draw water to wash with from the kitchen pump, heating it on the stove when necessary, and I was treated with decent respect, more as an employee than a slave.

Nevertheless, it was a lonely life and I worried about my family. I had heard nothing from my father since the German withdrawal from Ukraine. Sometimes, late at night, I tuned in to a Swiss radio station for news of the war's progress, although Ukraine was seldom mentioned. However, I learned about the liberation of France, Italy and the Low Countries.

The Gestapo called in at the farm once or twice to check up on me and received a glowing account of the improvements I was carrying out, which made me smile. As the farmer's husband was away fighting for the Fatherland, they had no choice but to congratulate her on the fact that the farm was being adequately maintained and would remain productive, and express satisfaction that she had someone in the house able to protect her.

The atmosphere was easy-going. Lots of friends called in to see Gretel, none of them Nazis, and their conversations were open and unguarded. Everyone talked about the war. With bombers coming over almost daily on their way to Graz and Vienna, and German soldiers pouring back from the Eastern Front, it was increasingly obvious that the Allies were winning. These country people just wanted the war to end, so their men could come home. They cared surprisingly little that they were on the losing side, though they must have known the region would probably be occupied by the Russians. They did not know as I did what a Russian occupation would mean.

Gretel – at her request I soon began calling her by her given name – sometimes asked me what I planned to do when the war was over. Would I consider staying on to help her husband when he returned? Not knowing what the world would be like when peace finally came, I could not commit myself. All I could say was that I had to go home to see my family and consult them before I could decide anything about my future, which she said she understood.

The nearness of liberation was hard to discern through the chill and the snow which fell in the months before spring. The days grew short. On these winter evenings, families from neighbouring farms often came to play cards and drink cider and dance, or we would visit them. There were cheerful young people of about my own age, and we had good times together. For the first time, I felt accepted among Austrian people as one of them, making that farm the nearest thing to a home I had known for years. This gave me an incentive to look after the place and take pride in it.

Finally the spring arrived and while hope sluiced the air, my *Ausländer* friends and I speculated, like everyone else, on which army would march into Voitsberg first. Needless to say, no one wanted it to be the Russians.

For the first time our employers showed some interest in what our lives had been like in 1939, when the Red Army occupied our countries. We could speak openly about this without offending the Gestapo, and told them how oppressive the Russian regime had been, how rough, unkempt and uncivilized the Russian soldiers had seemed to us, and how they had stripped our shops of consumer goods. No exaggeration was necessary when we recounted how farmers had had their land collectivized and confiscated without compensation, and how many of them were exiled to Siberia. It could be said that we were getting our own back on the enemy by frightening them with our gruesome stories, but we were only speaking the truth. Like us, they began to hope the other Allies would march into Voitsberg first.

It was strange, at church on Sunday mornings, to find that the Gestapo, instead of haranguing us with their propaganda, took little notice of the foreign workers. Some of them had even begun to make friendly overtures to us, dropping hints that we could take trains or borrow bicycles to visit our friends without fear of arrest, and asking if we were being properly fed and looked after by our employers. Our tormentors were plainly worried by the thought of what we might say about them to whoever assumed authority next.

As the snow melted from the mountains, I felt physically lighter; lighter on my feet, just from knowing that the end of the war was near. No longer did I feel subservient to anyone. I had no particular sense of obligation even to my farmer, though she was kind and I continued to do my work. Neither officials, administrators, nor Nazi sympathizers held any terrors for me now. Fit, and with the ability to defend myself, I considered myself a free man at last, on the brink of a wonderful journey. No one could stand in the way of my return to Ukraine.

Meanwhile, the problem for the entire population was to survive the turmoil. Voitsberg and the surrounding country were in imminent danger of military invasion from both east and west. No one knew better than I how little distinctions of nationality counted at such times! Bullets rake streets with absolute impartiality. A strange mixture of expectancy and apprehension hung over everything we said or did.

Deserters from the German Army who had avoided surrender to the Russians turned up at the farm almost daily in search of food. They openly admitted they had deserted and hoped to escape through the hills and forests to somewhere behind the British or American lines. They declared it would be only a matter of weeks until Germany capitulated.

Some of them were Austrians, Czechs, Hungarians, but I avoided contact with these men, unable to fraternize with any person, officer or man, who had worn a German uniform. Who knew what atrocities they might have committed, even in Antoniwka, during their time on the Eastern Front? With my mother dead and no knowledge of what had befallen my father and sister, full of bitterness as I recalled my own experience in a Nazi gaol, I could not look them in the face. I would not have turned them in to the authorities, but I would not help them either. Let them fend for themselves! They were, however, welcome harbingers of Hitler's imminent collapse.

When, on 8 May 1945, the German surrender was finally announced and Voitsberg still stood, my friends and I met one another with tears of joy streaming down our faces, Peace at last! Home was on all our lips. Some of us had suffered brutality from farmers, factory owners or the local Gestapo, who now feared retribution, but we were not concerned with plotting revenge. No one wanted anything but to pick up the small bits of luggage we had brought with us and go back where we had come from.

It was a relief to have the blue skies above us silent, cleared and cleaned of bombers, and to hear fewer reports of shootings and destruction. Everywhere we went people were drinking together to celebrate the end of the war and the defeat of Nazism. Every *Gasthaus*, however solemnly it had claimed there was not a drop of drink in its cellars, unearthed bottomless supplies of wine, beer and schnapps. People reserved their proclamations of allegiance, however, until it became clear which nation was to be the occupying power.

I told Gretel I wanted to leave for home as soon as possible. In tears, she begged me to stay at least until her husband returned, so that she would have some protection from the occupying army. Without me, she said, she could not manage the farm or feed herself and her children. Though sorry for them, I was adamant. I couldn't allow pity to hamper my movements now. My prime duty was to go home and find out what had become of my own family.

Anxiously we waited to see whose forces would march into Voitsberg.

My friends and I prayed that it might be the British or Americans. However, we heard that the Russians had occupied Graz, so it would be no surprise to see the Red Flag flying over Voitsberg, and the NKVD installed in the Gestapo headquarters. The Austrians grew apprehensive, with reason, since many of them had been loyal Nazis, but we were uneasy, too. The Russians might accuse foreign workers of having collaborated with the Germans. Slaves or not, we had helped produce food and factory goods, including ammunition.

Our worst fears were realized: Russian soldiers marched into Voitsberg. We had never guessed that so many Austrian Communists had stubbornly remained underground! Now, these ran up the hammer and sickle on public buildings. No one could say whether they had been part of a genuine resistance force or were mere opportunists, swift to capitalize on events.

We abandoned our farms to meet in Voitsberg and watch what was going on. Would the soldiers be any different from those we had known in Ukraine in 1939? Would six years of contact with the cultures of central Europe have improved their manners and their respect for life? Had they been civilized at all by the example of the people whose countries they had invaded? We asked these questions in deadly earnestness, feeling that, as our liberators from the evil of Nazism, they must be an improvement on the Russians we had known in the past.

The hell they were! The sons of Stalin were true to form. Straight away the soldiers, in groups of a dozen or more, started looting the shops, sweeping down a street on stolen or confiscated bicycles, in stolen cars, or driving horses and carts they had grabbed from their owners, and breaking the windows of a shop. If it was a jewellery shop, they would go in and emerge with a dozens of watches strapped to their arms and stuffed into their trouser pockets. Laughing uproariously – for they were often drunk as well – they would roll up the sleeves of their shabby uniforms to display them to bystanders. Clothes shops were also looted; I saw with my own eyes Russian soldiers stealing armfuls of men's and women's clothing and shoes. They raided the hairdressers and chemists for bottles of perfume and all other kinds of toiletries. We once saw them actually drinking eau de cologne, proud to be smelling good, and preening themselves before the local girls. If they could not seduce them, they would resort to brute force. Recalling my indoctrination at school, I wondered if Father Stalin would be proud of his sons behaving like this, or whether he would rather execute them on the spot.

Several hundred foreign workers who had been scattered throughout the area began to assemble in and around Voitsberg. We wanted to put our case for repatriation before the Russians, but did not know how to go about it. Only a high-ranking officer, such as a commissar or *politeruk*, a political indoctrination officer, would have the authority to take positive action on our behalf. His underlings might well be drunk or malicious, and amuse themselves by labelling us traitors or collaborators. Furthermore, if our first request were refused, what then? Some said we would be wiser to walk off right away and seek sanctuary with the British, whose army was only a few kilometres to the west in Köflach. Would we be allowed to cross over into their zone of occupation? Probably not. No one knew what to do for the best. If we made our approach too soon, the officer might be too busy to deal with us. On the other hand, if we delayed too long before putting our case, it might look suspicious, as though we were not genuine victims of the Nazis with a perfect right to be sent home.

The more of us there were when we made our appeal to the Russians, the more likely it was to succeed, we decided. If we went in small groups, they might try to trap us into informing on local people or incriminating one another. We knew how such interrogations were conducted. Although there were people we would be glad to see locked up we did not want anything to delay our departure.

On a given day, more than 100 of us assembled in Voitsberg, from Poland, Byelorussia, the Baltic States, Ukraine, Georgia, Turkmenistan, even Kazakhstan. So many of us went walking down the main street that people looked nervous, fearing some sort of demonstration, but the Russian soldiers took no notice of us, perhaps imagining we were volunteers wanting to join the victorious Stalin's Red Army. Since I was fluent in Russian, I assumed the role of spokesman and asked one of them where we could find his superior officer. 'We are a delegation representing people of at least a dozen different nationalities, all of whom were brought here against our will by the Nazis,' I told him. 'All we want to know is how we can return home.'

After a little hedging, he said, 'Follow me and I'll take you to Headquarters.'

Some of us were alarmed when we learned that this Headquarters was in a military camp outside the town, which might turn out to be the sort of camp you went into but never came out of again. 'Is it necessary to go to your Headquarters?' I asked. 'Isn't there an officer somewhere in the town, in one of the shops, perhaps, who is well enough informed to tell us what we want to know?'

He gave a sly grin. 'There are no officers in the shops, Comrade. There's nothing left worth buying. The shops are empty. We made sure of that.' An admission of what we knew already: everything had been looted.

By a stroke of good luck, however, three officers came walking along the pavement towards us at that moment; the soldier was obliged to salute. He asked permission to speak and repeated what we had told him. Seeing how young most of us were, the officers regarded us with interest, and we immediately gathered round them. In answer to their questions, I told them what ordeals we had endured. The girls who had been working in brick factories held out their scarred hands for them to see. I described our working conditions on farms, in coalmines, in factories and on *Arbeitsdienst*, digging trenches. Assuming an air of wide-eyed simplicity, I expressed our delight at having been liberated by the Red Army and our confidence that Father Stalin, ever mindful of the welfare of his people, would make arrangements for us to return home and be reunited with our grieving families. Those around me nodded in fervent agreement. For once, I was deeply grateful for my indoctrination by Russian teachers.

Though I laid it on thick, this approach made an impression. The officers told us that arrangements were being made for all slave labourers to return to their respective countries. They promised us that our turn would soon come.

'An announcement will be given out over the radio,' said the one whom I recognized as a political commissar, with responsibility for communicating with the local populace. 'When the time comes, you will be asked to gather here in Voitsberg and will be taken to an assembly point in Graz, where you will be put on trains that will take you home.'

A huge sigh of relief rippled from front to back of our delegation as this news spread. Nothing, it seemed, could be simpler or more satisfactory. So why, we wondered, did the officer who had told us this find it necessary to stand on tiptoe, stretching his neck and throwing back his head, in order to deliver a speech?

'Dear young people of the Soviet Union. You have suffered terrible persecution, oppression, and deprivation under the Nazis of the German Reich. You have been deprived of your freedom. You were separated from your families, deprived of your home life and your education, of food, of clothes, of sleep. The only things you were not deprived of were heavy toil and the sweat of your brows.

'Just look at you, so young, so thin and poorly dressed, you whose whole future is still before you! Father Stalin would shed tears to see you. From today, however, he welcomes you back into the open arms of Russia, where your mothers and fathers, sisters and brothers, relatives and friends are still weeping. Their tears have never ceased to flow for their lost children. You will go home and be reunited with your families. Once again you will plough the fields, sow the corn, and reap the rich harvests of your native land, happy in the loving care of Father Stalin. Adolf Hitler is dead and never again will you be allowed to suffer fascist tyranny and oppression.'

The faces around me remained politely blank. Apart from the welcome news that Hitler was dead, we were quite unimpressed by this absurd and all-too-familiar peroration, but we did not want to offend the officer in case he withdrew his promise of repatriation. It was astonishing to hear the same trite phrases of the political commissars as we had been subjected to at home. Through six years of war the story had not changed. We were expected to respond with joy to the same seductive words as those that had briefly won my father's allegiance in 1939. We were not so naive now, but of course we applauded and nodded our heads in agreement, crying, 'Bravo! Bravo! How true!' when all we actually wanted to know was when and where transport would be available to take us home.

Afterwards, as we dispersed to our respective places of work, a friend turned to me and said, 'Thank goodness you said all that about being delighted to be liberated by the Red Army. It went down well. If you hadn't given them all that guff, who knows what might have happened to us!'

I returned to the farm in a state of such impatience and expectancy that it was impossible to concentrate on my work there. Every moment of the day, I was on edge, waiting for the call to assemble in Voitsberg, after which I was convinced it would be only a matter of days before I was reunited with my family. I kept picturing how everyone in the village would turn out to greet me, and how each of us would look, and what we would say and do, as I went through the motions of tilling the land and tending the crops.

Much of my time was spent protecting Gretel from the harassment of Russian soldiers who turned up at the door demanding that she fry them eggs and *speck*, and went away carrying smoked *schinken* or a chicken or a duck, and some wine or schnapps to take back to their barracks. These were not casual demands, made in a polite or friendly way, but were delivered at the point of a gun. She was naturally timorous and did not speak Russian, so she could not even plead with them, yet it was plain that she and her children would starve if she kept giving them everything they wanted.

One day four Russians came asking for bicycles, which we did not have. Then they asked for food. I said we had only enough food for the children, and were going without food ourselves to feed them, but one man took his revolver out of its holster and, pointing it at me, repeated his demands louder than before. In the end we had to give them whatever they wanted to get them off the farm.

Another day, when Gretel and I were working together in the fields, two soldiers came demanding food. After translating what they said, I told her, 'I will say we simply haven't got any, because so many soldiers have been here already and taken it.'

She agreed and, at first, the Russians appeared to accept what I told them, but then they went up close to her and said, 'We know that you've got a revolver and a double-barrelled shotgun – we know you have – and you'd better give them to us or we'll make sure there is not a scrap of food left on this farm for your children to eat.'

Gretel had to wait while I interpreted what they said. 'I have told them there are no guns,' I added. I had never seen one and was convinced that was the truth. The Russians ignored me. They grabbed Gretel by the arm and shook her, threatening to starve her children if she did not hand over the firearms. I could not intervene, for the soldiers were evidently in earnest and she was trembling with what looked like guilt as well as fear. Her face had gone white and she was in tears. I was about to protest at their bullying when she became so terrified she could hold out no longer and said, 'All right then. Look under the floorboards in the kitchen.'

As I translated her words, I felt so angry and betrayed I could cheerfully have strangled her! She had put me in the position of telling lies to the Russians, which could jeopardize whatever chance I had of going home! At once they turned on me and growled, 'We knew you were lying. You denied that the revolver and gun were there, yet you obviously knew they were all the time. And you are a Ukrainian! You're one of us! You're one of those who's had the privilege of being schooled through the Soviet Education System, and yet you lied to us.'

'That is not true,' I said. 'I know nothing about any guns. Frau Gretel never told me. Why would she? I might have used them against her. I would not deceive you. I was a member of the Komsomol. I fully understand that it is my duty to assist the victorious Russian soldiers.'

'Where is your Komsomol membership card?' they demanded. 'Where is your Komsomol membership card?'

The question froze me to the spot. It was aimed, this question, in my direction, but *question* was not quite right – there was a kind of stupefied arrogance to the demand, which choked the response in my throat. As an answer, silence would not have sufficed; but no words would have satisfied my interrogators either.

Mere seconds into my interrogation at the hands of those NKVD soldiers, I was under no illusion that things would be cleared up quickly. Far from it. Nor did I treat the demand, now repeated – What have you done with your Komsomol card? – as a joke; but time, I remember thinking, will make this amusing; will make this silly scene into comedy.

'What have you done with your Komsomol card?' the Red Army soldier asked, and I learned how to breathe again.

'I don't know. I had to leave it behind when the Germans took me from my home into slave labour,' I managed to reply.

One of the men looked horrified. 'You left it behind? Your Komsomol card?' he stressed. 'I was a Komsomol member as well, and do you know what I did? When the Germans invaded the Soviet Union I *swallowed* my membership card, that's what I did – so now it lies close to my heart!' He laid a hand on the point where the stomach joins the chest. He looked disgusted, as if the taste was still fresh in his mouth. 'And you have the nerve to say you simply *lost* your Komsomol card?'

I closed my eyes. In fact, I expected to be shot, since that was the usual outcome of arguing with Red Army soldiers. And now I really had lied, since I would have been too young to join the communist Komsomol youth group even if my father had consented. However, good luck was with me – they did not take the trouble or time to work that out. The young man whose Komsomol card lay close to his heart must have felt some sort of kinship with me, for all they did was prod me (it hurt, but pain I could live with), using the barrels of their guns as they pushed me in front of them into the kitchen.

Gretel showed them exactly which floorboards to rip up. Perhaps she was even relieved to have been found out; it was impossible to say, as her face was free of expression.

Underneath the floorboards the soldiers found a German army revolver, a double-barrelled shotgun and some ammunition. Evidently her husband had brought the revolver back when he came on leave. He would have had the shotgun in his possession already, as most farmers had, for shooting rabbits, pigeons and wild birds. The soldiers' hunch – if that was what it was – had paid off, and now we were both in trouble. As the men left, taking the firearms and some *speck* and other food they forced her to give them, they turned to me and said coldly, 'You should know better than to try to protect the Fascists. They are Nazis and you are not one of them. Do it again and you will end up underground.'

So disgusted was I by what had happened, I was tempted to leave the farm straight away, although there had been no summons on the radio as yet. Friends on another farm would have taken me in. However, Gretel apologized so sincerely, and she and her children looked so pitiful and distressed that I relented. She swore she had not meant to lie to me. The less I knew about weapons concealed on the farm the better it should have been for both of us; if only she had not panicked and told the Russians the truth. I conceded that that was a valid point. I could also see what difficulties she would face once I had gone, so I agreed to stay, but only until the announcement came to pack and go.

About a week later, a rumour, later proved correct, circulated among the slave workers, to the effect that we should go to an assembly point in Graz to be registered and sorted out by nationalities before being assigned a place on trains that would take us home. This was the best news any of us had heard in three years! For the first time since my mother died, I ceased to sing the sad song *Verlassen, verlassen*, to myself. The Russians, whom we had seen only as lying, drunken, noisy, intimidating brawlers, thieves and uncivilized bullies were going to be as good as their word after all.

Gretel and her friends, who had become my friends too, threw a farewell party which lasted the best part of a week, though the routine work of the farm was not neglected. We ate *speck* and pork dripping, preserved somehow from the Russian soldiers, and drank schnapps though I, at least, needed no alcohol to be in high spirits.

Chapter 10

Summer 1945
Russian Deceit

I left Voitsberg in perfect June weather taking with me a memory of sunshine and wildflowers. I even bought a bunch of edelweiss, the little white alpine flowers so reminiscent of Austria, to take to my loving sister Lywosi. I was not yet eighteen.

In Graz, thousands of us converged on the registration centre, and there were shouts of joy as friends found each other again after three years of slavery for the Nazis. We were all euphoric at the prospect of going home. Three days later, our registration completed, we marched to the railway station. A shudder went through the crowd when we saw that the only transport they had found for us was cattle trucks like the ones we had been forced into by the Nazis. They were packed almost as tight, too, when we had all climbed in, but what did it matter? This time it was different. In two or three days we would be home. The train was so long it took two locomotives to pull it, and it moved very slowly. Jokingly we blamed the pregnant women among us for that, telling them it was their fault the train was overloaded, since more of us were going home than had come. Meanwhile we amused ourselves by singing, exchanging stories of all that had happened to us, and telling jokes. We were feeling irrepressibly cheerful.

Our train suffered constant stops and delays, but that did not surprise us. We had heard the bombers. We knew railway lines and bridges had been damaged and destroyed and that trains were constantly diverted. It was inevitable at the end of a war. We also knew we were in the hands of the all-conquering Red Army, which had the means and skills to repair the tracks and could easily whistle up road transport if the railway lines were irretrievably damaged.

What surprised us very much, however, was to find ourselves, around noon the following day, outside Budapest in Hungary. In our imaginations we had plotted this journey so many times, we expected Bratislava to be our first stop. Now we opened the wagon doors and looked up and down the train to see how many Hungarians were getting off. There were none. The platform was full of Hungarian gypsies, who serenaded us on their violins, guitars and accordions with songs celebrating our new-found freedom. They begged for money, food, or clothes in return. 'You will soon be reunited with your families, so give what you have to our children, who have nothing.' We gave them some of our food, or a few coins. It would have felt mean not to share our good fortune and we knew better than to invoke the gypsies' curse. On the other hand, we could not be generous; none of us knew how long our journey would last.

While the train remained stationary at the platform outside Budapest, we joined in their songs and dances to pass the time. They taught us new songs, improvising appropriate words about the joys of returning to one's homeland. We were there for six to eight hours before Russian soldiers ordered us back into the wagons and our train very slowly moved on.

Some twenty-five kilometres from Budapest, the train stopped in the middle of nowhere. When the doors of the wagons were opened, all we could see was the platform of a wayside halt, not even a station, with fields and widely scattered farmhouses stretching far into the distance.

'What are we stopping here for?' we demanded.

Our Russian escorts became busy checking the rifles on their shoulders and would only tell us to get out into the fields and stay put. There were no toilets or anything like that, because this was only a halt. Though we begged them to tell us why we were no longer heading east the Russian soldiers just shrugged their shoulders, saying nothing. Until now they had been reasonably helpful, even sympathizing with our discomforts. Now they looked grimly forbidding, as though whatever instructions they had received would annoy us but would nevertheless have to be obeyed.

Towards evening they announced that we were to spend the night there, where we were, under the open sky, and would move on the next day, adding that, since they knew no more than we did, we might as well all make the best of it.

We were desperately perturbed. There was much angry murmuring, and a great deal of frantic conjecture as to what was going on. Pregnant women were among us, and girls, some of them quite young, so their husbands and boyfriends made arrangements with the other men to protect them from the soldiers. We did not feel we could trust the Russians not to accost them during the night. Even then, it was difficult to sleep. All of us were speculating anxiously as to why we had been stranded in such a place. We were also hungry and thirsty. We had been given nothing to eat or drink since the start of our journey and though some of us still had a small amount of milk and bread with us, the milk had gone sour. We asked if we could approach local farmers with requests for milk, or even water, for the pregnant women, whose plight worried us all. We were told, with a waggle of their rifles, *'nelzia'* – not allowed.

In the morning we refreshed ourselves by washing our faces in the dew on the grass. Then, still without nourishment of any kind, we were roughly sorted into columns and marched off in a westerly direction, expectant mothers and all, back towards the Austrian border. After fifteen or twenty kilometres we came to a Hungarian village where we were told we were to stay for a time. No one would say how long.

There, sleeping in the orchards, fields and gardens around the village, we remained for over a week. A Russian army field kitchen arrived and served us with cabbage soup and slices of black bread – almost inedible but better than nothing. There was also the usual ersatz coffee, black and unsweetened, which was at least warm. Some nights it rained, drenching us all, but luckily it was June and we could dry ourselves next morning in the heat of the summer sun.

By now we were all in a state of extreme apprehension. Our confidence in the Russians had never been high, and it was plain to see we were heading in the wrong direction. We had received no adequate explanation, been offered no apology or information as to our future movements. Other ominous signs were present, too. The military escort that had set out with us from Graz, whom we presumed to have some responsibility for our welfare, had been changed so that there were no longer any familiar faces among the Russian soldiery. What's more, its numbers had greatly increased. Were they there to protect us or to prevent our escape? In desperation, we clung to the hope that it was just a mix-up – that the travel arrangements made for us had broken down or gone haywire, and that we would eventually be provided with road transport of some description to get us home. If that proved to be the case, we could put up with almost anything.

The worst thing was being kept in the dark. After all we had been through, and after our honest jubilation at finding ourselves actually on the train, it was almost too much to bear. We had come of our own free will, yet were treated like cattle; told nothing. Though I walked up and down the encampment, talking to as many among those many hundreds of people as I could, I found no one who had any precise notion of what was going on, or who could satisfy me that we were really safe and on our journey home. If you trust a Russian, you trust the devil, so the saying went.

Eventually, we were mustered and marched off again, still in a westerly direction and guarded by still larger numbers of soldiers. We crossed the border on foot from Hungary into Burgenland, in Austria, some 100 kilometres from our original starting point in Graz. There we camped, as before, under the open sky, with no protection from the heat of the daytime sun or the frequent chill of the night-time hours.

As the days turned into weeks, our hopes crumbled to ashes. More and more soldiers arrived to patrol the camp and watch our every movement. The food doled out was barely enough to keep us alive, much less satisfy our appetites. The whole area had a strangely desolate air. Many of the farms and farmhouses were empty, apparently abandoned by their owners as the Germans retreated and the Russians advanced, and there were a lot of unoccupied houses in nearby villages. Their owners could well have been Nazi sympathizers, who dared not stay. These were now commandeered by the Russians.

One morning, we were ordered to assemble in a large field. When everyone was present, a Russian officer announced that the men and women, even those who were married, were henceforth to be accommodated in separate quarters. The women would be lodged in some of the vacant houses, while the men would occupy various farm buildings. We men were to find suitable farms, clean out the cowsheds, stables, and barns, and take up residence there.

The officer then demanded to know how many of us could read and write German, Polish, Ukrainian, or Russian. A few of us – not many – raised our hands. 'Give your names to Captain Markov,' he commanded, pointing to where the captain sat at a folding table.

Captain Markov had the approachable but serious manner of an experienced apparatchik, a political commissar or personnel manager. He questioned us, one by one, about our backgrounds, wanting to know where we were born, who our parents were, who our grandparents were, what schooling we had received, when and how we were taken as slave labourers by the Germans, where we had ended up working in Austria, what kind of work we did, and how we were treated by our employers. Then, at his request, we recounted our life histories as far back as we could remember. The captain wrote down details of my grandparents, parents, our home village, and my father's occupation and political leanings. The interrogation was conducted in a fairly low key, but it was clear that the Russians were intent on acquiring a very detailed picture of those who had raised their hands.

Meanwhile the women gathered their things together and were taken to their allotted houses. Many were weeping and distraught in spite of repeated assurances that they would be properly looked after. Among the Russian troops there were no women soldiers, and deprived of our protection, none of us knew how the women might fare. However, we were powerless to do anything but comply.

The men who now remained, about 600 or 700, were separated into national, or language, groups. Those of us who had already given details about ourselves were then asked to select fifty or sixty men each and record their life histories in the same way that had been done with us. Paper and pencils were distributed and we set about this task straight away.

I chose fifty-odd men from western Ukraine and moved them to one side, preparing to proceed in the same way as Captain Markov had done. They were all very worried and fearful. Why did the Russians want all this information? Would it be used against them or their families? A trap? Many of them had the added anxiety of having been separated from their womenfolk.

I felt that we had no option but to answer the questions, and I shared this opinion with them. The war in Europe was over and our homeland was under Russian occupation. The Russians had a legitimate interest in knowing who they were sending home, and it was in our interest to cooperate with them. The main thing was for us to stick together, being frank with one another, but speaking to the Russians with one voice.

I began taking down the particulars of the first man. Even as I did so, others were asking my advice as to whether or not they should tell the truth or make up the facts. Suppose the Russians went investigating their families and found something contrary to their liking and prosecuted them, not for any crime they had committed but simply for having had to work, as everyone had had to do, with the Germans. I advised them to tell the truth, since lies are often easily found out, but the problem for them was that a number of them could not read or write. They had to rely on me absolutely. Could they trust me to write exactly what they told me? I tried to reassure them that I would certainly do my best.

It took two days to register every one of the fifty-odd men, reading back what I had written, and altering anything with which they were not satisfied. I had to be very patient, to make sure I did them justice. When I had finished, I gave the complete list to Captain Markov, keeping a copy for myself.

'Do you think any of these men collaborated with either the German or the Austrian Nazis?' he asked me.

I vehemently denied the possibility of any such thing. 'They did the jobs they were made to do, as we all did. That's all.'

'What about their physical fitness? Are they quite strong? Are there any disabilities? Do any of them require medical treatment of any kind?'

This struck me as an odd question. 'No, Captain. Not as far as I know. No one is complaining of any illness. They are just disturbed by this long delay. We all are. No one tells us anything, and we are extremely anxious to know when we are going home.'

Markov brushed this aside. 'We do not know yet. When a decision has been reached, you'll be told and can inform your men. Till then, I don't wish to be questioned about it.'

He then began to interrogate me in greater depth about my political views. Did I believe in the teachings of Lenin and Stalin? I replied that I had been educated by the Russian education system to think of Stalin as my father, and was well aware that the twelfth paragraph in his constitution says that those who do not work shall not eat. That seemed to satisfy him.

'The military political commissars will be giving instruction in our recent history, so that when you reach home, you will be fully aware of the magnificent victory the Red Army won over the Nazi Germany, and give your wholehearted support to Father Stalin. The rebuilding of our shattered nation depends on it. Do you understand? Your aim, therefore, in the next few weeks, must be to absorb fully the lessons the Military Political Commissars have to teach you. Make that clear to your men.'

While I was still reeling from the shock of hearing that we could expect to be in that place for some weeks to come, Captain Markov surprised me by offering me a Red Army tunic. It was too big for me, smelt peculiar, and the insignia on the shoulder tabs conveyed nothing. I tried to refuse.

'I have some clean shirts in my case which I am saving to wear on my arrival home,' I told him. 'I don't need another.'

He looked at me pityingly, then, with a wry grin; he told me: 'You will wear it all the same, and at all times. This is the tunic of a Red Army officer, a Hero of the Soviet Union. You should be proud to be seen in it. It means I'm putting you in command of four platoons. You'll carry out my instructions at all times and make sure that they are understood by all your men.'

I was aghast. What on earth was happening to me? How could a shirt with shoulder tabs make me, a Ukrainian some months short of his eighteenth birthday, into an officer of the imperialist Russian Red Army? What would my men say when they saw me? Would they think I had betrayed them and had been working for the Russians all along? That I was deceiving them when I took down their life histories and they had, after all, fallen into a trap? However, I controlled myself and asked what the insignia represented.

'Don't you know?'

'No, I don't. I've seldom been privileged to be in the company of soldiers of the Red Army.'

'The shoulder tabs indicate that you have been commissioned as my lieutenant, in charge of a company. Congratulations! We're going to impose a curfew – and it's your job to see it's observed. No one is to wander around the streets, orchards, or fields, or visit the women at their houses in the area, while the curfew is in force. Is that clear? If they do, they'll be severely punished. Take a roll call this evening, at midnight, and again in the morning, to make sure that all your men are present.'

He did not tell me the penalty for breaking the curfew but made it plain that he would come down very hard on anyone disobeying orders. Nothing he said brooked any argument.

With the four platoons now under my command, I set up headquarters on a farm. We cleaned up the barn and laid out bundles of straw for our beds. As we worked together, I felt assured that the men still trusted me and understood that the shirt was simply the mark of leadership. It soon appeared I was not the only man to have been suddenly created an officer and made to wear a Red Army uniform. Our situation had become clear to us all. A military camp was being set up in which we were the soldiers.

Each morning at six I got my men up and into line in four platoons, four abreast, to march to the cookhouse for a breakfast of clay-like black bread and ersatz coffee. During the march to breakfast, and again to lunch and dinner, every man in the platoon had to sing such Red Army songs as *Katusha*, a love song, or *Strana moya, ridnia moya* – My destiny, my homeland – this was compulsory, a part of our indoctrination, instilling in us not only unswerving devotion to Stalin but military habits and ways of thinking. If I had reported any man for not singing, he would have been punished with three days in a coal cellar on bread and water. So I made sure that my men sang loudly at all times.

I spoke to them not as an officer but as their friend. We were united in our distrust of the Russians, whom we had hated ever since they invaded western Ukraine in 1939. We did as we were told against our will, out of fear of punishment. We were as much their slaves as we had been slaves of the Nazis.

Before long, quite a few of us were dressed in army uniform. Later I realized it was to get us used to the idea of being in military service, though no one was yet prepared to say this was so. The impression they tried to give was that we were being organized in military fashion simply to make the camp run smoothly.

When I met a superior officer I had to stand to attention and would be told to identify myself as a *zwodnay*, or company leader. I resented having to do so. Everything that was happening to us was a betrayal of the promises made by the Russian officers in Voitsberg, whom we believed had liberated us. Everything in me rebelled against being trained by Russian officers; my every movement controlled by Russian guards with rifles on their shoulders and revolvers in their holsters. They fared better than us. They rode bicycles and went on horseback, and they were better quartered and better fed than any of us.

While I did what I was required to do, I had the full support and understanding of my men. I did not stop them going to meet their wives and girl friends at night, though I warned them not to get caught. They reported that the women were all right, and were not being molested. Having registered, they were being re-educated along Stalinist lines, much as we were. I longed to get acquainted with some of the local people, especially the girls I saw walking in the villages or picking fruit in the orchards. If I could meet a nice Austrian girl, it would make life pleasanter. Perhaps she would tell me what the villagers were saying about us. Having radios, some of the local people were probably well informed about recent events in the world and might have understood our situation better than we did.

One day I paid a visit to a house in whose orchard I had slept during our first few days in the neighbourhood. A pretty blonde girl named Helga lived there. She and her mother and father had kindly invited me into their house and offered me water and bread and even a bit of smoked ham when I was hungry. I had to eat it in the house where I couldn't be seen or they would have had hundreds of men asking for food and the Russians would have confiscated what food they had as a punishment for befriending us. The behaviour of Russian soldiers in the areas they occupied – looting shops and stealing people's wristwatches or bicycles – had turned most of the population against them.

I became friendly with this family, and especially with Helga, who sympathized warmly with my plight. Her father appeared well educated – he may have been a teacher or government official – and, as an Austrian patriot, rejoiced at Hitler's defeat. On the other hand, he was no fan of the Russians, and was horrified to hear of the treatment that we, who had been deported into slave labour as children, had received at the war's end. They offered food, comfort, and moral support whenever I went there.

One day a rumour went round the camp that we were going to be taken to the Far East to fight in the war that Russia had recently declared against Japan. We were devastated, shocked and, frankly, terrified. We knew next to nothing about the war in the Far East, but the possibility made sense. Why else had we been kept in Austria instead of being sent home?

None of us had ever been soldiers, but we were of military age, and had been easily conned into wearing Red Army uniforms and singing Red Army songs. We were receiving basic military training and political indoctrination. It explained, better than anything else we had heard, why we had been deceived and lied to from almost the moment our train left Graz. At last we had a clue to what it was all about and it made my blood boil!

The rumours had an instant effect on me. I did not even wait for official confirmation before I began to plot my escape. Under no circumstances would I go and fight for Stalin in Japan. My distrust of the Russians was absolute. Six years earlier we had hated them but, in our delight at being freed from the Nazis, we had momentarily seen them as our saviours. What blandishments they had heaped on us in Voitsberg! My mind was made up beyond any shadow of doubt.

I felt particularly angry with Captain Markov who had so recently commissioned me and yet told me nothing. Yet I realized I could not now demand that he tell me the truth because, if he suspected my intentions, I could be court-martialled. I would not be regarded as a mere runaway; I would be a deserter.

My escape plan was already half formed. I had the revolver Captain Markov had presented me with a week or two earlier, and I was friendly with an Austrian family whom I believed I could fully trust. All I needed now was a companion to escape with me. More than one might make us conspicuous or slow us down when we had to act quickly and decisively, so I was looking for just one man – courageous and reliable, as keen on escape as I was – who would be certain to keep our secret. I began to review the faces of the men in my company, aware that I would have to be very careful in my approach. At worst he could report me to Captain Markov. Even if he didn't do that, he might gossip, spreading word of my disaffection that could destroy the morale of my men.

I was absolutely bent on escape, but so full of youthful optimism, I took little heed of the likely consequences. I did not reckon on having to give up all hope of seeing my father and sister whom I had been dreaming of meeting again within days, for the foreseeable future. I reasoned that if I went back to Voitsberg, I could simply make a fresh start. When everything settled down – even if it took months, or a year – I could write to my father and find out how things were at home, then work out new plans for my return. Surely the Russians would not be tolerated in western Ukraine forever! For the time being, I concentrated on making my escape.

I soon had the details worked out. I would tell Captain Markov I was not well, that I had stomach pains, a terrible headache, and no appetite for food, and request a few days sick leave, promising to get well quickly and return to my company. The volunteers in the field hospital were friends of mine and would not give me away. I would tell them that what I actually wanted to do was to spend three days hunting for food in some of the nearby villages, since my men were permanently hungry. They knew this was true, for they were hungry themselves, and I'd agree to share any provisions I obtained with them on my return. They wouldn't betray me. So I should have three days in which to get away before anyone's suspicions were aroused.

Before I could put this plan into effect, there were other arrangements to make. First, I took Helga's family into my confidence. They were not surprised at what I told them. They said they had heard that more and more young people like myself were being brought into the area, where there were already thousands of Russian soldiers.

'We see them drilling the young people, marching them up and down, and holding political meetings, just as you say they are doing with you,' said Helga, eyeing me with affectionate concern. Her blonde hair hung in plaits on her shoulders, her blue eyes were full of tenderness, and she grasped my hand tightly as she said, 'You're absolutely right. Don't go to Japan. Go back to Voitsberg. You can hide in the hills and in the mountains anywhere in Austria and you will be protected and given food, but you couldn't run away from Japan. Even you can't walk on water, Stefan!'

Her father offered practical advice. 'Tell me when you are ready to go, he said, and I'll prepare a map for you that will keep you out of the way of the Russian patrols and their manoeuvres. You'll have to avoid all bridges, main roads and railways, because Russian guards are everywhere, and it would be disastrous if you fell into their hands. Keep to the hills and forests, or follow the course of rivers, avoiding villages and towns as much as you can.'

I was so grateful for help and advice from someone with local knowledge that I dubbed him Herr Glücklich – Mr Lucky – but his help didn't end there. 'You can have my leather trousers and hat with the thistle in it, and my jacket, which will be the perfect disguise for you. As a young Austrian you'll find it easy to walk through the countryside. If you're spotted by the Russians, they'll certainly think you're an Austrian. So long as they don't ask you for your passport or any identification, you should be all right.'

'What about the friend he is going to take with him?' asked his wife. 'What will he wear?'

'Ordinary clothes, just long trousers and a jacket. That's a perfectly normal sight, two young men dressed differently but looking very much like Austrian boys.' Getting more and more interested in the project, he went on, 'We'll have food and water ready for you. I have a canvas shoulder bag you can put your spare clothes in. You won't be able to carry much. It'd be obvious you're going a long way and you could be stopped and be made to open the case and answer a lot of questions.'

I had to agree to abandon my old rucksack and the precious little wooden case, which my father's friend had made for me. It had been with me since 1942 and I kept everything I owned in it. Many memories were attached to it, but this was no time for sentiment. Herr Glücklich's family promised to keep those and another small case for me, so that I could go back for them if and when the Russians retreated. They treated me like one of their own family – to be welcomed, helped and protected in any way they could.

I had one great advantage, in that I spoke the Austrian dialect perfectly.

I also spoke grammatically perfect Russian and Polish, which I'd had to learn at school. I would be able to understand and converse with Austrian officials or Russian soldiers without giving myself away. As for civilians, I had decided to trust them, telling them exactly who I was and where I came from, and I hoped whoever escaped with me would do the same. We would only tell lies if we fell into Russian hands.

I felt highly exhilarated by what I was planning to do. Deserting from the Red Army would be a kick in the pants for Marx, Lenin and Stalin. I was making a resolute protest against everything Russia had stood for in my life – and Hitler, too – demonstrating that I would never remain a slave.

No doubt it was naive to imagine that a young boy could take on the Red Army or make a journey of more than 100 kilometres across land occupied by them and get away with it. But, once the decision to abscond from the camp was made, I was so confident that I would reach my destination that it never crossed my mind that I might be caught. Armed only but powerfully with a secure faith in God and a considerable belief in my own resourcefulness, physical strength and speed, I believed that whatever I undertook must turn out well. I believe that still.

My mind was so busy with plans that I couldn't eat or sleep. I had to move quickly, before my company could be marched off to a Black Sea port and sent on the long sea voyage to Japan. My search for a man to desert with me, however, took time – lots of time. I knew my own men well and could not think of one of them I could approach with such a desperate and dangerous proposal. On the other hand, the right fellow was bound to turn up somewhere among the hundreds of men in our camp. With God's help I would surely find him.

To avoid suspicion, I asked each man I spoke to an innocent question, convinced that I could assess his likely attitude to my proposal by his response. I said, 'Have you heard the rumour that all this military training we have been doing, and all these daily lectures we have been hearing, could be preparing us to be shipped off to fight the Japanese? You know, of course, that Russia declared war on Japan after conquering Germany.' Then, if he spoke of running away rather than be press-ganged into the army in such a way, I would ask if he thought he could make his own way home to Ukraine, Poland, Byelorussia or wherever, or whether he would wait and hide somewhere until such time as the Russians were gone and he would be free. From this I hoped to judge whether the man was ready, then and there, to desert the army and return to the town or village in Austria he had recently left.

I spent most of a week in what seemed like a fruitless search and was beginning to feel very frustrated when I suddenly found the man I was looking for. He was a very disgruntled Ukrainian of about my own age and his name was Ivan. With his curly, blond hair, blue eyes, and rather slight build, he could easily pass himself off as an Austrian youth. Before I could even ask my preliminary questions, he began complaining about everything that had happened to him since the day the Russians reached the part of Austria where he had been working, in reasonable contentment, on a farm. He cursed the Russians, swearing angrily that no Russian, least of all Stalin himself, could be trusted. At the same time he admitted it was foolish to say such things openly, since we could land in Siberia if we spoke our minds to the wrong person. He ended by saying with deep conviction, 'If I knew of any conceivable ways or means by which I could get away from here, I would go today!'

Good enough for me! In fact, it was music in my ears. At once I knew that he was a man I could trust, so rather than delay any longer, I decided to be frank with him and outlined my plan on the spot. He, of course, would have to find his own alibi for an absence from his unit that lasted three or four days. How would he excuse himself to his superior officer?

Ivan said that was no problem. 'I'm a carpenter by trade, Stefan, and everyone for miles around needs a carpenter to do repairs. I'll say I've found a job in the village.' All the villages were without their men folk, who had not returned from the war, so there were plenty of jobs to be done. 'I'll tell my company commander that the work will take three or four days, and that I'll be paid in food, which I can bring back and share with the men in my company. He should have no reason to doubt that.'

I rushed off at once to the field hospital and explained my intention of pleading illness and then going round the villages searching for food, making quite sure my friends there would stand by me if they were questioned. I then went to tell Herr Glücklich and his family that I had found the man I needed and would be ready to set off the following morning. Their relief that I would not be going to Japan showed in their faces and they assured me that the map, the clothes, the food and the bag they had promised me would be ready whenever they were wanted.

'Will it be all right,' I asked, 'if Ivan and I come here – very discreetly, making sure no one sees us – tonight? We could sleep in the barn and take off first thing in the morning.'

Without a moment's hesitation, Herr Glücklich said, '*Ja*, that's all right,' just glancing at his wife and daughter to make certain they agreed. 'When you come, we'll go over the map, so I can show you what you need to know. It's not a proper map, but I know the area all the way to Graz and can point out roughly where the hills are and the rivers, and where the railway lines lead. If we go over it several times, you'll be able to memorize it. After that you'll be in the hands of God.'

With everything settled, I thanked him and returned to the camp.

Chapter 11

1945
Red Army Deserter

Our getaway plan worked without a hitch. Our alibis were accepted without question by our superior officers – Ivan's that he was going off to do carpentry work in exchange for food; mine that I was ill and going into the field hospital for a few days. We gathered our belongings together and, as it began to get dark, left our units and made our separate ways to the home of my friends.

It wasn't only Ivan and I who were taking a tremendous risk. If anyone had reported seeing two men going to Herr Glücklich's home carrying luggage, the Russians would have had no mercy on this generous and compassionate family. Until we were gone from their house the following morning, and the things we were leaving with them for safekeeping were hidden without trace, all of us were in mortal danger.

As we sat in the kitchen of their home, eating the delicious meal Frau Glücklich set before us, we pored over the map her husband had prepared. Ivan and I studied it eagerly, tracing out our journey over and over again to make sure we knew exactly where we were going. Fortunately, Ivan had a basic education and could read and write. We were both able to commit many important landmarks to memory.

The clothes Herr Glücklich brought for me to put on were too big, but not obviously so. In wartime, plenty of people went about in clothes that were not an exact fit. We stuffed the band of his hat with paper so it would stay on my head and decided it would do. In the time that remained, Ivan and I wanted to concentrate on the details of our escape.

We decided to get moving at about four in the morning, when no one but a few Russian soldiers, with perhaps some of our own men, would be out patrolling the village. Everyone else would be fast asleep. We had been told which paths to take, and how to avoid the roads and lanes where we might be spotted. Once clear of the village, it would not take us long to reach a stretch of forest. Then we would be truly on our way.

As we finished supper, Herr Glücklich brought out a bottle of schnapps and we drank a toast to our mutual health and good fortune and embraced one another with deep affection. Frau Glücklich declared, with tears in her eyes, 'You boys are like my own sons. God bless you and save you from the Russians. We pray you will reach your destination safely.'

After a sleepless night, we were up and ready well before the appointed time for our departure. In my leather shorts and Tyrolean hat I looked so much like a typical Austrian that Ivan and I could not help laughing. He wore an ordinary jacket and trousers and no hat. We looked like any two country lads who might be going out for the day. With our revolvers (Ivan had acquired one too) and the few precious papers we carried with us at all times (our map, family letters and photographs, and identification documents we hoped we would never have to show) tucked securely in the inside pockets of our jackets, our bags held only a change of shirt and underwear, a small blanket each, and a little food. It was late July or early August; there was food ripe in the fields and the days were still long and warm. After brief, grateful farewells to our host and his family, we were on our way.

We got clear of the village without incident and, perhaps thirty minutes later, had just reached a cart track in the shelter of the forest when we heard the sound of horses whinnying, somewhere in the forest itself. We stared at one another in dismay. Who would bring horses into the forest at this time of year? Not local farmers. The horses might just have been left out to graze, but we agreed in whispers to proceed with the utmost caution. Before long we heard voices and, peering through bushes at the side of the track, saw Russian soldiers moving about, their rifles on their shoulders, keeping guard while other soldiers were cutting down trees. They were stacking the wood on wagons pulled by the horses we had heard. The cart track was leading us straight to them!

I gestured to Ivan to follow me, and we crept away from the track we were following into deeper undergrowth, bending low and keeping our heads down, careful not to disturb branches or make any sound. There was an overgrown path veering off to the right and, when we were far enough away to feel sure we could not be heard, we stood up, stretched, and grinned at one another in relief. What a beginning! What a stroke of beginners' luck! We had nearly walked straight into the arms of our enemy.

Once through the forest we checked our route on the map and found that it went up a hill where we would be out in the open and very exposed. Our near-encounter with the Russians had put us on high alert, so we kept a sharp lookout in all directions. It was perhaps just as well we had been faced with the dangers that threatened us right at the start, rather than being lulled into a sense of safety, for the sun was shining, the fields and forests looked calm and serene, and, though we could see around us for a considerable distance, there was certainly nothing sinister in sight. Nonetheless, we remained watchful.

When we reached the top of the hill we were startled to see several hundred Russian soldiers drilling in the fields below us, crossing and re-crossing the dirt road we were following. Our immediate reaction was to turn tail but, before we could do so, we realized we had already been seen. This left us no alternative but to keep going, strolling as unconcernedly as possible straight towards them, as though making contact with them was part of our plan.

'Let me do the talking,' I muttered. 'If we both talk we may contradict each other and then we'll really be in trouble. I'll make up some sort of story and you just look stupid and nod your head in agreement. Just that – no more, no less.' My Russian was better than his and I reckoned I was fairly good at talking my way out of difficulties.

'Make it good!' said Ivan, grinning amiably.

By then I was so nervous that I doubted if I could find my voice, much less think of anything intelligent to say. I knew the Russians were shrewd at assessing people. If we got involved in a long interrogation, one of us might blunder. The only thing would be to say as little as possible, hailing the Red Army for its heroism, and lauding Lenin, Stalin, and anyone else I could think of, and hope to get away with it.

A Russian officer, older than me but also a lieutenant, stopped us and asked abruptly, 'Who are you? Where are you going? Are you German or Austrian?'

I replied in my best Russian, with as much eagerness as I could muster, that we were neither Germans nor Austrians but from western Ukraine. 'We have been slave workers on a farm twenty or thirty kilometres from here, and have heard that there is some sort of Russian headquarters, or camp, or assembly point, for all of us who were oppressed by the Nazis, and we are going to join this camp, because we want to go back home. We don't want to be slaves any longer. Thank God Hitler is defeated! Thank God he is dead and we can now return to our homeland!'

The Russian lieutenant regarded me with amazement, touched by our simplicity and pleased that his men should hear this condemnation of the Nazis. He congratulated me on my command of Russian. 'What a youth we have here!' he exclaimed. 'Where did you learn to speak such perfect Russian?'

I smiled broadly and declared, 'Father Stalin taught me Russian in my school in Halychyna, western Ukraine, between 1939 and 1941.'

'What about your friend?' he asked.

'Oh, the same. We are both the same,' I declared. While Ivan stared at his shoes, I chattered on breathlessly, telling him all about my Russian teacher and how I was an enthusiastic Pioneer at school and how I danced in a school folk-dancing group, and how we were told by our Russian teachers that one day would be dancing in Moscow in front of Father Stalin. Unfortunately, the Nazis invaded and our hearts bled at missing that wonderful opportunity. Worse than that, my friend and I, like many others, were taken by the Nazis as slave labourers. So now the only thing we wanted in the world was to go home.

I fed the lieutenant whatever I thought he might swallow, fervently reminiscing about my schooldays under the Russians, and leaving him no time to ask questions, until it was clear that he was convinced. Meanwhile, Ivan kept nodding, murmuring, 'Yes, yes' or 'That's right' to anything that seemed to require his confirmation. The lieutenant then told us how to find the camp we were looking for. We feared he might direct us back to the one we had just come from, but evidently there was another. Having pointed the way, he stood aside to let us pass. It made us wonder how many camps there were of that kind.

Having shaken hands with him, thanked him, and smiled as he saluted, we made our way through the ranks of drilling soldiers and continued on our way – as easy as that! We felt as light as feathers, as though the slightest breeze would make us fly, after the ten or twenty minutes during which we had felt as if nailed to the ground in shoes of lead, holding our breath in panic. Best of all, the route he had pointed out to us was the very one our map recommended.

Several kilometres beyond the point where the Russians would be able to see us even if they were following us through their binoculars, we turned off that road – so as to put them off our trail. They might, after all, decide to check up on us. We knew we could not get lost in relation to our map, because there were plenty of hills providing vantage points where we could climb a tree, look around, and get our bearings once again. We were in no hurry, much as we wanted to get back to familiar surroundings. It seemed best to take our time, hiding by day in the hills and forests, and doing our walking in the very early morning, late afternoon, and evening. Herr Glücklich had told us the Russian army was most active during the day and that those times would be the safest.

Considering how, in our first few hours, we had experienced two situations where we could easily have been captured and sent back either to the camp we had come from or to another, we had already learnt prudence. The thing now was to relax, talk things over, agree on our story, lay very careful plans, and stick to them. We had had two close shaves and might not be so lucky a third time.

We sat down to rest and eat on a hill, high enough that we would know if anyone was coming, and with bushes for cover. If we rationed it carefully, the food we had would last for four or five days. Water could be a problem, but much of our route followed the course of the River Raab and its tributaries, and the river water was generally clean and safe. One day soon we would have to go to a farmhouse for food or water, or for directions from local people, and trust them not to betray us, but till then we would just move cautiously and take our time.

Our first night was spent in the forest, which was the safest place to sleep. It was cold at night but the weather was dry and we had blankets, so the temperature did not bother us. We were young and healthy and used to sleeping outdoors.

The following day we were walking through open fields when we saw four elderly women and a boy cutting the hay and, sure they could not do us any harm, went closer.

'Can you tell us if there are any Russian soldiers in the vicinity?' I asked them.

They stopped working and gazed at us with some alarm. 'Oh, yes! There are a lot of Russians around here. Be very, very careful where you go: we've been told they've set up camps for young fellows like you. If the Russians catch you, they'll put you in one.'

'What do the Russians do with the people they catch?' I asked, though I already had a pretty good idea.

'Who knows? All we know is that the young men are taken away and aren't seen again.' Ivan and I exchanged looks. We could guess the rest. 'Make sure you don't walk on the main roads, or alongside the railway. Keep to the hills and forests, or follow the river,' our new friends warned, confirming the advice Herr Glücklich had given us. We thanked them for this useful information and went on our way, hearing them call 'God bless you!' after us.

On another occasion, when we were unwise enough to be out on the hills at midday, we found a cherry tree with ripe cherries on it and decided to climb up and pick some. God must have been watching over us, for we took our bags up into the tree with us, securing them among the branches. We were busy picking and eating the fruit when, all of a sudden, two Russian soldiers on horseback appeared out of nowhere, trotting straight towards us on a path up and across the hillside.

Terrified, we reached for our revolvers and clung as tightly as we could to the tree, flattening ourselves against the trunk motionless, so that not a twig moved. If the soldiers looked up and saw us, we should have no choice but to shoot them both and run. On the other hand, if they merely rode on, we would have been saved once again.

God was with us - and even more so with the Russians! The horses, for reasons perhaps not unconnected with our presence in the cherry tree, could not keep their heads still and kept tossing them up and down, jerking their riders forwards and backwards. Or they may have been bucking and swaying to keep their footing on the sloping pathway, which was not very wide. Whatever the reason, the two riders had to concentrate hard to keep them in line. Keeping a tight hold on their reins, they walked their horses under the cherry tree and past it, continuing on over and down the hillside. Ivan and I put our guns back in our pockets, gasping with relief, and went on picking and eating cherries until our stomachs could hold no more. I don't believe I have ever eaten cherries that tasted so good!

We had many enjoyable moments in those days, in spite of the perils that surrounded us. The countryside was sparsely populated so, as often as not, we wandered along in perfect peace. Sleeping in the woods was blissful, especially if we could find moss to make a springy mattress. The grass, full of wild thyme, gave off a wonderful aroma and, provided that no ants or snakes disturbed our rest, we slept soundly, safe and secure, knowing no one could find us before the sun rose. Moreover, the weather was superb – bright sun and blue skies by day and at night the moon beamed down on us with its friendly face.

Exulting in our freedom after years of slavery, we roamed at will, bathing in streams, deviating from our route sometimes to approach a farmhouse and ask for food. When we told the farm people who we were and what had happened to us, they were almost always kind.

Ivan and I could also speak freely to one another, with no need to guard our tongues, as we planned our route and devised our strategy. Ivan was a quiet fellow, without much to say for himself; he mostly followed my lead but neither of us was under orders. Like the birds in the trees and the rabbits in the fields, we lived each day as it came. We were moving south through rural areas and only had to be on guard when we came upon the Russians unexpectedly. Being seen by Austrian civilians did not worry us because we knew, deep in our hearts, that the Austrian people were as disillusioned with the Russian occupation as we were, and were on our side.

We went out of our way to find isolated farms, far from the main roads where the Russians might be undertaking exercises or scouring the neighbourhood in search of food. When we told the farmers our story and asked for help, they would give us food and fresh water to take with us on our journey. Sometimes they invited us to stay on the farm and work there until the Russians pulled back towards their own borders, as people expected them to do. We thanked them but said we preferred to go on. No one could say when, if ever, the Russians would withdraw. It sounded to us like wishful thinking – knowing the Russians, they do not shift very quickly.

A few weeks had passed, and we had covered less than half the distance we had to go. We decided to look for a village where there were no Russians in sight, and try to find out what was happening in the world. Perhaps they would be able to tell us whether it was safe now to walk on the main road, or take a train, if there was a railway station nearby. We had some Austrian money and could afford to buy tickets. Herr Glücklich had given us some, and so had a friendly farmer we met along the way. 'As long as the Russians are here, money won't buy anything, anyway,' he told us, 'so you might have more use for it than I do just now.'

From a hill high above fields full of wild flowers, we began to keep a close watch on a little hamlet of fifteen or twenty buildings – houses, barns and stables. Moving closer cautiously we scanned the place for several hours, checking the comings and goings to see whether any Russians were about. While I lay on my back looking up at the blue sky, Ivan would be on watch duty, then he would rest while I took my turn. We saw people going about their daily work within the village, but no one arriving or leaving. We decided to slip down into the village and go into the first house we came to, trying to avoid being seen by anyone, lest we rouse the villagers' suspicions. If too many people saw us, they might start speculating about what we were there for, which might make it difficult and dangerous for us.

I am absolutely convinced that God was by our side, guiding us, planning our route, saving us from peril, every hour of the day, wherever we went and whatever we did. When we finally walked into the village and tapped softly on the door of the first house, it was a very special sort of young woman who opened the door to us. She drew back in alarm at the sight of strangers.

'What do you want? Who are you?' she asked.

We couldn't afford to linger on the doorstep answering questions, so we pushed past her into the hallway of the house and closed the door behind us, in what must have seemed a very threatening manner. However, I tried to reassure her.

'Don't be frightened,' I said. 'We won't hurt you. We need your help. We're on the run from the Russians and need some information about the locality. If you'd be kind enough, would you please tell us the things we want to know?'

She relaxed at once when she realized we were fugitives, not rapists or marauders wielding guns, and she led us through a doorway into a delightfully sunny room, where a smiling baby was sitting up in its pram.

'This is Pepi,' she said proudly, brushing the child's cheek with her finger. We wondered if the baby's father was at work elsewhere in the village, and might come in at any time and be angry, or if he was away in the German army. She didn't appear to be a widow. Widows, at that time, usually made their status plain.

We told her briefly who we were, where we had come from, and where we were going, imploring her not to give us away. All we wanted were reliable answers to certain questions concerning the location of the village in relation to nearby towns, and the whereabouts of Russian contingents who might otherwise intercept us. For that we would be eternally grateful. Since her manner suggested she was as afraid of the Russians as we were ourselves, we vowed we would not tell anyone that she given us her assistance. In the event, she showed herself to be anything but fearful. On the contrary, she proved courageous, intelligent and resourceful.

She told us her name, Marianne, and then her story, while her eyes filled with tears. Her husband was a soldier and had been serving on the Eastern front. Now that the war was over, she had been expecting him to come home, but he had lately been listed as missing. She prayed daily for his return. He had never had the joy of seeing his baby son, who had been born since his last home leave.

Relieved at having someone to tell her story to who listened with concern – Ivan and I were visibly moved – she invited us to make ourselves at home and went to fetch food and milk. 'You're quite safe for the time being,' she told us. 'There are no Russians in the village, and it's such a small place, they rarely bother to come and check up on us.'

Given that information, we began to relax and contemplate staying there with Marianne for an hour or two, enjoying the company and attention of a lovely young woman. We could then return to the hills under cover of night. Stiffly we sat on a small wooden settee, eating the lunch she had prepared and minding our manners, while she perched on a chair by the pram, gently rocking the baby and eyeing us with lively interest. She was clearly excited by the arrival of two very young strangers out of the blue to break the lonely monotony of her days and seemed eager to share in our adventure. After turning the matter over in her mind, she suggested, 'Why don't you stay with us here in the village for a little while, at least until we see what the Russians are going to do? At the moment they hardly ever come here, so I could hide you and feed you, and it would be wonderful for us villagers to have you here, lending a hand with the work and looking after us. All our young men are either dead or missing in the war, and we have only a few old men to protect us.' These older men, she told us, had been made *Strassen Polizei*, or road police, by the Bürgermeister. 'He issues them with a signed certificate with his seal on it, which they have to carry with them at all times, as well as an arm band which they always wear on their sleeves. My father has one. It's a red band, printed in Russian and German with the words STRASSEN POLIZEI. In the centre of the band is the Bürgermeister's seal with his signature, so the band signifies that you are an Austrian citizen and also that you are an authorized road policeman.'

I exchanged glances with Ivan, certain that the idea of us two becoming authorized road policemen had occurred to him as soon as it had to me. Not that we wanted to stay on in the village, as she suggested, but it would certify our Austrian citizenship so that no one would feel it necessary to ask for our papers. It might even enable us to walk on the main roads, or travel by train, with some confidence. That would simplify our journey considerably.

'Thank you for your invitation,' I said, 'but, much as we would like to stay on here and help you, Ivan and I are determined to get back to the places where we have friends as quickly as possible, and would prefer to continue our journey.' I looked to Ivan for confirmation before adding, 'If, however, you can think of anything that might help us to pass ourselves off as Austrians if we are confronted by the Russians – something official, perhaps, like the arm bands of the *Strassen Polizei* – that would be a tremendous help to us.'

At first Marianne seemed disappointed. Having made two new young friends, she was reluctant to let us go but the idea of disguising us clearly appealed to her. She began to consider ways and means.

'I'm quite clever with my hands, especially when it comes to sewing or doing lettering. I could make you the fake arm bands and forge two likely-looking Bürgermeister's certificates, but of course they wouldn't stand up to close inspection. The arm bands would look perfect from a distance, so long as no one got too close, and you could probably show the certificates to the Russians and get away with it, since half of them can't read, but neither the arm bands nor the certificates would fool a genuine Austrian policeman.' She laughed, picturing the scene.

Ivan and I were overcome with admiration. She did not seem to consider the danger to herself and her baby, yet she must have known there would be no pity for either of them if she were found out. She was engrossed with the practicalities of her project. The baby watched us intently, gurgling from time to time, evidently amused by the two strange faces. 'I've got a Nazi flag somewhere, which contains red and white material that would do. I'll tear it up and make the arm bands on my sewing machine and you can have them in no time. As for the official seal, my father will lend me his to copy. I can use a round ink bottle to make a black ring on each arm band, and then print STRASSEN POLIZEI in German and Russian in black ink.'

Ivan and I were really excited. We looked enough like Austrians in the clothes we were wearing, which we had been given by Herr Glücklich, so that we would not stand out in a crowd, but the arm bands would provide a further camouflage. The Bürgermeister's seal might prove difficult to reproduce, however.

Marianne brushed our fears aside. 'I know the kind of heavy notepaper with old-fashioned lettering on it that they use for official documents in the

1. My parents, Olena and Oleksa Terleckyj, on their wedding day.

. My mother as a young woman in service
with a Prussian noble family.

3. My sister, Lywosi, in traditional
Ukrainian dress.

4. The men of the Terlezki family. I am the boy standing between my father and my Uncle Dmytro at the brickworks. The other man is their boss.

5. Some fifty years later, the family is reunited in Antoniwka. My Uncle Roman is standing behind me. *(Helena Terlezki)*

6. Nazi Germany's advance through Ukraine in 1941.

7. Slave Labourers arrive in the Reich, dishevelled and filthy after their horrific journey.

8. Deloused and cleaned up, the human cargo on its way to slavery.

9. The man who bought
me, Hansel Böhmer.

10. His brother,
    Anton ('Toni').

Gefreiter
Stering Anton
geb. 1924, ist infolge schwerer Verletzung 1945 i. Bayreut verst

11. 'Mutti', the matriarch of the family.

12. Her daughter, Frieda.

13. The British occupy Graz in 1945, liberating me from the Russians.

14. Voitsberg 1945. I am in a jacket, standing next to a fellow slave labourer, who was murdered on his return to Ukraine.

15. El Alamein Transit Camp Catering Corps. I am wearing a chef's hat!

16. Villach 1947. We were all 'displaced persons' hoping a country would accept us.

17. On my way to a new life, towards the end of my time in Villach.

18. Ukrainians going to Britain pray at the graves in Münster of their countrymen who killed themselves rather than be forcibly handed over to the Russians.

19. Family life: with my mother, cousin and aunts just before the war.

20. Staying true to my roots, wearing Ukrainian dress with my wife Mary. (*South Wales Echo*).

21. A family of my own. With Mary and our daughters Caryl and Helena and dog, Sandy!

22. Telling the truth about the Russian empire, at the 1973 Conservative Party Conference.

23. The Aldermen and councillors of Cardiff are addressed by Her Majesty the Queen.

24. A more informal moment in City Hall. The Lord Mayor, Sir Charles Hallinan is flanked by Cardiff City Football Club's chairman, Stefan Terlezki, and manager, Jimmy Andrews.

25. Vote Stefan Terlezki! My Ukrainian Youth supporters during the 1983 Election Campaign.
(South Wales Echo).

26. Victory! Caryl and Mary with the new MP for Cardiff West.
(South Wales Echo).

27. With Emily Philips after she received the medals won by her son Leon.
(South Wales Echo).

28. Prince Charles meets me (right) and my predecessor as MP for Cardiff West, George Thomas (left). *(South Wales Echo)*.

29. A meeting with the Prime Minister.

30. I am forever grateful to Sir Geoffrey Howe (Lord Howe of Aberavon) for his help in reuniting me with my father.

31. Father and I hold an impromptu press conference in my kitchen!
(South Wales Echo).

32. Shopping for the Siberian winter (and summer!) in Marks and Spencer.
(South Wales Echo).

33. A proud moment for all the family: after receiving the CBE from the Queen at Buckingham Palace.

34. An audience with His Holiness Pope John Paul II at the Vatican. My daughter Helena is on the left.

(L'Osservatore Romano)

35/36. Fellow cold war warriors: Henry Kissinger and Ronald Reagan.

37. Viktor Yushchenko, centre, Ukraine's first truly democratic President meets representatives of the Ukrainian Association of Great Britain.

38. Visiting the site of the destroyed nuclear reactor in Chernobyl.

39. A nostalgic moment in the ruins of my old home in Antoniwka.

40. Antoniwka 2002. The traditional Easter blessing of the *Paska* baskets.

41. I was allowed to address the congregation.

42. No visit is complete without paying my respects at my parents' graves.

43/44. The whole television crew enjoyed my relatives' hospitality.

45. Reunited with Hilde on the farm near Voitsberg in Austria.

Bürgermeister's office, and I think I can find some. My father had a letter from the Bürgermeister and I remember exactly what it looked like. Don't worry.'

We spent a nervous fifteen minutes while she dashed out to borrow her father's arm band and certificate, but she left the baby with us, and we were convinced she would not betray us. When she got back, she found the Nazi flag she had mentioned and laboriously tore it up. Then she opened her sewing machine and got to work, enjoying the chance to demonstrate her skills to appreciative spectators. We felt like members of a theatre audience, absorbed in the performance of a highly accomplished actress. She knew exactly what she wanted to do and did it.

A few hours later, the arm bands were ready. Then she began on the certificates. She appeared to have all the materials she needed, and we were spellbound by her efficiency and skill. After living rough and in danger for so long, about as welcome in most places as stray cats, we could hardly believe that a beautiful young woman would go to such trouble on our behalf. We were strangers, and little more than schoolboys. The Almighty had certainly led us to the right place, into an angel's hands.

When she put the bands on our arms, and declared herself satisfied that they looked genuine, we embraced her for joy. Ivan and I had agreed on what I should say. 'In appreciation of all you've done for us, we'll be glad to stay on for a day or two, if you'd like us to, just in case the Russians come to the village. If they make any trouble I'm sure we could persuade them to leave. I speak Russian and have talked us out of awkward situations before. After that we must really be on our way.'

To cement our friendship, Marianne produced a bottle of schnapps she had hidden just in case the Russians turned up at her door demanding some, and we drank to her husband's safe return and our own successful journey, and relaxed.

For the next couple of days, we chopped wood, cleaned stables, mended bits of machinery and performed any other chores beyond the strength of the villagers to do for themselves. Everyone was welcoming and grateful for our help. Then, late one afternoon a few days later, we thanked Marianne from the bottom of our hearts for all she had done for us and said goodbye.

We returned to the hills, not yet sure enough of ourselves to start walking on main roads. We had to get used to our arm bands, which we admired as we went along, and we wanted to study our certificates and be sure of what they said. It was important for us to get accustomed to our new identities and agree between ourselves on exactly how we should behave if we were stopped by the Russians, or by the real *Strassen Polizei*, so that we could feel confident enough to walk into a railway station and buy tickets for a train journey. Meanwhile, the kindness we had encountered made us walk tall.

Chapter 12

1945
On the Run

At this stage of our journey, with the armbands on our sleeves and the certificates in our pockets, we felt considerably happier than we had in the first week after our escape. Walking along in a leisurely fashion, we built up the courage to go down onto the main roads and considered the pros and cons of travelling by train.

We talked about what we would do when we reached the safety of the British, or American, Zone, but the idea of a future outside the constraints of a totalitarian regime was so alien to our experience, so clearly in the hands of the Almighty, it was difficult to imagine. We told each other our life stories, sharing memories of our families and our childhood in Ukraine. Ivan spoke affectionately of his younger brother and sister, Bohdan and Marijka, but like me he had heard nothing from home since early in the year. We compared notes on the farms we had worked on in Austria, what we had learned and how we had been treated. Ivan had spent all of his three years on one farm, where he felt very much at home. His farmer was a man he respected, a good employer who made him feel like one of the family. He had never been in trouble with the Gestapo. Ivan was a country boy to the core. He had not had much formal education, but he could recognize and imitate the whistles of birds, trilling back at them as if they were old friends. He had a copious knowledge of the properties of wild plants, knowing which ones were edible or could be used for medicinal purposes. He had a pleasant voice and used to sing and whistle a tune as we walked along.

Our route was bringing us close to the area, on the other side of a range of hills, which Ivan knew best. We scrambled up to the highest point we could find, to get a clear view to the south-west. On our map we found the small town of Feldbach, which was near the farm where Ivan had worked. Little by little, Ivan ascertained where these were on the landscape spread out below us. Gradually we got our bearings. Over on our left, to the south of us, near the Yugoslav border, lay Radkersburg, where I had nearly frozen to death doing my *Arbeitsdienst*. Graz was almost due west, some sixty to seventy kilometres beyond Feldbach, and Voitsberg was another fifty to sixty kilometres beyond Graz. Eventually, we decided that the road we could see at the foot of the hills was the one Herr Glücklich had pointed out on the map, the one that would take us to the farm where Ivan had worked. By now, I looked forward to that as much as he did.

'You'll like the people there, Stefan,' Ivan assured me. 'Once we reach the farm, they will tell us what conditions are like now, and what the Russian army is up to. Then, depending on what they say, we can decide whether it is safe to use the main roads. It's a pity I didn't stay there. I only left the farm because I was longing to see my family and workers from Poland and Byelorussia told me the Russians had promised to take us home. We'll be safe once we get there.'

That sounded good to me. 'Can we tell them the truth about what has happened to us? If we explain how disillusioned we are with the Russians and say that we just want to head for the British Zone, will they still help us?'

'Yes, of course,' Ivan said. 'I'm sure they will; they're generous, kindly people.'

As we started our descent, he pointed to a bridge he recognized, which spanned a narrow stretch of the River Raab. 'Unfortunately, we're going to have to cross that bridge when we get there,' he said. 'Let's hope the Russians aren't guarding it.'

It was a vain hope and we knew it: every bridge was patrolled and, sure enough, as we drew near, we saw three or four Russian soldiers, rifles on their shoulders, marching stiffly to and fro. There was no way we could slip across the bridge without them seeing us.

'If we follow the river a little way, staying on this side, and try to cross it further up, we might not be spotted so quickly,' muttered Ivan. 'We might find a place shallow enough for us to wade across, and there are dense woods on the opposite bank which would give us plenty of cover. The farm is only a little way beyond those woods.'

We headed along the riverbank in the direction he indicated, not confident enough, even with our arm bands, to brazen it out with the soldiers on the bridge. The question remained, however; what on earth should we do if the Russians noticed us and stopped us? Would we identify ourselves then as *Strassen Polizei,* and show them our Bürgermeister's certificates? Or would that be too risky?

There was a place where we could wade across, screened by trees from sight of the soldiers, or so we thought! Taking off our shoes and trousers, we waded in up to our waists, carrying our clothes and bags above our heads. We were on the other side in no time and were hurriedly pulling on our trousers when we heard, loud and clear, the command '*Pastoy! Pastoy!*' 'Stop! Stop!' Somehow the soldiers must have caught sight of us through the trees.

Beyond a shadow of doubt we would be crazy to stop. It was too late now to pretend we were legitimate travellers. If the soldiers saw our arm bands, they would want to know why we hadn't crossed the river by the bridge, as any ordinary road policeman was entitled to do. Having roused their suspicions, anything we said would only make our position worse. We were in a trap of our own making and there was nothing we could do about it but to ignore the call and take to our heels. The soldiers were perhaps a kilometre or more behind us. If they followed, as they were sure to do, we would simply have to outrun them and try to throw them off our track, or fight them off as best we could if we were cornered.

Hearing another shout, we picked up our bags and began to walk very fast towards the woods, playing stupid, pretending we had not heard them shout, or did not understand Russian, or did not realize it was us they were calling. When they yelled at us a third time, we ran, and at that point they opened fire. We couldn't wait to find out whether they were firing directly at us or sending warning shots into the air. Our revolvers were no match for their weapons. We raced off and plunged into the woods, hoping to hide or climb further up into the hills if we had to. It didn't matter how far we had to run. We were in good physical shape and running was our only hope.

No sooner had we reached the woods than, to our absolute amazement, we saw vast piles of munitions of every kind – hand grenades, machine guns, Sten guns, revolvers – all dumped together in heaps, an enormous armoury that must have been abandoned by the Germans as they retreated from the Eastern front. Though we could hardly believe our eyes, we could see at a glance that the weapons were German.

For boys raised in Ukraine, making use of this heaven-sent arsenal presented no problems. We had always been fascinated by military equipment. We prided ourselves on being able to identify each type of gun the soldiers carried and on knowing how they were operated. I remembered seeing Russian soldiers throw hand grenades into the river in Antoniwka trying to catch fish.

Ivan and I didn't hesitate. We picked up hand grenades with both hands and hurled them behind us to stave off pursuit. If the Russians gave chase, we had ammunition enough to hold out there for a month, provided they came after us on foot! Grabbing up one grenade after another, we tossed them indiscriminately in all directions, making as much commotion as we possibly could with our bombardment, to give the impression that there were many more than just two of us hidden among the trees. We must have made enough noise for twenty or thirty men at least!

The bushes and trees filled with smoke, so that we couldn't see whether the soldiers were still on the bridge or close on our heels. We just kept throwing the grenades, picking them up as casually as if they were potatoes and pitching them into the distance, until Ivan said, 'Come on, Stefan! Let's run for it. The smoke is hiding us.' He started to move. 'I know the way to the farm and we can hide there until the fuss dies down.'

No further suggestion was necessary. Within seconds we were tearing as fast as we could through the tangle of trees and undergrowth when Ivan, who was leading the way, glanced back at me and said urgently, 'Stefan! Look at the blood on your foot! Look at your leg! You must have been hit! You're wounded!' I looked down and saw that my ankle and foot were streaming with blood, although I didn't feel any pain. It frightened me but I didn't dare stop.

'It's nothing,' I gasped, not slackening the pace. 'Don't worry about it! I can run! Doesn't hurt.' I was pretty sure I hadn't been hit by a bullet. It was probably a piece of shrapnel from the explosions we ourselves had created.

Moments later we were in the farmyard, surrounded by people, with Ivan desperately trying to impress the urgency of our situation on the old farmer, Rudi. He and his family had heard the explosions in the forest and now overwhelmed us with questions, agog with curiosity as to what was going on. They were shocked to see that one of the fugitives was Ivan.

'Please, Rudi, we can't talk now. Just hide us somewhere quickly!' Ivan begged. 'Our lives are at stake! The Russians may come looking for us at any moment! We threw some hand grenades we found at a Russian patrol, they'd started shooting at us when we wouldn't stop. We stumbled on this pile of ammunition and tried to stave them off by hurling grenades at them. That's what all the noise was about'

Rudi hustled us into the barn at once and told us to dig as deep into the hay and straw as we could. 'Even if they come to the farm, they won't find you there,' he said calmly. 'We'll pretend we know nothing. We're good at that. We'll say we were busy working in the fields and haven't seen you. They won't hurt us.'

His wife saw the blood pouring from my ankle and pulled off her head scarf and pushed it into my hands. 'Here you are,' she said hurriedly. 'Wrap this around that bleeding foot before you hide yourself. Quick now!'

With hearts beating so fast with terror we were hardly capable of thinking for ourselves, we did as we were told and burrowed deep into the straw. We were hot and exhausted and my wounded leg was beginning to throb with pain. What concerned us most just then, however, was the trouble we might have brought down on the farmer and his family. They were now deeply implicated. If the Russians came looking for us, they would put a lot of pressure on them with their questions. Had they heard the shooting? Had they seen two men? And what if the Russians started doing as we had seen them do before – threaten to harm the women and children – or took out their revolvers and announced that they would shoot them all, one by one, until they got the answers they wanted?

We imagined them searching the farm. They would be bound to use the farmer's pitchforks, plunging them deep into the straw and into our heads and bodies – stomachs, faces, eyes, or legs. Or, if they didn't kill us that way, they would surely shoot us when they found us, without even asking our names, since we had committed the unforgivable crime of firing live ammunition at Russian soldiers. We lay there trembling uncontrollably.

At first we remained silent, straining our ears for the approach of soldiers, but, as time went on, we made a little tunnel in the straw through which we could whisper to one another. Ivan was worrying about my wounded ankle. Could I breathe? Was it giving me pain? He was afraid I might pass out. We had no air and it was very hot, buried deep down in the straw. If the Russians didn't find us, it seemed possible we might just suffocate staying where we were.

I don't know what Ivan did but, true to my Greek Catholic upbringing, I prayed. We were, after all, only two innocent lads who had been duped into joining Stalin's Russian army and, through no fault of our own, were wandering in the wilderness. Surely the Almighty would protect us and keep us safe from harm. If we could be patient and withstand the pressure of the terrible heat and fear, and our ignorance of what was happening around us, I believed we would survive. Sweating it out deep in the straw, I forced myself to relax.

Even at that depth we were aware that the barn was growing darker. Night had fallen without any very ominous sounds in the yard outside. There had been no shouts or stamping of feet. No one had come into the barn. Cautiously, we parted the straw a little and began to breathe more freely. We should have to sleep where we were that night and see what the following day would bring.

It was the middle of the next morning before we heard a woman's voice softly calling, 'Ivan! Stefan! It's all right. You can come out now.'

She told us her name was Tina and that she had come to get us so that we would know it was not a Russian soldier, or the farmer being marched out at gunpoint by the Russians, hoping to trick us into showing ourselves. As we struggled up through the hay and straw, she said comfortingly, 'Don't worry, lads. Safe now. The Russians came to the farm last evening, but they didn't stay long. They asked if we'd heard the noise of shooting in the woods or seen anybody running away. We told them we hadn't seen anyone, and that we assumed the shots were the Russians themselves. Weren't they always loosing off firearms, out on exercises, or shooting rabbits or pheasants for food? We hadn't taken any notice of it.'

'And they believed you?'

Tina tossed her head. 'Why not? We heard this morning that two lorry-loads of soldiers were out searching the forest late last night, but they evidently didn't find anything. They seem to have called off their search now. As far as we know, the only Russians left in the area are the three or four on patrol on the bridge.'

We followed her into the farmhouse where the farmer's wife, a short, elderly woman with a round, wrinkled face and kind smile, gave us a truly sumptuous breakfast. There was plenty of milk to drink and bowls of *sterts*, the thick porridge made of ground sweetcorn, followed by bread and sliced speck. We relaxed, finding ourselves the focus of friendly attention from the five or six people of the house. Rudi's old eyes twinkled as we described our heroic stand in the forest. He sucked at his meerschaum pipe, elaborately carved in the shape of a Turk's head, and waited till we had finished eating. Then he announced that he had sent for the local doctor to come and see to my leg.

'Oh, no,' I protested, alarmed. A local doctor might feel obliged to report us to the Russians. 'There's no need for that. It's just my ankle and it's only a flesh wound. It won't give me any trouble. I'd rather manage without a doctor. If anyone mentions our presence here, we'll all be in the soup, you and your family as well.'

Rudi looked unperturbed. 'Don't worry. I thought about that before I sent for him. This is our family doctor, who's looked after us for more than twenty-five years. He cared for the children when they were young. Ivan knows him. He can be trusted. He'll just look at your ankle and make sure it's all right, bandaging the wound for you so it doesn't get infected.' Hearing that, and seeing Ivan's nod, I felt better.

When the doctor came, he examined the wound and bandaged it, complaining meanwhile of the shortage of drugs and medicines that continued even though the war was over. 'I don't think you've broken anything, so it's not too serious, but it's rather a messy wound and I don't have the right sort of ointment to clear it up quickly. I'll give you some spare bandages. If you keep the wound clean and change the bandage at least once a day, it should heal all right. It would be better still, however, to get yourself into a hospital where they have a good supply of drugs. Failing that, there's a leaf you can find in the fields that has antiseptic properties: a thick leaf called *hubka*, about the size of the palm of my hand, and it grows close to the ground. Ivan will know it. Cover the wound with it before you put the bandage on and change it once or twice a day. Don't forget, though the best cure would be a week or so in hospital.'

I expressed my gratitude for his help and advice, but he brushed it aside, gazing at Ivan and me with deep sadness. 'Don't mention it,' he said, ' I'd do anything in the world for boys like you. My own son was about your age when he was killed on the Eastern Front.'

Expecting to leave the farm as soon as the doctor had paid his visit, I was surprised to hear Rudi say: 'Don't start out yet. Wait a day or two. The Russians might start investigating again. Or you might walk away from the farm and find that one of the Russian patrolmen has spotted you.' He shrugged. 'Out of the frying pan into the fire.' Good advice, we thought, and we were glad to rest up on the farm for a few days, recounting the whole story of our adventures to an appreciative audience. We described our escape from the Russian camp in vivid detail. The farmer was unsurprised when he heard how the Russians had tried to trick us into going to fight for them against the Japanese, just when we had thought we were on our way home. There was no love lost between him and the Red Army.

After two or three days, it became plain that Ivan was tired of being on the run, though he hesitated to say so. He was glad to be back among people he knew and they seemed overjoyed to have him with them again. They were warm-hearted folk, unlike the people on my first farm, to whom I could likewise have become attached if they had demonstrated the same degree of human kindness. Ivan was fond of them and they had succoured us, at great risk to themselves, when we were in mortal danger. In addition to all that, the farm was a pleasant place to live, set in peaceful rural surroundings pervaded by sunshine, and far removed from the tensions of war.

It was disappointing but no great surprise when Ivan at last said, 'I think I would like to stay here on the farm now, Stefan, and carry on working until things get back to normal. Perhaps the Russians won't occupy the area for very long. They might even hand it over to the British, which would make it safer for me. Meanwhile, Rudi and his family have agreed to hide me, if need be, and take care of me while we wait to see what happens next.' He waited for the blow to be absorbed and then added: 'Would you like to stay, too? Rudi says he would be pleased to have us both.'

'No thanks! Not on your life, Ivan!' I declared vehemently. 'I've had three years of farming and that's enough.' Not even a man like Rudi could lure me back into farming, endlessly ploughing the fields and sowing and harvesting the corn, getting up at four o'clock in the morning in the summer and working until nine or ten at night. 'It's too much like slavery, and doesn't appeal to me one bit. No doubt I could claim now to be a professional farmer, fully qualified, but in the future I will only follow that career if I can be a gentleman farmer, a squire with hundreds, or even thousands, of hectares of land.'

The fact was, I had different aspirations. I wanted to take command of my own life, and complete my interrupted education. I wanted to go to college or university, become better read and really well-informed, so that I could speak my mind on controversial issues that mattered to me. I hoped to make a home and settle down somewhere. My immediate priority was to find out what life was like in either the British or American occupied zones of Austria. I felt sure the people of Britain and America enjoyed opportunities we lacked and that their system of government would suit me. Once there, I could perhaps make plans for the future. I could not contemplate living under the Russians, whom I would never trust again. In fact, I was more resolved than ever, if I fell into their hands, to fight my way out with my revolver, leaving it to God's judgement as to whether I should die myself or kill someone else in the attempt to survive. Nothing would induce me to linger on longer than I had to in the Russian zone.

Rudi and his friend the doctor were greatly amused to hear that we had planned to pass ourselves off as *Strassen Polizei*. At the same time, they were full of praise for Marianne, who had taken the risk of forging arm bands and documents to help us on our way.

'Now that Ivan has decided to stay on with us and you are going on alone, will you continue to pretend that you're a road policeman, Stefan?' they asked me.

'Yes, I will,' I replied. 'If we'd had the nerve to brave it out on the bridge back there, it might have saved us all a lot of trouble!'

My three days' rest on the farm had given me time to think about that. My ankle was giving me less pain and as my strength improved, my confidence returned. Taking to the hills and forests again might make my injured ankle worse, so I preferred to walk on main roads. I was bound to be confronted by the Russians at some point but, if I wore my arm band and walked with a firm step, trying not to limp, they would have no reason to doubt I was a young Austrian road policeman going about his legitimate business. It was my best bet for getting to Voitsberg quickly, and I could always use my revolver as a last resort. My mind was made up. I would opt for the main road, and to hell with the consequences!

Rudi gave me all the help he could. 'There's an alternative route into Graz which you might like to take but, if you want to reach Voitsberg, you will have to cross the River Mur by the bridge near the airport. That could be dangerous because it is always patrolled by Russian soldiers, much more regularly than the bridge near here. The airport itself is also heavily guarded, so there is no way you will be able to keep out of the way of the Russians altogether. However, Graz is a big place and there will be plenty of people heading there. Provided you just keep walking, you may get by unnoticed in the crowd. Avoid the centre of Graz, if you can. It is stiff with Russians. You will just have to weigh up the chances as you go along.'

I estimated that, since I could never travel in a straight line, it would take me from five to ten days to reach Graz, perhaps much longer. I didn't want to make my foot worse by overdoing it. If I tried to walk too far and began to limp, the Russians might suspect that I was unfit to be a road policeman. Then they would really start asking questions.

Leaving Ivan behind on the farm brought a moment of wrenching heartbreak. I felt perfectly composed as I thanked Rudi and his family for all their hospitality and help but, when I turned to embrace Ivan, there was no way I could restrain my tears. He had been a true friend and brother to me – we had relied totally on one another and I could hardly bear to leave him behind. From now on I would be on my own and facing increasing danger as I approached more populated areas. To ease the pain of parting, I gave him an address in Voitsberg.

'That will find me if I succeed in getting through,' I told him. 'And I'll leave messages wherever I go, in case you decide to follow.' Sad to say, I never saw Ivan or heard from him again. You get used to such partings far too easily during wartime.

My clothes were clean and well-brushed. As I strode off in the strong black shoes I had been given, I was assured that I looked every inch the typical young Austrian road policeman. The August weather was glorious. The sun shone, the air was fresh and clear, and the meadows were ablaze with wild flowers. I decided to avoid going through towns and to sleep in the open rather than be obliged to tell my story to anyone who might get suspicious and report me to the Russians. I would still take the risk of calling in at farms on the outskirts of villages during the day. Farmers rarely refused a request for a little food and milk, and they were usually too busy to ask questions.

The main obstacle to my peace of mind was the thought of that bridge at Graz, which loomed larger and larger in my imagination. On the third or fourth day, when I was only a few kilometres from the city, I decided to call in at a farm and seek advice about the best way to cross it safely.

Talking to strangers, always risky, had become more frightening now that I no longer had Ivan's support and encouragement. Furthermore, my injured ankle was a worry. I was not sure I could run for my life if an encounter went wrong. Keeping a stern grip on myself, and saying a silent prayer, but with my heart thumping heavily, I turned into a farm where a man was just coming out of the barn. As I approached, two more men emerged from the stables, and three women and a little girl came towards me from the orchard. For several moments, I had the impression they were bearing down on me with their scythes and pitchforks, to surround me and take me captive. They stared suspiciously at me, without smiling. No one spoke.

I greeted them with the words, '*Grüss Gott*', or 'God's Greetings'. 'Will you be good enough to help me?'

'Are you lost, Herr Polizei?' came the response, 'how can we help you?'

In my confusion, I had forgotten that I was masquerading as a policeman! Now I saw that they were not hostile, simply mystified by my presence, and uneasy on account of my official badge. When I explained that I was not a genuine road policeman, they began to ask questions, all talking at once. Was I Austrian? Russian? Where had I come from? Where was I going? I was trying to answer everyone at the same time while, without waiting for my replies, they escorted me into the farmhouse, urging me to sit down at a table in the large, well-equipped kitchen; then, seating themselves close around, they put bread and milk, smoked ham and cider, in front of me.

I expressed my thanks but told them I needed information more than food, and did not want to waste their time. However, they were determined to hear my story. Before long, I had divulged everything. They listened, amused and incredulous, especially intent on examining my arm band and the Bürgermeister's certificate.

'You are attempting to fight the Red Army single-handed?' the farmer cried. 'You, a young lad not yet eighteen? You are taking them on all on your own?'

He assured me I was safe on his farm. They had, he said, heard of boys like me being forced into the army by the Russians and quite understood my predicament.

'There are no soldiers in our immediate neighbourhood,' said one man, 'but at the airport in Graz, and around that bridge you plan to cross, there are masses of them.'

The word masses sent cold shivers down my spine, but I tried not to show it. Their anxious concern could become infectious and work me up into a panic. Then another man made it worse by saying, 'The Russians are in Graz in their thousands, with tanks, guns and aeroplanes. Crossing the city will be like trying to penetrate the Eastern front itself! It'll be a miracle if you get through!'

'What you must do, if you're determined to try it, is stop at a farm just short of the bridge and make sure you've got the latest information,' added the farmer. 'Then you will know exactly what you are up against. The situation changes from day to day.' Put like that, the prospect seemed manageable, even if terrifying. They urged me to stay with them for a day or two, but I knew I had to remain resolute and press on or lose my nerve altogether. After a few hours' rest, I thanked them, promised to heed their advice, and left. They embraced me and wished me God's luck.

I got away into the fields, so as not to attract the attention of anyone at all, even the local people, and slept under a tree that night. I wanted to get as near to the bridge as I could before making my final enquiries. Finding it hard to sleep, I lay gazing at the stars, identifying the ones I knew and counting them, like sheep. I told myself that under the constellation furthest to the west lay Voitsberg, on which all my hopes were pinned. That helped to calm my fears.

The people at the last farm before the bridge were in the kitchen, having their mid-morning break, when I walked into the farmyard. They saw me coming from the window and opened the door before I could knock, greeting me as 'Herr Strassen Polizei' and pouring me out a cup of coffee before asking me my business. Once again I told them the whole story. They jumped to the conclusion that I was returning to Voitsberg in order to find employment on a farm again, and could not understand why I should take the risk of going so far. The daughter of the family was an extremely vivacious girl, about my own age, called Trudi. She immediately pressed me to stay there and work for them instead. She did not even bother to consult her parents or seek their approval.

I was embarrassed and did not know how to reply. If anything could have shaken my resolve to continue on my perilous journey, it would have been the pleading of this very attractive girl. She had caught my eye straight away, as I had obviously caught hers. Her indulgent father pointed out the dangers I faced in trying to get through Graz, as emphatically as the men on the previous farm had done. He did not hesitate to second his daughter's invitation.

'You'd be welcome to stay here for a time,' he said. 'In a few weeks or months the Russians may leave the area, and then you could go on to Voitsberg. At the moment, though, there are tremendous numbers of soldiers everywhere. They leave the keeping of law and order mostly to the local *Strassen Polizei*, but your credentials could be challenged at any time.'

Nothing could make me change my mind. It had been firmly made up from the day Ivan and I deserted the Russian camp. Even if it was love at first sight for Trudi – as her tender glances seemed to indicate – I had more pressing matters on my mind than courtship just then. Trying to avoid meeting her eyes, I only agreed to stay long enough to have lunch with them. Farm work was abandoned for a few hours.

'If you're lucky and get across the bridge, you'll still have to walk quite a distance along one side of the airport to get to the railway station,' the farmer told me. 'Once there, however, your problems will be over. You can ride the rest of the way to Voitsberg in a comfortable train'

They gave me conflicting advice about whether to wear my arm band. If I were found out and forced to tell the truth, the women warned me with a shudder, I could endanger everyone who had helped me, right down the line. Marianne, who had made it for me, Ivan, and Ivan's farmer, Rudi, and they themselves, all could be compromised and sent to Siberia! The farmer, however, insisted I had a realistic chance of deceiving the Russian guards, so long as I kept them at a reasonable distance. Unless it was examined closely, the badge looked perfectly convincing. I should have to present some sort of identification before crossing the bridge, and I had none except the Bürgermeister's certificate, so his advice was simply to show that and keep my left arm away from the man who was examining it. It was a chance I would have to take. Otherwise they might search me and find my gun.

The gun was not the only thing I was carrying that might incriminate me. I had photographs of my family, and letters, and a full list of every man who had been in the Red Army company under my command, with their biographical details. I was preserving that for posterity! Clearly it would be safer to destroy it, but I felt I had a duty to notify their relatives in Ukraine, if I were ever given the chance, so they would know what had happened to their boys. My own family photographs and letters were simply too dear to my heart to be destroyed: I had to keep them even if it cost me my life. Discussing all this, however, made me more and more terrified.

Straight after lunch I bade everyone farewell. Each one hugged and kissed me, but it was Trudi who flung her arms round my neck and held me tight, whispering in my ear, 'Please don't go. Stay with us. I love you. Please don't go.' Sad to see young people, so obviously taken with one another, forced to part, the older women wept sentimental tears but by now I was impatient to be gone. My journey had reached its climax. The bridge at Graz had still to be crossed. Once on the other side, I should be within reach of friends in the comparative security of Voitsberg, which I had often cursed myself for leaving in the first place!

Chapter 13

1945
Bridge Over the River Mur

The road led to the airport, but it was not the main road into Graz and was, I thanked God, all but deserted. Had it not been for my situation, I would have been content enough to be walking along this particular thoroughfare. After all, it was a beautiful hot day, without a cloud in the clear blue sky. Fields of ripe wheat and barley, sweetcorn and potatoes, spread around me in a magnificent panorama that stretched away to distant mountains but this somehow made my own sense of danger more acute. Feeling about the size of a matchstick, I was unprotected on every side. Each step I took, frequently glancing back over my shoulder, brought me nearer to the bridge near Graz, which could no longer be avoided.

My heart was pounding painfully in my chest and my throat was dry, for I was well aware that my situation was desperate. My chances of bluffing my way past the guards without showing any documents were slim indeed, even though I wore my arm band. Since I could not produce papers, and dared not risk being searched, I would then have no recourse but to shoot my way out – kill or be killed. There was a very real possibility that this might be my last day on earth. I sang again the old song: *Forlorn, forlorn, forlorn am I, like a stone on the road.*

Nevertheless, I still had my faith in the Almighty. I did not know where help would come from but I believed it would come, being convinced that God had a plan for me. It might not preclude fear and suffering but would surely take me through in the end. Why else should I have survived this long? The impassioned prayer I murmured as I walked was quite simple: 'Dear God, in this hour of peril, save me! Deliver me not into the hands of my enemies. Protect me from the Russians. Help me to cross the River Mur in safety.'

Suddenly, as I looked back, a man and woman appeared on the road behind me, pushing a bicycle between them. At first I was apprehensive and walked more slowly, for the man – aged between thirty and forty – wore military uniform. It might be safer if they crossed the bridge before me. Snatching a second glance, I judged the man to be a Polish soldier, from the colour and cut of his uniform. Then, when they were perhaps twenty metres behind me, I decided he was British, and a heavy weight seemed to drop from my shoulders. I breathed a quick thank you to God. Here were my deliverers, in answer to my prayer.

I had met British soldiers at the prisoner of war camp near Voitsberg but was astonished to find one walking freely along the road here. The woman was much younger than he was, hardly more than a girl, and almost certainly Austrian. The bike was loaded up with bundles and suitcases of various sizes. As they drew near, they eyed me – to all appearances an Austrian road policeman – with polite curiosity, since I had obviously hung back in order to speak to them.

'God's greeting to you!' said the girl in the local dialect.

'God's greeting to you!' I replied, adding, in a direct appeal to the soldier, 'Excuse me for stopping you, but I desperately need your help. Do you speak German?' It was the first time I had seen a British soldier in full uniform, with a sergeant's stripes on his arm. For all I knew, he might have come straight from England.

'*Ja,*' he replied amiably, continuing in a way that showed him to be fluent in the local dialect, though with a noticeable foreign accent. He explained that he had spent some time in a prisoner of war camp near Voitsberg.

My face lit up. My guardian angels! Already I wanted to confide without reserve in this couple. I said that I'd had friends in the very same camp and described how I had been arrested and imprisoned by the Gestapo for unwisely recommending increased rations for them. As we compared notes on our experiences and mutual acquaintances in the Voitsberg area, the girl looked on admiringly. We were clearly heroes in her eyes. She could not know that, in my eyes, she and her companion had been sent by God himself! The bridge was only a few kilometres ahead.

'What are you doing here?' I asked the sergeant, forgetting that he and I no longer faced a common enemy. 'Isn't it dangerous for you? Aren't you afraid the guards on the bridge into Graz will arrest you? No Russian can be trusted.'

The sergeant laughed with total unconcern. Everything about him, his jovial manner, his considerable height and bulk, conveyed a strong self-assurance. Perhaps he imagined he could take on the Russians with his bare hands! 'Why should they? We're not dealing with the Nazis now, laddie,' he said. 'The Russians are our friends. We defeated the Nazis together.' Then, while I digested that fact, he explained his presence in the neighbourhood of Graz. 'I came here about a week ago from Köflach, where I am stationed, to see Mitzi. She's been working at Köflach but she lives near here, and she wanted me to meet her family.' As they say, he glowed with pride. 'She's coming back with me now so we can get married. Quite open and above board.'

I'd have liked to ask if I could be best man at his wedding – the most plausible excuse I could possibly have for crossing the bridge with them – but didn't dare. I did, however, tell them the whole sad story of what had happened to me since leaving Voitsberg. Like most people who heard it, they were appalled by the treatment I had received at the hands of the Russians.

The sergeant scratched the back of his head, tipping his khaki beret over one eye. 'You must be an extremely brave and resourceful young fellow, if you managed to desert from the Red Army and get this far without being caught! But you do realize, I hope, that you'll be court-martialled and almost certainly shot if they do get onto you! What's more, now that we and the Russians are all on the same side, there aren't many people who could help you.'

To me, that sounded as though he, my last and only hope, had no intention of putting himself in such a compromising position, and I cried out in protest. 'Friends or not, the Russians lied to us – not only to me but to *thousands* of us! Promising to take us home! We were all people who had suffered horribly under the Russians in the past, but we made up our minds to trust them and were betrayed. After that, I certainly wouldn't go to Japan to fight for them. Would you? And you're a sergeant. I'm not even a *soldier*.'

'Calm down, laddie, calm down. Remember, Britain is still at war with Japan,' he pointed out reasonably. 'I could be sent to the Far East even now, though it's not likely to happen. I was only pointing out what the Russians will do to you if they learn who you really are and what you did.'

'I know very well what they will do to me!' I almost sobbed, in my frustration. He studied me with compassion. 'You can trust me. I won't allow it to happen,' he added.

He exchanged looks with Mitzi, who had followed my story with anxiety. Proudly she squeezed her fiancé's arm, pleased by his response. In my desperation I was hardly aware of the enormity of what I was asking them to do for me, a stranger newly met on the road. Befriending a deserter from the Russian army could imperil their whole future. But these were risky times and the sergeant was not one to flinch from danger. Nor, apparently, was his bride-to-be.

The plan was quickly outlined. 'Look here,' he said. 'Mitzi and I are all right; our papers are all in order. You can pose as Mitzi's brother, Hans, an Austrian road policeman who has come with us to Graz to see her off at the railway station. You are representing her family, so to speak, because it's an occasion of great importance. Mitzi is leaving home to be married to a British soldier.'

Mitzi joined in eagerly: 'Moreover, you are obviously intending to go back over the bridge and return home, since it's your bike we are using, purely for transporting the suitcases, and you are going to take it home again. If they open our cases they'll see it's true. They're stuffed full of wedding gifts.'

'You are Hans, Mitzi's brother,' the sergeant declared again, his eyes twinkling with satisfaction at the prospect of putting one over on the Russian guards, 'and, whatever they say to us on the bridge, I'll back you up. I'll say you'll be cycling home again as soon as you've kissed us both goodbye and the train doors have closed. Seeing some doubt still in my eyes, he added, 'Trust me, laddie. Don't worry: I won't let you down. If the Russians decide to take you somewhere for questioning, Mitzi and I'll come with you. They won't want to take on the British army. They'll have to take my word. Otherwise, I could make things uncomfortable for them.'

If it had been my own father speaking, I couldn't have felt more confidence in him. I had an Englishman's word that he would stand by me whatever happened, even follow me to prison if need be. For the first time that day, I felt much less tense. Road policemen, after all, must be a common sight crossing and re-crossing the bridge. We walked on, behaving as much as possible like a family group, in case we were noticed by anyone, telling each other the stories of our lives. I even managed to smile at some of the comic incidents Mitzi and her sergeant described. When I asked him his name, he said, 'Just call me Jock.' I assumed Jock was his baptismal name.

We were still some way short of the bridge when a horse-drawn carriage driven by two Russian soldiers came clattering along behind us. Jock muttered, 'Keep calm and walk on. They'll go past.' However, he was mistaken. Seeing that one of us was a soldier in His Britannic Majesty's forces, they stopped and offered us a lift, speaking to us in Russian, which I pretended not to understand, though I was the only one who did. As their intention was quite plain, Jock smiled, signifying our acceptance and said to me, 'You and Mitzi get in and take the cases, and I'll ride behind you on the bike.'

There was no time for discussion. We did as we were told. After hundreds of kilometres on foot, avoiding all sight or sound of Russian soldiers if I possibly could, I found myself riding like a king in a carriage drawn by two fine horses, with Russian soldiers in the driving seat! The carriage had no doubt been confiscated. At the same time I was paralysed with fear. Hearing Russian spoken, having Russian soldiers, revolvers in their pockets and rifles on their shoulders, in such close proximity, even though they were smiling at us, unnerved me completely. If they knew who I was, they would shoot me without a second thought! As they didn't, however, they simply drove with a flourish up onto the Graz bridge, then over it and down the other side. I could hardly believe what had happened. All in an instant, while I was struggling to control my shaking knees and keep calm, the bridge, which had loomed so large and threatening in my imagination had been crossed. My second pair of angels wore Russian uniforms!

I had kept my eyes open, observing everything about the approach to the bridge and working out where the airport lay in relation to it. Not difficult; the bridge itself was elevated, providing a good viewpoint, and there were aeroplanes taking off and coming in to land. On the far side of the bridge the road forked. There the Russians brought the carriage to a halt and my euphoria to an end. They pointed to a guard hut on the road to our right, casually indicating that we should go and show our papers there, while they branched off to the left. My stomach began to churn afresh. The bridge with its sentries had not, after all, been the greatest hurdle; I still had to face up to the guards at the checkpoint.

As Mitzi got down from the carriage, she murmured softly, 'Don't worry, brother, it'll be all right,' and gave me an encouraging smile. Jock caught up with us while we were lifting their luggage down into the road, hailing me as Hans and ordering me about in brotherly fashion. All three of us paused to smile and wave the Russians goodbye, looking as relaxed as we knew how. Then, while Mitzi and Jock loaded their suitcases back onto the bike, I looked around us. What on earth could I do now?

The carriage disappeared in a cloud of dust down the road to the left, passing a horse and wagon loaded with hay, a farmer and his wife perched tranquilly on top of their load. Surely they would not be stopped. I had only a split second in which to decide whether to wait for my newfound friends and face the Russians in the guard hut with them, ready to use my revolver if I were forced to show my papers, or, now that I was safely across the bridge, to fend for myself and relieve them of my company.

I sprinted across the grass to the wagon. If the Russians noticed me at all, they would only see an Austrian road policeman hitching a ride on a hay wagon with fellow Austrians – probably friends. I levered myself onto the back of the slow-moving wagon, saying urgently, 'Please don't ask me a lot of questions. I won't hurt you. All I want to know is the way to the railway station. Which road do I have to take?'

They looked startled but not alarmed, assuming from my armband that I was a genuine policeman, a stranger but travelling on legitimate business. The woman said, 'Just stay where you are for a moment. We'll tell you when to get off.'

I only travelled thirty or forty metres with my third pair of angels. Then I jumped down as directed and started walking on the pavement alongside the airport, following the directions they gave me to the railway station. I wasn't yet out of sight of the checkpoint when I heard Jock's voice calling, 'Brother, come back. Come back, brother.' However, I feigned deafness and walked on, certain that he would realize that I was now in the clear and knew what I was doing.

I have often wondered how he explained the sudden departure of Mitzi's brother to the Russians. Given the story we had prepared, he probably told them I had gone ahead to check the train times, assuming that, as a road policeman, I had no need to show my papers. Anyway, he would say, I wasn't going to stay in Graz. I had only come to see them off, so I could show my papers on my way back. Then, to divert their attention, he would tell them how he had met his girlfriend Mitzi and come to be introduced to her parents, who lived in the Russian zone. Now they were going back to Köflach to get married! Mitzi would shine with excitement and fill in her part of the story. Then, as a fellow soldier and ally, the sergeant could expect not only to be believed but to receive congratulations on his great good fortune. Mitzi was a very pretty girl.

It was four in the afternoon. With the Mur behind me, I walked quickly but not so quickly as to arouse suspicion. Red Army trucks rumbled to and from the airport, but no one took any notice of me. Theoretically, I had only to go to the station and buy a ticket to Voitsberg, but I was still too keyed up to do that. Could I be absolutely sure Jock and Mitzi would not give me away if they were grilled at any length by the Russians? What experience, after all, did they have of such interrogations? Even now, there might be a search for me. After all, young though I was, I was a dangerous man, an exile who had dared to resist the mighty Stalinist Empire.

Seeing a young woman pushing a pram a little way ahead, I walked faster and caught up with her, hoping, at the very least, to pass the time of day with her as any other citizen of Graz would do. At best, I might enlist her help.

Falling into step beside her, I tipped my hat with a conventionally polite greeting, which she returned, expecting me to pass on. I lingered, however, as if to admire her baby, and quickly outlined, in as few words as possible, the danger I faced.

'*Mein Gott!*' she exclaimed, looking me full in the face. 'Then watch your step!' She was not very many years older than I was and extremely attractive – as lovely, it seemed to me, as the film stars I had seen on my only trip to the cinema. At any other time in my life I'd have fallen head-over-heels in love with her. Cool-headed and quick-witted, she gave no outward sign of shock at my sudden appearance. Smiling as if entering into conversation with an acquaintance met by chance, she said, 'Listen: whatever you do, don't cut across this airfield. There are thousands of Russian soldiers everywhere. I live nearby. Walk back to the house with me and talk to my mother. Between us, we'll find a way to get you to Voitsberg.'

As we walked, my latest guardian angel told me that she had been born in her present house and knew the area well. Her father, a mechanic, had worked on the airfield until he was drafted into the army. Both her father and brother were now reported missing on the Eastern Front. Sad to say, so too was her husband, to whom she had been married for only three years. It was a tragic and all-too-familiar story. 'There is only my mother and the baby and me at home. We'll take care of you. Enough young lives have been lost! Lay your bag on the pram and just keep walking.' The further we walked, the safer I felt, until we heard a motorbike approaching from behind and looked back to see two well-armed Russian soldiers riding towards us, beginning to slow down and veering off the road as if to stop.

'I'm off,' I said, reaching for my bag. 'I'll make a run for it. Don't worry. I'll be all right. I've got a gun.'

She seized my arm in a steely grip. 'No, you don't. Put your hand on the pram and push. You're my husband. This is our child. I'll swear to it. You're not going anywhere.'

'I may have been reported by someone who knows I'm a deserter,' I muttered. 'They'll shoot me on sight.'

'Just keep walking,' she almost shouted, clutching my arm tight. 'You're my husband. We're walking the baby home.'

As the soldiers drew abreast of us, they looked sideways, then halted just ahead of us. My heart stopped and I froze as I waited for their next move. Had I been recognized? Would I be asked to identify myself, then be dragged back to the checkpoint hut to confront Jock and Mitzi? The soldier riding pillion got off the bike first, giving us a sharp look, but the driver seemed more concerned with his machine. I was grateful for my grasp of the Russian language for, to my relief, I heard him swearing copiously, not at his companion or at us but at the motorbike. He was furious because it had broken down and would take them no further. Hardly breathing, my 'wife' and I pushed the pram past them, giving them a nod and a very wide berth, and left them grumbling and cursing at their predicament. My new friend looked at me with tears of triumph in her eyes.

'You see? I told you to keep your nerve and nothing would happen!' We walked the rest of the way close together, bodies touching, like the husband and wife we were supposed to be.

Her home was a bungalow set in a small garden bright with summer flowers. I waited while she told her mother my story, wondering how the older woman would receive it. Perhaps she had borne so much grief she was past caution, for all she said, unable to hold back tears, was, 'Young man, you are so like my son!' After bringing me a glass of milk and offering food, which I was too worked up to accept, she told me again what I had already learnt from her daughter – that her husband, son, and son-in-law had all been reported missing. Then, wiping her eyes and becoming severely practical, she offered me the use of her son's birth certificate and his apprenticeship papers as an aircraft mechanic. 'I will adopt you as my son,' she said. 'If you're stopped by the Russians, you can show these papers, and we'll stand by you. Good luck with your journey to Voitsberg.'

Gratefully, I embraced them both and left for the station, promising to return the papers if I ever got the chance. I hoped to meet Jock and Mitzi on the way, but reached it without seeing any sign of them. I was now in a place called Lieboch, at the junction of the line from Graz to Voitsberg with another route running further south.

The railway platform was packed solid with Russian soldiers. Austrian travellers seemed to have sought sanctuary in the waiting room, where I joined them as soon as I had bought a ticket for a train to Voitsberg that was due in shortly. Slouched down on a bench with my hat pulled over my forehead, I pretended to take a nap while observing my fellow travellers closely.

When the train came in, I boarded it instantly, with as little sign of agitation as I could manage, but was no sooner on my way than I realized that it was the wrong train. Frantic, I searched out the guard, who told me not to worry. If I got off at the next station and returned to the one I had just left, I might still catch the last train to Voitsberg, if I was lucky.

I scanned the landscape anxiously as we approached the first stop, and was relieved to see that it was a mountain village, with woods all around, so that I could run for my life if anyone ventured to question me. Climbing down onto the platform, I had to make my way again through hordes of Russian soldiers. However, they seemed intent on their own affairs. I soon caught a train and returned to Lieboch without incident.

Fortunately for me, the train to Voitsberg was still expected, being half an hour late. When it arrived, it was very full, with standing room only, but the passengers were all civilians, with not a Russian soldier in sight. For the first time in months I felt positively light hearted, like an ordinary human being instead of a hunted creature. I was among normal people going about their daily business. Full of the confidence engendered by having escaped so many dangers unscathed, I took a positive delight in entering into conversation with them, exchanging the brief, dull civilities of everyday life. No doubt they took me for a road policeman, since I still wore my illegal arm band, but no one commented on the fact.

One pitfall still remained, however, that could easily have turned all the triumphs of that day to nought. When the train reached Voitsberg, the station was deserted and the streets of the town were very dimly lit. Passengers who lived there sighed and explained, 'It's the curfew: imposed from nine o'clock every night, and God help you if you're out on the streets after that! But we can't help it tonight. It's not our fault the train is late, is it? It was half an hour late when we caught it. So it's now nine-thirty. Whose fault's that?' I started walking through the town in near darkness, in the direction of the farm I had left several months earlier. Luckily for me, a dozen or so other men, women, and children were going in the same direction. Halfway through the town we were stopped by two Russian soldiers on horseback. They ordered us to halt and enquired where we had come from and where we were going. Though someone explained at once that we had come from the railway station, having arrived from Graz on a train that was half an hour late, they chose not to believe us. 'Come with us to the *komendatura* and identify yourselves,' they said roughly. 'Then, if you are telling the truth, you can go home.'

I nearly died on the spot. After risking my life so many times for so long, and surviving until now, to be arrested in a town where I had expected to feel safe would be the last straw! Everything would be against me if I had to explain myself. I had a gun in my possession, was carrying false papers, and I was wearing a spurious *Strassen Polizei* arm band. My ankle was still bandaged and causing me pain. If questioned, how would I account for the injury? Once in Russian hands, I would never walk free again.

The people I was with kept protesting, 'We've broken no rules; done nothing illegal. We didn't want to break the curfew. The train came in late and we're walking home!'

'We'll believe you when you've been identified,' the soldiers told us. 'So hurry up. Get walking. We'll follow you.'

We had no alternative but to move on, with the Russians on horseback close behind us. Some of the old people and small children were very tired and began crying, begging the soldiers to let us go and not take us out of our way, until one soldier finally said to the other, 'Wait while I check up. I'll ride back to the station and find out if the train really did come in late.'

Meanwhile, the other soldier urged us forward. The command post was only about half a kilometre away, so we took care to drag our feet, making sure we did not reach it before the first soldier returned. I was hoping to escape, now that only one man was guarding the lot of us. It was fairly dark and I knew the streets and alleyways quite well. There had to be somewhere to hide. Ordinarily I was swift-footed, too, but I had been on my feet all day and wasn't sure how well my swollen ankle would support me. Before any opportunity presented itself, the first soldier galloped up to us again.

'Yes, it's all right. They were telling the truth. These people came off the Graz train, and the train was half an hour late, so we can let them go. But make sure it never happens again,' he said threateningly, swinging his horse around to face us and shining his torch in our eyes, 'or you won't get off so lightly next time.'

Relieved to have escaped interrogation, we went our separate ways through the ill-lit streets. Eventually I found my way to the farm I had left in June. It was strange to think that it was now July and I was right back where I had started from. I felt as though I had aged by several years in the interval!

The farm was in total darkness but it seemed unlikely that everyone was asleep. If the house was shuttered on a late summer night, it was probably because of the curfew. Were even country people not allowed to congregate after dark? I could see it might offer welcome protection from Russian soldiers out on the scrounge! A sense of tremendous excitement welled up in me as I reached the front door, almost as if I were to be reunited with my own family. Provided nothing had changed and Gretel was still in charge, I knew I would be welcome, and safe. She would not report me to the police or to the Russians, that was for sure! I had protected her too often in the past. The big moment arrived, and I knocked on the door.

When no one came to open it, I called out for someone to let me in, taking the precaution of shouting in Russian, since no one else had permission to be out of doors. My heart leapt when I heard Gretel reply. She said, quite correctly, that she was not allowed to open the door after nine o'clock at night. All the same, I must have given her quite a fright because, if it had been a soldier, or one of a party of soldiers, she could not have kept me out. After making a few threatening remarks, just to tease her, I said, 'Don't worry. I'm not going to shoot my way in. Just open the door to me, Gretel, because it's Stefan outside. Remember Stefan?' Could she have forgotten me so quickly?

After a second or two she recognized my voice and I heard her cry of astonishment as the door burst open. When she saw me, she threw her arms around my neck, kissed me, and began to cry. So did the children. It was a warm welcome from people normally so undemonstrative, and brought a lump to my throat. Even Karl showed pleasure at my return. Seeing Gretel again, with her pale, freckled face, her neck thickened by goitre, and her slender build, so unlike the stout, red-faced farmers' wives I had mostly come across, I was struck by how young and defenceless she looked. However, that night she had the support of friends. Inside the house, the neighbours I knew so well were playing cards, just as when I had last seen them. A joyful reunion! Everything was comfortably familiar. For the first time in weeks, I felt safe.

Gretel noticed my bandaged ankle and persuaded me to bathe it and change the dressing before joining the others. I was so full of happiness at their caring and compassionate welcome that the ankle hardly hurt at all. Then we sat up into the early hours of the morning talking. Everyone wanted to know everything that had happened to me since June. How on earth did I come to be back in Voitsberg instead of home in Ukraine with my family, as they had fondly imagined? I had a long, sad story to tell, and they heard it from beginning to end.

Then food was produced and we drank wine and schnapps. The farmers still managed to bring something out on special occasions, sharing whatever they had with one another and so creating a veritable banquet in the midst of scarcity. I enquired after Gretel's husband. Had she heard when he would be coming home? No. It appeared that none of the local men who served in the German army had yet returned. What about the Russians? Did they still come to the farm confiscating everything? Would it be safe there for me? We talked and talked; there was so much to talk about.

'If you stay on the farm and don't go into Voitsberg, you should be all right here,' they told me. 'Keep an eye out for Russian soldiers, though. Discipline has improved, but they still come and demand food occasionally. You can hide in the woods or hills while they are around.'

The border between the Russian and British sectors was now only two or three kilometres away, between Voitsberg and Köflach. It should have been ridiculously easy to slip through to the British side, but everyone advised me not to try it. It was heavily patrolled and had begun to take on an air of permanence. 'The Russians are setting up guard huts on the border just a few hundred metres apart and there are tanks and anti-aircraft guns, all pointing into the British sector, not to mention the barbed wire fence that marks the border. We're totally cut off from Köflach now.'

Crash went my dreams! If the defences were as impregnable as all that, I didn't have the heart, though I still had the burning desire, to attempt an escape from the Russian sector. I had walked from Hungary but the events of the past day had stretched my nerves to breaking point and my foot was still giving me pain. My luck had very nearly run out that very night, right there in Voitsberg! If I tried to cross the border in defiance of all warnings, it might desert me altogether. Kaput! After talking it over with the farmer and her friends, I decided to wait for a time at least, living and working on the farm and praying to God, as before, while we waited to see what happened next. It might have been wishful thinking, but none of the people present seemed to think the Russians would be around much longer.

Voitsberg was not as I remembered it. None of the friends I had met at church and on Sunday afternoons were there any more. Had any of them reached home? Homesickness overwhelmed me. There was still no news from my family and friends and I constantly worried about them. Were the people of western Ukraine being allowed to carry on with their lives, or were they being transported to Siberia in cattle trucks, like animals, or liquidated, as in times past? I worried too about the men I had left behind in the camp, especially the men from my company. Had they been taken to fight Japan? Had any of them been killed? Would they ever reach home? What had happened to the women and children? The more I thought about it all, the more depressed I became, for I knew I might never learn the answers to any of those questions.

I moved around from farm to farm, not staying anywhere long enough to arouse suspicion, working to earn my bed and food, often sleeping in the safety of the forest. The farmers I worked for had known me in the past and were good to me. Aware that I was in constant danger, I spied out the land, climbing trees so as to gaze all around, and into the British sector, to get an idea of the Russian military strength at strategic points along the border. I looked regretfully at countryside that had been wide open to me before it was 'liberated'. My ankle stubbornly refused to heal, but was no great problem provided I kept the wound clean.

We heard rumours of a Russian withdrawal. People claimed that the Russians had originally agreed to pull back to the east of Graz, but became reluctant to do so. They said the British, perhaps Churchill himself, had now given them an ultimatum – '…retreat within thirty days or we will attack and drive you back'. All I know is that, to our immense relief and astonishment, the Russians gradually dismantled their guard huts and barbed wire and moved their tanks and guns out of the neighbourhood. Eventually they withdrew to well beyond Graz.

Almost at once, for the first time in my life, I saw large numbers of British soldiers. They marched into Voitsberg on foot and rode on the backs of lorries, with some on horseback. Cheerful, relaxed, almost happy-go-lucky, they went past as though we were old friends. The people welcomed them with a spontaneous warmth quite different from the greeting they had given the Russians. Women waved their kerchiefs and the girls ran out to present them with armfuls of flowers, including edelweiss. Their uniforms were not as well-cut or immaculately pressed as those of the Germans, and their boots, though well polished, did not look like military boots at all. Their belts were of some rope-like material, painted white, unlike the stiff leather belts the Germans wore. They seemed too casually dressed to be soldiers, yet we all knew their armies had emerged strong and victorious, and we felt extremely proud of them – our liberators!

The troops handed out bread and cigarettes to bystanders, and sweets and chocolates to the children, with a friendliness we did not expect to last. The Russians had once done much the same in Antoniwka! However, these men did not immediately deliver propaganda speeches to which everyone was obliged to listen. Their demeanour was good-natured, and seemed genuine. I think it is true to say that I have never in my whole life felt greater inner contentment than I did the day the British soldiers marched into Voitsberg. As I waved back at them, I searched every face in the hope of finding my good friend Jock, who was frightened of nothing! I longed to meet him again, and Mitzi, whose brother I had almost become. For an hour or so on that day near the bridge over the River Mur, they had been my family. My joy would have been complete if I could have rejoiced with them, thanked them for their kindness, and joined them in celebrating their marriage and my newly acquired freedom. I had fantasies of becoming part of their actual family, living and laughing with them for the rest of my life.

That day, the fear I had lived with for so long evaporated. My peace of mind was guaranteed. I thanked God for a future that promised to be infinitely better than the past.

Chapter 14

1945-1946
Magdalein Refugee Camp

Now that I was no longer a 'wanted' man, I wasted no time getting myself onto a waiting list at the local hospital, the *Krankenhaus*, so that my injured ankle could be treated. A few weeks later they sent for me, and I was admitted for about ten days. The medical treatment was spartan – they sponged the ankle with a disinfectant that stung – and the discipline was severe. We were badly fed but when I asked for more food, a nurse boxed my ears and told me to shut up; there was not enough food to go round. By that time there were terrible shortages even in agricultural areas. The wound finally healed over, to my great relief, though it has caused me occasional twinges ever since.

That autumn I listened to the radio news and read the papers avidly, hoping for an announcement that would tell me what was being done to help people like myself. As a Red Army deserter, I was in a particularly vulnerable position but masses of refugees had flooded into Austria and were likewise in need of assistance and advice.

I soon learned that there were camps for political refugees, or 'displaced persons', not far away in Carinthia, at Judenburg, Klagenfurt, and Villach. The camps in Villach apparently housed thousands upon thousands of people, old and young, who chose not to return to their own countries and remained under the supervision of the British military authorities. The camps were run by the United Nations Relief and Rehabilitation Administration, UNRRA, which fed and looked after everyone who came to them. Straight after the war, there were up to one million officially recognized refugees in Austria.

Desperately anxious to join up with people who spoke my own language and were in a similar plight to my own, I discussed the matter with my farmer friends, who advised me to go to Villach at once. They provided me with adequate clothing and footwear to make myself presentable, (though my socks did not always match), and I had earned a little money, so I packed my few belongings, bade Gretel and her children a poignant farewell, and set off by train for Villach.

When I arrived at the station there, I was thrilled to hear the many different languages being spoken, among them Polish, Czech, Ukrainian, Hungarian and Romanian. But the sound of anyone speaking Russian scared me to death. To this day, I do not like the Russian language. I can speak it but I still do not like having to do so. I waited until I could identify some Ukrainian speakers. They told me at once where to go and how to get there.

Shortly afterwards I walked into Camp Magdalein, a great sprawl of wooden barracks beside the River Drau, and reported to the main office. An assortment of officials speaking various languages sat in hastily constructed cubicles behind battered desks, and took down the personal details of each new applicant. A Ukrainian looked at the papers I carried and filled in a form with my name, nationality and most recent address. I answered his questions as clearly as I could, with nothing to hide and no reason to be ashamed of a thing.

'Married or single?'

'Single,' I replied, holding up one finger. 'It's better to be poor alone.'

Smiling very slightly, he nodded in agreement. The account of my treatment by the Russians after their offer of repatriation caused him no surprise. Many people he had received into the camp had told the same story. The Russians had not only falsely promised to return people to their own countries, they had shot people too. They claimed that their victims had worked for the Nazis, even though their only crime was to have laboured under compulsion as I had done. The only difference was that they had been forced to work for people known to be members of the Nazi party.

Having filled in my details, he assigned me to barrack number 7, and sent me to the camp store to collect a few basic necessities – a thick brown sheet with which to cover my mattress, two blankets, a pillow and towel, a small piece of soap, and two pairs of socks. Leaving the store with a load on my shoulder and my personal belongings, I went to find barrack number 7. The camp was huge and I felt lost and bewildered. The crude wooden buildings brought back memories of the ghastly military encampments in which I had been imprisoned as a deportee three years earlier. As I looked into the faces of the people who drifted about, apparently with nothing to do to kill the time, I could see that many of them were seriously disoriented, confused and depressed, and wondered how long I should be able to bear living in such surroundings. Having been admitted, was I free to leave?

I greeted any folk I could identify as Ukrainians or Poles in the appropriate language, but hurried past those speaking Russian. Most likely they were simply victims, like myself, but Russian spies could have infiltrated the camp, posing as refugees. Who would know? How could anyone tell? Even before I had reached the camp I'd heard that Russian soldiers sometimes came from their sector in lorries, to seize people they claimed were Russian nationals and take them away.

When I found barrack 7 and opened the door, the first thing that hit me was the fearful stink! It was compounded of the smell of unwashed bodies, clothes, and bedding, of hoarded foodstuffs like garlic, salami, and cheese, of mouldy tobacco and wood smoke, I inhaled it and gasped. About twenty double-decker bunks were on either side of a broad central aisle, and a wood-burning stove was in the centre. It seemed to me only pigs or horses could make a place smell like that, and I wondered whether anyone ever swept the floor or made any effort to keep the place clean. Were the windows ever opened? Was disinfectant ever used? Apparently not.

On Gretel's farm I had enjoyed a room of my own for the first time in my life, and in recent months I had lived largely out of doors, so the prospect of sleeping in this overcrowded, foetid barracks appalled me. Was this the best I could hope for in the immediate future? For how long? My first impulse was to turn and run, but that was not a realistic option. Deliberately leaving the door ajar so that I could breathe, I looked around carefully before setting down my load, having had plenty of practice in staking out a claim to a piece of territory I could call my own! A bunk near the door would get air, but the door creaked and there would be endless people going in and out, making it difficult to sleep. I looked, instead, for one near a window and not too far from the stove, for warmth in winter, but there were not many bunks left to choose from. As I slung the things I was carrying onto an upper bunk by a window, a man grumbled, 'Shut the door, will you? And don't try to open that window. It gets cold in here and we can't always have a fire in the stove – there's not enough wood. We have to keep everything shut to stay warm.'

'But the place stinks!' I exclaimed, as I climbed up onto my bunk to make the bed and sort myself out. The smell was so intolerable I felt perfectly justified in saying so.

'You're young, with plenty of blood in your veins,' said another man, 'but the nights are cold and you'll soon see that you haven't got many bedclothes. Don't worry. You'll get used to things in a week or so; you won't have any problems.'

Once I had stowed things on the shelf above my bunk, I surveyed the scene around me. There were beds for eighty men, and nearly that number were in the hut, playing cards or chess with one another, talking, or just lying on their bunks. Though they spoke several languages, they seemed to understand one another, and I found I had no need to ask questions to find out who they were and get acquainted. They talked endlessly about their homes and families, where they had come from and what had happened to them during the war. I was not the only one there who had deserted from the Red Army, having been forced to join it against his will, but I was the only one to have achieved officer rank. Some of them had actually gone into battle against the Germans. Others had been unwillingly recruited into the Wehrmacht and had deserted at the first opportunity. There was no love lost for either the Russians or the Germans.

Then there were the central Europeans who had simply moved out of their respective countries as the Germans retreated from the Eastern front. Fearful of the Russian backlash, whole families – married men with wives, children and old people – had packed their belongings into prams, push carts, or horse-drawn carts (if they were lucky enough to have them), and abandoned their homes. Then they just kept going, fleeing further and further without ever being stopped, until they were in Austria and the war was over. When the Germans capitulated, the fugitives finished up in this camp.

My initial horror at the state of the building lessened, as the days went by; this was largely because of my fascination with hearing all the astonishing stories of survival. Many of them were tragic, yet for the most part the men kept cheerful. There was no point in being otherwise, so they whistled and sang to themselves as they went about their daily chores. There were men two or three times my age, who had their families with them and little hope of ever leading a normal family life again. I tried to imagine how my mother and father would have coped in their situation, deprived of their home and daily work, robbed of even the limited choices that had been open to them in Antoniwka.

There was little hope in store for these people but come to that, how much hope was there for boys and girls my own age? None of us was master of our fate; we were all at the mercy of forces over which we had no control. Even in my years as a slave labourer, I had still imagined I could somehow shape my future. I was wrong.

When they heard my story, the men considered me very lucky to have been promoted to the rank of an officer in the Red Army. Who wouldn't live like an officer! They said they would never have deserted if they'd had an officer's privileges, and had been able to make other people do their dirty work! That I had done so seemed particularly heroic to them, since they knew that I would not have been given a second chance if caught. I'd have been shot without mercy there and then! Sympathy for all I had gone through was always concluded by saying: 'You are fortunate, all the same, being single. At least you don't have to see your family suffer when you are helpless to change anything.'

There were no special arrangements for married couples or families in the camp. Our barrack had only men in it, but in some of the barracks family members managed to get bunks close together and contrive a sort of room for themselves by screening them off with blankets. Couples sleeping together might have to endure a certain amount of ribald mockery, but it was always good-natured, and no offence was taken. In any case there was always a fair amount of noise, and plenty of singing and laughter, to drown out the love-making.

In the Klagenfurt region of Carinthia there were now about half a million refugees, who had found safety, freedom and security under the protection of the British Army, which occupied that southern part of Austria. The refugees did not want to return to their respective countries for fear of the Russian communist regime, the NKVD and the Siberian labour camps, the most feared of all fates. What scared me rigid in those days was the knowledge that the British military authorities did not prohibit Russian soldiers from entering camps under their control. Stories abounded of Russian soldiers driving into the Picalo, St Martin, Warmbad, Kellerberg, Judenburg and Magdalein camps and forcing people onto their lorries to be taken to Klagenfurt, where they would be loaded into cattle wagons and sent to Russia. It did not matter whether you were from one of the newly occupied countries or from Russia itself, and it was widely believed that these people would not live long once they reached their destination. 'So you be careful!' the men would say to me.

'Doesn't anyone put up any resistance?' I asked.

'Oh, yes. There have been many demonstrations. We have organized ourselves to collect paper and cardboard boxes, and a reserve supply of petrol, and have actually set several Russian lorries on fire to show how strongly we feel. The British didn't prosecute our people but the Russians are their allies and they won't keep them out, either.'

I had proof of this the following year, when I was living in St Martin's Camp and I was asked to collect newspapers. The Russians brought a lot of their own newspapers with them with which they were hoping to lure people home. In the event, we put a match to it all and burned their lorries down. But we had to be alert to such situations all the time.

Cooking in the camps was done by people of all nationalities, so we all got a taste of some of our own native dishes. For this reason alone, the camp authorities preferred to have people from different countries in separate camps, but this was not always possible. Generally speaking, the food was good and well cooked, and we did not complain, provided there was enough of it. Unfortunately, that was not always the case. That first winter after the war, food was in very short supply.

The people of Camp Magdalein got on well, in spite of their differences and difficulties. We knew that we were assembled there through no fault of our own and were very likely better off than the people we had left behind in our native lands. At least we had the good luck to be living under a British administration.

Everything was communal. We queued to get into the toilet and took our own toilet paper with us, if we were lucky enough to have any. Otherwise, tough luck! There were no flush toilets, just buckets which had to be emptied by one of us when it got full, but we were used to that. Few of us had ever known anything different.

The camp was like a village, with church services on Sunday, and dances three or four times a week. I was eighteen and very keen on dancing, and the canteen was large enough to hold hundreds of people, some of whom had their own violins, guitars, accordions, mouth organs, drums and clarinets. They played waltzes, polkas, mazurkas, *colomyjkas*, and *huzulkas* and made a magnificent sound. For a few hours young and old could forget their anxieties and the misery of all they had lived through.

We got up teams for football and folk-dancing, formed friendships and flirted with the girls. My relations with girls were entirely platonic – my future had still to be worked out – but people met, fell in love, and, to the joy of everyone, got married. It was a good life, albeit in bad circumstances. As winter came on and the first snow fell, we had snowball fights. People of all ages piled out of the barracks and tumbled about like young children, laughing and pushing one another into the snowdrifts. Apart from anything else, it helped to pass the time.

Trading went on in the camp, too, even though most people had little or no money. In that immediate post-war period, barter was the rule. UNRRA provided what clothing it could to those in need and, if you became friendly with the staff, you could sometimes obtain an additional garment, or a length of material, which you could sell in the town, or dispose of in return for fresh food, wine or schnapps to a farmer out in the country. If people owned anything they did not need, or anything that could be cut up and remade into something else, they knew its market value. The black market was largely supplied by soldiers, as a British transit camp had ample stores less than half a kilometre away.

Many items could be bought: cigarettes, spam, sardines, chocolate or soap, all of which were scarce and expensive in the town and you could pay with other commodities such as a loaf or two of bread. The British soldiers had access to things totally unobtainable elsewhere. This black market operated on quite a large scale without anyone objecting. We saw it simply as a way of helping one another. If people had something you needed, they were willing to swap it for something you had. If people had money, they were glad to pay. Everyone had to trade things in order to survive.

The camp had a medical centre to which we could go with our coughs and pains. The Red Cross nurse in charge had little equipment and not much in the way of medicines, but she inspired confidence, could call in a doctor in an emergency, and get any seriously ill patient into hospital.

The day after our first snowball fight I went down with a feverish cold and began to shiver and shake uncontrollably. I could not remember ever having felt so ill. Normally, my health was good, so I was convinced I was on the point of death. Finding I had a high temperature, the nursing sister first gave me some powders to drink, then told me to go into an adjacent room and strip naked. 'I'm going to give you a cold wrap,' she said. A moment later she came towards me carrying two large, white, dripping wet sheets that had been soaked in ice-cold water. I jumped about a metre in the air when the icy sheets came into contact with my bare skin. 'You're killing me! You'll give me a heart attack!' I cried. But the nurse was a powerful woman and simply pushed me back down onto the bed, wrapping me up swiftly in the wet sheets, then in one thick blanket after another. Eventually the powders took effect and I relaxed and fell asleep.

When the sister came to see me next morning, she could hardly find me under the cocoon of bedclothes. Tossing off the blankets, she began to tap at my body, on which the sheets had stiffened like cement. 'You've had a good sound sleep, and your temperature is back to normal,' she announced. Then, as she started to roll me back and forth to unwind the sheets, I remembered that I was naked and got very embarrassed.

'Don't be ridiculous, Stefan! You're not the first man I've seen naked!' she scolded. As the last sheet came off, releasing my arms, I lifted them up and threw them around her neck, casting shyness to the winds and kissing her on both cheeks. 'Thank you! You have saved my life!' I cried. My fever had left me and I felt fine after my first and only experience of the cold wrap.

The men there teased me unmercifully, asking if I was game for another snowball fight, but one of them brought me a mug of ersatz coffee from the pot brewing on the stove, while another handed me a slice of toast and said he might be able to get me a bowl of hot soup from the cookhouse if I wanted one. They alternated between treating me as a boy, to be petted, and as an erstwhile lieutenant, which still evoked a certain awe. Either way, I knew I was part of the family.

It was not easy to get a night's sleep in the barracks. Men went out in the evening to play cards or chess in other barracks or other camps. They would have schnapps to drink and return in high spirits in the early hours of the morning, fumbling for the door catch, switching on the dim night lights, stumbling in their attempts to find their beds, all the while laughing and telling jokes. If one of them slept in the bunk below you, he would, like as not, kick at your mattress to wake you up so you could join in the fun. It strained the patience of those longing for sleep, but rarely resulted in a fight.

I enjoyed their stories, as each one capped the one before to raise a laugh. Occasionally I told a joke of my own, or someone would start singing in German or Polish or Ukrainian, it didn't matter what, and others joined in until everyone was singing. Whether you enjoyed it or not depended on how tired you were. Mostly we tolerated one another, grateful for the gifts of laughter and song. It was no good being a misery! I learnt a lot of songs and jokes in various languages, not all of them suitable for a young man's ears, and grew up fast in the company of these older men.

One day some of us wandered into Villach to take a look around, passing a brothel on the way. We had already been told that it was regularly checked by health inspectors, so that no one need fear infection from the prostitutes, but none of us had visited it. The girls waved and smiled at us, however, and showed off their bosoms, and we waved back, laughing and making rude remarks but so far as I know, that is all it ever came to.

As Christmas – my first in the camps – approached, I was full of apprehension. How should we celebrate it? We would, of course, keep it, as in Ukraine, on 7 January 1946, but would it be any different from other days? I doubted it very much. In the past, I had never given a thought to the preparations for Christmas. Now I was among friendly folk, all of whom were remembering earlier, happier times in our own countries, with our own families, so we were thousands of kilometres apart in our hearts. I soon learned that each of the barracks would organize its own Christmas meal, but how, I wondered, would we resolve our differences? Each nationality would have its own customs. The Ukrainians would certainly expect to have their traditional twelve dishes to represent the twelve apostles.

I wanted to wipe out the memory of my Christmases as a slave labourer, which had not been like Christmas at all. No one had sung the Ukrainian carols or cooked the traditional food. Now I was among my own people again, a free man, but for such a big festive occasion one needed money to buy food, drink, soap, new clothes and of course some toys for the children. How on earth did people manage? Was there any work to be had?

I visited some of the other camps in the neighbourhood of Villach to find out what plans people were making. Everyone gave different answers to my questions but the situation seemed to be that no one was making plans for either the near or distant future. Everyone was living on hope but the situation sometimes seemed hopeless. Nevertheless, it lifted my heart to see how many of us there were in the same boat, trying to keep our spirits up. I resolved to be as cheerful as possible in the circumstances.

A week before Christmas, a crowd of us went out into the forest and cut down a large evergreen tree to erect in the centre of the camp. Immediately all sorts of people began to make decorations for it. The camp authorities helped us by laying an electric cable out to it and producing strings of lights. Soon a magnificent Christmas tree stood glittering in our midst. Devout older men and women never passed it, day or night, without crossing themselves.

On Christmas Eve, preparations began for the Christmas feast. To make the occasion festive the kitchen workers and storekeepers turned out all sorts of unheard-of things. The Ukrainians were to have their banquet in our barrack and when morning came, it was astonishing to see how white tablecloths, the traditional bundle of hay and barley, and special kinds of food and drink, hoarded secretly through recent weeks, appeared as if by magic. That evening we sat around a long table in the centre of the barracks, while men and women brought food from the kitchens. It was a time of joy as each of us remembered our loved ones and raised a silent prayer for the living and the dead. Once the food was eaten, and we began toasting one another in schnapps, singing carols and dancing in what little space we could find, the Christmas spirit took over and the world beyond ceased to trouble us. The war was over and we lived in comparative peace and freedom; reason enough to celebrate. I was young and optimistic and felt sure that somewhere, somehow, I would find happiness.

As time went on, I made good friends in the camp; mainly young Ukrainians, though our particular group included a Romanian, a Hungarian and a few Poles. Our ages ranged from about sixteen to twenty-five. We had many things in common – our wartime experiences, our interest in literature and politics, our love of sport and of singing and dancing and exchanging jokes. A band of us swore undivided loyalty to one another – 'All for one and one for all' – and that solidarity did much to overcome individual loneliness, as well as being of practical help in many small ways. If it was your turn to have your weekly hot shower in the wash house, and you had no soap, friends would always lend you theirs.

The peace of the camp was periodically shattered by the arrival of Russian lorries. The British assured us they would never divulge the nationality of any one of us to the Russians, but the soldiers had their permission to 'persuade' the people they found in the camps, if they could, to return to the countries they had come from. That meant going with the Russians to Klagenfurt to be shipped off somewhere; no one knew where. Those of us with experience of Russian offers of repatriation felt sure that their destiny was a Siberian labour camp and an early death, but there were always a few people homesick enough, or desperate enough, to go with them. We were never sure when force would be used. Every time a Russian lorry drove in, we would see men, women and children run away screaming and trying to hide, while others were caught and presumably pressurized in some way. I was thoroughly frightened whenever this happened. The peace treaty had ceded my homeland to Russia, making me currently one of its citizens, and my heart bled for those who failed to escape.

We set the lorries on fire when we could, and eventually the Russians stopped coming to Villach, apparently convinced that no one remained who would go home voluntarily as long as Stalinism held sway. I remember going into Klagenfurt one day with my friends and seeing the 'death trains', as we called them, standing in the station there, patrolled by Russian soldiers. Having travelled on such trains in the past, we shuddered and recoiled in horror, and resolved to speak no language but German so long as we were in the town.

As the sun melted the snow around Villach in the spring of 1946, the people in the camps grew increasingly frustrated. Food was desperately short and we were often quite hungry. We depended entirely on UNRRA for food, clothing and every basic necessity but there were shortages of everything everywhere and our needs were not always met. To have money, one had to trade on the black market or find some kind of work, and work was virtually unobtainable. There were plenty of Austrian ex-soldiers looking for work as well as the thousands of people in the camps. Though we would willingly have accepted any kind of heavy manual work, like repairing the roads or railways, that kind of work was reserved for ex-Nazis as a punishment.

Even if you had money, it hadn't much value. Items such as soap and cigarettes, tinned meat or fish, sugar, bread, chocolate, tea, coffee, biscuits and dried fruit were luxuries beyond price; worth more than money itself. I remember times when up to ten men would share a cigarette, taking a puff and passing it on while women would take in washing for a month in return for one good-sized bar of soap. The children had no toys or any decent clothes except for the things people contrived or cut down for them. If people had jewellery, or anything of value, they traded it for food. As for anything like a bicycle, radio, camera, or a good quality suit – these were beyond the reach even of those doing a flourishing trade on the black market.

I was occasionally invited to a Polish or Ukrainian wedding. The camp administration would bring out a few extras, and everyone would chip in with whatever money they had to make the occasion a happy one. Musicians would offer their services free, so long as they got something to eat and drink. I loved the music and dancing and was, of course, adept at performing the traditional steps I had learnt in my schooldays. On one occasion, I nearly got married myself, inadvertently, having drunk one schnapps too many and proposed marriage to one of the beautiful girls present. When I sobered up enough to learn from my friends what I had done, I had to retract my offer with abject apologies. Fortunately for me, the young woman was either very forgiving or had not been greatly tempted by my proposal.

Married or not, one of life's greatest pleasures was going to the cinema in Villach. However, it was important to avoid films in which food and drink played a prominent part. To see people guzzling and stuffing themselves amid scenes of real abundance was more than we could bear. We formed the habit of sending someone to the cinema to check from the film clips outside whether there were any restaurant or banquet scenes, and if there was any doubt, to enquire at the ticket booth about this. If we had accumulated enough money for tickets, and the messenger returned saying there were no scenes in the film of people eating, we would say, 'All right, let's go tonight.'

Films were not just entertainment, nor a formerly forbidden pleasure that was now allowed. They were not even just a way of escaping the hardships of life for a few hours. For me, at least, they were crucial to my education. I learnt a great deal about polite forms of behaviour, particularly those that governed the delicate relationships between men and women. I observed the graceful little courtesies that people, brought up in good society, showed to one another; their restrained manners at table, their gracious ways of addressing one another, helping one another into a carriage or car, and of looking into each other's eyes.

Those films were my window on the world. There were romantic films in which the characters were impossibly beautifu; sombre tragedies which filled my eyes with tears. There were grim portrayals of the heroism and sacrifices of war, realistic films showing how people suffered from poverty and oppression, brave films in which ordinary individuals emerged victorious, overcoming every obstacle to win love, happiness, fame, or justice. A fictional world, no doubt, but there was much of value to be learned by a young man on the brink of adulthood.

Sometimes my friends and I visited a dance hall. We had dances in the camp of course, but we liked meeting people from the town. The Austrian girls were beautiful and good dancers. There would be a live band of ten or more musicians, who played almost continuously from seven or eight in the evening until two or three the next morning. If we had any money we would try to bribe them to go on even longer, until four or five! Someone would ask the bandleader if they were prepared to play, and for what price, and then pass a hat around until the necessary sum was collected. If that happened, no one went home; everyone just carried on dancing.

Evenings like these kept young people sane and in good heart but everything we enjoyed cost money. If you had no job and nothing to sell, the only way to get money was to steal it. But if you did that and were found out, your life was at stake. Not only would you be reported to the police, the people in the camp would deal with you even more severely. No one I knew resorted to stealing, or certainly not more than once! So, by the summer of 1946, I felt I simply must obtain a job. Without one, my situation was becoming more desperate. Though friends helped one another out with money if they could, any cash or possessions people had brought with them into the camp had long gone. Besides, I was bored doing nothing. The more I saw films of well-fed, well-dressed people with money to spend, the more I felt determined to acquire that kind of freedom. As I lay on a top bunk mattress so thin I could feel the boards through it, getting more and more frantic and depressed, I would ask myself, 'How do they get started? How can I make a beginning?'

One day I decided to go looking for work. I would go to every single shop in the town, every butcher, baker, delicatessen, and tailor; every factory, every barber shop – and ask for work. I had done this once or twice without success, but this time I meant to keep going, covering as many places as possible, knocking and knocking on doors. Surely somewhere a door would open for poor Stefan.

Furthermore, I decided that I would look so immaculate that no fault could possibly be found with my appearance. A good wash, with plenty of soap, a neat haircut, a clean, carefully mended shirt, clean shoes, freshly pressed trousers, newly washed jacket – even in the life I led, it would only require a bit of effort and self-discipline. Embarking on this positive project gave me a useful incentive. When my friends saw me doing so much washing and polishing, and sewing on of buttons, and darning of socks, they began to ask questions. Where was I going? Was I going to a wedding, a funeral, to see some gorgeous Austrian girl? I would not tell them.

I said I was going somewhere special and was making myself presentable so as not to let down the people in the camp. I would give the impression that all of us were neat and tidy and particular about our appearance. I said this to shut my friends up. I couldn't bear to say I was going to look for work and then come back reporting I hadn't found any. For although we were allies, if I returned empty-handed they would laugh and think me a failure. Such is the atmosphere that develops in situations of penury and scarcely-tempered panic. The less my friends knew about my endeavours, the better.

For four days, from morning until evening, I knocked on the doors of restaurants, butchers, bakers, factories – even the cinema. I did not care what I did. At each place I would bow and say *Guten Morgen* or *Guten Tag* in my most polite and dignified manner, tell them my name and address, and say that I was looking for employment and would do whatever was required of me. But, as soon as I gave my address as Camp Magdalein, by the River Drau, I would see their faces change and immediately I would be told, 'No. I'm very sorry. We do not need any workers.' For four days, I heard nothing but the *Nein, Nein, Nein* of total rejection, which added to my despondency.

With plenty of Austrians looking for work, why employ anyone from a refugee camp? This was how the logic seemed to run. Personally, I could understand their reasoning. All the same, I was glad I hadn't mentioned my plan. There wasn't any work for people like us. For the next few months I didn't even bother to go searching. I filled the time playing football, joining the camp's team and competing against other camps. I was much admired when our team won and booed when we lost. I helped produce plays, as I had once helped Uncle Dmytro to do. Some of them were both interesting and well acted. I even managed to get involved in the black market, to avoid being hungry.

Then, in the autumn, I heard that some people in our camp had got work in the British Army Catering Corps at the El Alamein Transit Camp, not far away. The idea of a Red Army deserter working for the British Army appealed to my sense of the absurd. In fact, my imagination ran riot! If I told them I spoke perfect Russian and had the Red Army's whole political indoctrination programme down pat, they might recruit me into British Intelligence as a military spy! I could become a secret agent and report on Russian troop movements. I decided to go and try my luck.

Once again I said nothing. If there were any vacancies I wanted to be the first one there. But I told the man in the bath house, because I needed a hot shower and it was not my turn. I said I had to attend a very special interview at the El Alamein Transit Camp. If I had just said I was going to look for work, he'd never have let me jump the queue, but he knew that I had deserted from the Red Army and presumed I was in possession of military secrets, for he said at once: 'Of course, Lieutenant, whenever you are ready.'

Thoroughly spruced up, I presented myself at the El Alamein Camp. Two soldiers with Sten guns were on guard at the entrance. I asked if either of them spoke German, to which they replied, '*Nein*', so I resorted to body language, employing every miming skill I possessed to show someone hard at work, repeating the word *Arbeit* as I did so. The soldiers understood. They nodded and said, '*Ja, ja. Arbeit*'. Then, to my astonishment, instead of turning me away as I expected them to do, one of them pointed the way to a small building immediately next to the entrance. I couldn't believe my luck. '*Ich danke Ihnen herzlich*,' I said, as effusively as I knew how. 'I thank you from the bottom of my heart!'

Chapter 15

1946
No More Hunger

A s I entered the building, I saw three men in an office to the right of the door, behind a long plate-glass window. Two were army personnel officers, a captain and a lieutenant, I learnt later. The captain's senior rank was obvious, since he was leaning back in his chair with his feet on the desk. The third man was a civilian. Seeing me, he came out and enquired in German what I wanted.

'I've been sent to ask for work,' I said. 'Is there a job?'

'Who sent you?'

'The soldiers,' I replied, trying to give the impression that I had been recommended for employment. The only soldiers who had sent me there were the ones on the gate!

'Wait a minute,' he said, and went back into the office. A moment later, he called me in.

I shook hands with the two officers and was invited to sit down. The first man, their interpreter, asked if I spoke English, to which I replied that, regrettably, I did not but was hoping to learn, since I already spoke excellent German, Polish, Russian, Czech and Bulgarian – and of course Ukrainian, which was my native tongue. This made a great impression. When it was translated, the two officers smiled but I could see that the boldness of my claim had sparked their curiosity.

'What, may I ask, is your profession?' asked the captain gravely.

I hesitated, terrified lest my lack of training for any particular profession might disqualify me altogether, then hastened to say that I knew how to cook and bake bread, do gardening work, was quite handy as a motor mechanic, and could turn my hand to almost anything. That was no lie. There weren't many things I hadn't done in my years on the farms.

Breaking in young horses might not be much use in the Catering Corps but my expertise in making cider and schnapps might be.

The amiability of the two officers amazed me. They treated me with unfailing courtesy, smiling encouragingly and offering me first a cigarette, then coffee and biscuits. Nevertheless, it was an interrogation, not an interview. Everything I told them was written down by the interpreter.

'Where did you learn all those things?'

'I learned cooking and baking from my mother and sister and from some of the Austrian farmers I worked for. On the farms, I was 'man-of-all-work'. As far as languages are concerned, I can read and write Polish, Russian, and German, because they were part of my education. The others I have picked up from people in the camps.'

Suddenly one of them asked, 'Who are you?'

As the interpreter put the question, the two officers observed me closely. Little by little, they extracted every detail of my past history. They were, I think, genuinely interested. Perhaps I was something of a novelty to them. The refugee camps around Villach housed many thousands of people in need of work – homesick, sunk in poverty, many of them ignorant and illiterate, grimy, shabby, accustomed only to doing other people's bidding, traumatized by torture and crushed by all the sufferings of war, disheartened by endless rebuffs, and finally too apathetic to do more than exist as cheerfully as possible from day to day. In contrast, here was an eager, self-confident young man from Ukraine who was literate and master, he claimed, of at least four languages, an ex-Red Army officer who had commanded a company of men, yet was unskilled in military matters. This fellow, threadbare but scrubbed shining clean and as neat as a pin, willing to learn and to turn his hand to anything, had the effrontery to attempt the impossible and seek a job with the British Army!

I answered their questions with absolute candour, telling them the whole truth. Had I not done so, they could easily have tripped me up. But they questioned me in a relaxed way; it was not at all like a cross-examination by the police. In the end, I spent several hours with them, feeling more and more sure there would have to be a job for me. No one from whom I had begged for work had ever offered me coffee before, or spent any significant amount of time with me. Therefore, I was bitterly disappointed to be told, when the interview ended, to come back at noon the following day. Perhaps the account of my training in the Red Army had alarmed them and they needed time to check my story.

The three men must have seen how crestfallen I felt as I thanked them, shook hands with them, and left the room. Getting a job had become a matter of life and death and I now wanted to work at the El Alamein Camp more than I had ever wanted anything. How could I survive the suspense of the next twenty-four hours? Walking back along the River Drau, I reminded myself of the old saying that goes, 'I've been soaked to the skin so often in my life, I'm not afraid of a shower of rain'.

When the man at the washhouse saw me back in the camp, he asked how I had got on. 'It's not over yet,' I told him. 'I've been asked to go back and see them again tomorrow.' He beamed. 'Would you like another shower tomorrow then?' he asked. Such a thing as two showers in two days was unheard of! I hesitated before accepting, since I was exceptionally clean already. However, it had to be a good omen, so I said yes.

When I arrived at the *Arbeit* building at twelve on the dot the following day, the interpreter greeted me with a smile.

'You've been accepted to start work in the cookhouse, Stefan. If you come back at six, the people there will tell you what will be expected of you.'

I clapped my hands for joy, jubilant from the crown of my head to the soles of my feet, and would have liked to hug and kiss the interpreter but, instead, just pumped his hand until he could stand it no longer, then ran back to wring the hands of the soldiers at the gate. They glanced at one another, grinned, and shrugged. 'Okay, okay,' they said. 'Okay' was my first English word.

The interpreter told me I was to work a twelve-hour shift, from six at night to six in the morning. He handed me a letter for Sergeant Major Tiger, in the cookhouse, which I was to present on my arrival. 'He'll issue you with a uniform, which you will wear at all times and will pay for out of your wages.' I nodded energetically, in full agreement with every condition, whatever it was. Everything was acceptable. He didn't say what I should be paid, nor did I think to ask.

My feet grew wings to carry me back to the camp. I had a job! I was going to earn British money, eat British Army food, drink British beer and smoke British cigarettes. Heaven had opened its gates! God loved me still! When my friends heard the good news, they congratulated me with great generosity, though they must certainly have felt envious, and said, 'The more food for us, if you're swilling beer and scoffing army rations! Don't forget your old friends, though, will you, Stefan.' I promised that I never would – and I never have.

At six o'clock, when I reported to the cookhouse and asked for Sergeant Major Tiger, the corporal who received me chortled with glee and asked if I spoke English. I confessed that I did not. 'You'd better just call him "Sergeant Major", not "Tiger",' he advised, setting me straight. When I learned the meaning of the word 'tiger' and met the Sergeant Major, I understood that it was a joke. His nickname, however, did not surprise me.

He was a tall, hefty Scotsman with a voice so loud it could only be called a roar. He carried a baton in his hand or under his arm, using it to rap for attention, or strike at any utensil that offended him by its lack of cleanliness or by being found in the wrong place. His spoken German was sufficient to make himself understood; it was punctuated with a copious flow of English swear words for greater emphasis. Since many of the kitchen staff were Austrians, most of his orders were delivered in this mongrel dialect, which meant that four-letter words formed the initial basis of my English vocabulary. I was soon peppering my conversation with them just as he did.

The young corporal showed me around the kitchens and told me what would be expected of me. At first I was merely to watch what went on. Before long, I would be assigned to a task for a certain length of time, then move on to another task until I had learnt how to undertake most of the kitchen work efficiently and could fill in wherever needed. As we inspected the kitchens and adjacent stores together, my jaw hung open in astonishment. Never had I seen so much food! Loaves of bread were stacked up in their hundreds. There were vast tubs of lard, layer upon layer of fresh eggs in special cartons, and countless enormous tins containing fish and spam, spaghetti and baked beans, reaching almost to the ceiling. As usual my stomach felt empty and I could not conceive how people could be busily working among such vast supplies without reaching out and grabbing the food and eating it. They just went about, whistling and singing some of the time, but concentrating on whatever jobs they were doing. Everyone wore white uniforms, but the soldiers and their rank could be identified by their arm bands. I was told to address them as 'sergeant', 'corporal', and so on. I couldn't wait to take my place in the team, certain that I could learn to do every job to perfection.

Having donned my white coat and hung my own in the appointed place, I was assigned to help the Austrian chef who was preparing soup in huge boilers. I learned from him that, because it was part of a transit camp, the kitchens at El Alamein never closed. Troops came and went at all hours of the day and night. They might come from Graz or Vienna, spend a day or two, and then go on to Italy, France, or England – or vice versa. As there was a ceaseless movement of soldiers through the camp, so the kitchen work went on continuously, though the staff was slightly smaller at night.

When it was time to have a break and get something to eat, the soup chef told me to go and help myself. 'Eat whatever you like,' he said. Even in my childhood I had never heard such an invitation, which was beyond my wildest dreams of self-indulgence. I considered the available options.

'Could I have something fried? Some spam or corned beef with an egg and slice of bread?' I asked tentatively, with what felt like great temerity.

'Sure. If you like scrambled eggs, take some egg powder and milk and butter. If you'd rather have fried eggs, take fresh eggs. Get a loaf of bread from the store. If you want tea or coffee, just help yourself. Have whatever you want.'

I couldn't believe my ears. It passed all reason. In some confusion of mind, I opted for scrambled eggs and made so much I could hardly pile it on the plate. 'Should I get a whole loaf of bread from the store or just cut off a slice?' I asked. It was white bread, too.

'Take two loaves, if you want,' was the reply. For the first time in my life, I could eat bread by the loaf and not by the slice.

It was the same with drinks. Having drunk a big mugful of tea, with creamy dollops of condensed milk spooned into it, I asked if I could have coffee as well. And it seemed I could, and it was real coffee, which smelt wonderful, not the ersatz stuff I was used to. I ate and drank with gusto, sitting down at a table with the first shift of workers to have their break, trying to remember not to appear too greedy. I knew it was important to observe how others behaved and follow their example. My first meal break had, however, been exactly what I had always dreamed of, and the realization was slowly dawning on me that I might never be hungry again.

On my return to Camp Magdalein, my friends were dying to hear how the first night had gone, dwelling on and luxuriating in every detail. They took heart from my account, for if one of their number had managed to find work, it was evidently not impossible for them to do the same. I described exactly what had taken place, declaring that I had been in Heaven, but even to me, it felt like a dream. It was hard to believe my luck. Thousands of people in the camps would have given their right arm for the privilege of working for the British Army and eating their fill in the army's kitchens.

The El Alamein camp was large, its main buildings solidly built of brick in the pre-war manner. What delighted me was the fact that it was scrupulously clean and tidy, indoors and out. Everything that could possibly be painted was painted white or whitewashed, even the stones and chain-link fences that lined the walks and flower beds. There was an agreeable sense of order about the red brick buildings with their white-painted trim, set amid handsome, dark green shrubbery. Though most of the sleeping accommodation was in tents and Nissen huts (or 'half-barrel barracks', as we called them), these likewise stood in even ranks, with the ground between them neatly planted and maintained. Everything was disciplined, nothing haphazard. Even the military vehicles were parked in a certain way and in certain places and were not left just anywhere. It was a great pleasure to find myself in a place that was so efficiently run.

My first pay packet was seventy Austrian schillings, or about £1 10s in

English money. Seventy schillings was virtually worthless – you couldn't buy a bar of soap or chocolate with it – but I was too happy in my work to mind. I got plenty to eat and learnt something new every day. It might be a new recipe, or new facts about the people I worked with, or about British life, or about the camp. Some of my fellow workers dropped mysterious hints about who could be trusted and who couldn't, but I paid little attention to such remarks, not wanting to be associated with one faction or another. I failed to notice anything strange or underhand going on. The only odd thing was the way Tiger would talk to certain people. I thought perhaps he had favourites.

Then, one day, when I received my pay, the young corporal, who was known as Pete, asked how much I was earning. He seemed shocked when I showed him my pay packet. 'With that money you couldn't even buy a packet of cigarettes!' he exclaimed. 'Are you willing to work so hard just for that?'

'Oh, yes,' I assured him. 'Don't forget I get very good food here and plenty of it.'

He laughed and made a comic face. 'I wouldn't say the food here is anything special!'

'To you it may not be. To me it is absolutely fantastic.'

He leaned forward then and said in a low voice, 'That's fine. But if you'd like to earn a little more, just let me know. I can arrange it.'

'I wouldn't want to do anything that might get me into trouble,' I said, beginning to get the drift. 'I'm really very happy working here.' So he shrugged his shoulders and went back to work.

We cooked a tremendous amount of food, much more than the soldiers in the camp could eat, because we did not always receive warning when a trainload of soldiers would arrive. Or we might have advance warning of a trainload, and find it was several hundred soldiers short. Either way, there would be a surplus. Everyone was offered a considerable choice of dishes, too, from roast beef and Yorkshire pudding, with gravy and boiled vegetables, to Austrian specialities cooked with a variety of herbs and sauces. There was always food left over. Every day, at lunch and dinner time, poor children and elderly folk were allowed to come into the camp with their metal containers and queue up outside the Mess. Instead of scraping their plates into waste bins, the soldiers could empty them into the containers – chunks of meat and potatoes, or portions of steamed pudding and custard. Sometimes there was a queue at breakfast time as well. If the children began to push and shove, a soldier would be sent out with a baton to keep order, but mostly the poor people stood docile, with three or four containers in their outstretched hands, hoping to get different kinds of food. If the soldiers were considerate, they would

159

separate their leavings into divided tins, but often the containers were filled with unappetizing assortments of whatever food was left. Beggars can't be choosers, and there were no complaints. Many people ate the food on the spot and queued up again for food to take home to the family.

The waste of food was almost inevitable given the scale on which the catering was done. Fortunately there were impoverished civilians who could benefit, so it was not simply wasted. We in the kitchens were glad to get rid of leftovers. The stores were full and we could always request fresh stocks with which to prepare meals for the next batch of soldiers to arrive.

There was, however, a less justifiable reason for this chronic glut of food in hard times – an absence of sensible control. Our supplies were ordered from Klagenfurt, the capital city of Carinthia and headquarters for the British Military Administration in the district. Lorries were regularly dispatched to Klagenfurt from our camp to draw rations for between 2,000 and 3,000 men. Each lorry would unload its contents at the storehouses serving the kitchen, bakery or NAAFI (which provided a shop and canteen facilities for servicemen) regardless of how well-stocked with stores they already were. It appeared that no account of stocks currently held had to be rendered – or it was rendered incorrectly – when new supplies were requisitioned. As a result, the stores were permanently overflowing.

It was this surplus that flowed into the black market in Villach in which, though I did not know it to begin with, our friend Sergeant Major Tiger played a significant part, lining his pockets nicely. It was clear that by getting involved I could add to my seventy Austrian schillings very considerably. However, my lapse into a new way of life did not come about immediately. It had to be prepared over the course of several months.

There was much discussion in the kitchens and during meal breaks about the relative merits of the occupying armies. Russian soldiers were considered backward, barely literate, less intelligent and less well-educated than the British and Americans, and certainly less well-informed, since most of what they knew about the world was drilled into them in their indoctrination classes – the world according to Marx, Lenin, and Stalin! People would say that Stalin was not much better than Hitler but that, all the same, he deserved credit for defeating the Nazis and driving the Germans back out of the eastern countries they had occupied, freeing people from Nazi concentration camps and slave labour. Whether they had freed them to live their own lives, or only to serve the state under compulsion was a question that was hotly debated. My own story became part of the argument.

Even at that time, people were aware that there were thousands of slave labour camps all over Russia too, mainly in Siberia, and that people sometimes spent their whole lives in them, while others died on the journey there. They were, however, reluctant to face the fact that most of those people were innocent of any wrongdoing. 'What do you think, Stefan?' they would ask.

By now it was an open secret that I had been a Red Army officer and that I had deserted. The story of my escape had made me friends among soldiers and civilians. I was only nineteen, and the soldiers liked to pull my leg, saluting me when I made a request and replying, 'Yes, Herr Lieutenant. Certainly, Herr Lieutenant.' I didn't mind their teasing – it made me feel part of the team – but it reminded me of times I preferred to forget. I had regular nightmares of being arrested by the Russians and marched out for execution.

My job seemed secure, since I soon became capable of most of the jobs in the cookhouse. People were sometimes moved from the kitchen to the bakery or NAAFI, and that was all right with me. I was ready to go anywhere so long as I was still employed in the camp.

One day Pete, the corporal who had spoken to me earlier, and with whom I had become quite friendly, asked me again if I was satisfied with my pay packet. While making the same reply as before, I understood what he was driving at. He said, 'With your cooperation, I could make it ten times what you are earning at present.'

Caution prevailed. His overtures might be a trap that would lead to instant dismissal but I was curious. I said, 'Before I ask exactly what you have in mind for me to do, let me think about it, since I presume it is something that could lose me my job. I need to consider it for a week or two before taking such a risk. I'll let you know.'

What tempted me most was the possibility of moving out of the wretchedly overcrowded conditions of Camp Magdalein into accommodation in a private home in Villach. After finding a job, it would be the next step towards independence, but it was hopeless even to consider it on my present earnings. I simply had to have more money.

I began to wonder whether any of the civilians on the kitchen staff could advise me. They might be less likely to report me to the sergeant major than one of the soldiers. Were workers ever permitted to take a little food out of the camp? I might ask. A little sugar, soap, fat, spam, or egg powder, perhaps? The sort of food the kitchen store was full of? Even half a kilogram or a kilogram of one of the foods that were so precious and expensive outside would sell for a good price, and taking it could hardly be enough of a crime to get me dismissed from my job. I did not approach anyone straight away: it was a delicate matter.

At the same time I began to make enquiries about accommodation. I wasn't choosy. I would accept almost any room that offered a little more privacy than was possible in the camp. Did anyone know of a family that might be prepared to accept an *Ausländer* as a lodger? It was sad to feel that I was still an outsider after so many years but many Austrians avoided all contact with foreigners, especially those from the UNRRA camps. On my side, I wanted nothing to do with people who had been strong adherents of the Nazis during the war, and they were not easy to identify. Like anyone else, they might be prepared to offer a room in return for a few scarce commodities, but I did not wish to make my home with them.

My friend Pete took me aside and told me how I could make more money. He assured me that all the Austrian staff took food out of the kitchen for their families. 'They don't earn much money, but their families eat well. They're not going hungry like many families in Villach. They can also make a little money on the black market.' Making sure we were out of earshot of anyone else, he added, 'Let me explain how they smuggle the food out of the camp.'

'How do I know you won't report me?' I asked. 'No amount of money would make me do anything that would lose me my job.'

'That won't happen, I promise. I swear to you, on my word of honour as a soldier! I'm only telling you this because I want to help you. I know you've had a rough time and are all alone in the world. You're young and should be having a little fun. I won't betray you, Stefan. I'll give you my hand on it.'

I believed him and shook the hand he offered, looking him straight in the eye, still unable to believe that an English soldier was offering to be my friend! Then, overcome by his sympathy for my lonely struggles, I embraced him.

'All right,' I said. 'Just tell me what I have to do. I know the rest of the civilian staff have families, but my friends are hungry, too. Look at them over there! Their clothes are almost worn out.' That day I was more conscious than usual that I was now comparatively well dressed, in clothes and shoes that had all been handed down by the soldiers. I was virtually in British uniform but for the insignia.

'Listen carefully,' said Pete. 'The first thing you have to do is get some bags made. They need to be long and thin, like a stocking. You'll need one or two for each leg and a longer one to go around your waist. You can get a lot of things – tea, coffee, sugar, flour, raisins – into such bags. And you can put fat and chocolate, in fact most things, into tins. You'll have to tie them tightly around your legs and middle, and wear trousers bigger than your usual size, with wide enough legs to hide the bags. Don't overdo it. If you go out looking like a circus clown or a pregnant woman, the MPs on the gate will stop you and search you for sure. So be very, very careful!'

The struggle with my conscience did not last long. I was, however, careful to take only modest amounts of food. Even so, each week's gleanings mounted up. Sold cheaply to friends, they soon raised money enough to pay for a private room. Before long, it became a way of life. I would greet the soldiers on the gate and chat and joke with them as I went in and out, so that their attention was on my face and not on my girth.

As the bitter-cold Austrian winter set in, in late 1946, I still had not found a place to live, and life in the camps was becoming more and more depressing. Nearly everyone planned to emigrate, but hardly anyone had actually gone. Camp officials would raise our expectations with information about countries that might accept immigrants, and we would listen to descriptions of England, America, Canada, Australia, France or Switzerland, but nothing seemed to happen. We wondered how many more winters we should have to endure right there. But hope kept us going – it was hope, and the special brand of fatalistic humour developed by people whose hopes were perennially crushed.

On the first day of the New Year, 1947, we made an effort to count our blessings as we prayed for the loved ones we had left behind and might never see again. We were at least alive and well and, with God's help, could look forward to a future that would be an improvement on the past, whereas many living under the heel of Stalin would freeze or starve to death in labour camps. We also prayed for ourselves – that the New Year might offer fresh opportunities to the people in the camps.

As our Ukrainian Christmas on 7 January approached, I was glad to find that I was on the day shift, and could therefore get back to the camp in time to celebrate the Holy Christmas supper with my own people. The barrack was decorated with astonishing artistry – stars, snowflakes, and all sorts of figures of people and animals cut out of coloured paper. Finest clothes were worn by everyone. That year we had guests from other camps and I was proud to be able to contribute smuggled bottles of whisky and cognac, packets of cigarettes, and boxes of chocolates to the festivities. Sergeant Major Tiger had acknowledged the importance of the occasion by excusing me from work the following day.

After prayers, a festive meal – during which everyone got at least a taste of all twelve traditional dishes – and many rounds of toasts that brought tears as well as laughter, we adjourned to the canteen for dancing. It was already full when we got there, with strangers as well as friends. As the band started playing, we moved our chairs back to make room for the dancers, and I caught sight of a man who looked exactly like someone I remembered from my Red Army company. He was deep in conversation with a Russian-speaking couple. My first reaction was one of alarm – even now I was not free of the fear that Red Army spies might infiltrate the camp and inform on me – but I knew that such a person, if identified, would be quickly and violently dealt with. I said to my friends, 'There's a man from eastern Ukraine I recognize. He could be a spy, so I'd like to ask him a few questions. Would some of you stand by the door, ready to stop him if he tries to get away? If he proves to be a genuine refugee, I'll give you a signal and you can come and meet him.'

Assured that my friends would do as I asked, I approached the man and said in Ukrainian, 'The season's greetings to you, Hrehor. What are you doing here?'

His face lit up with amazement as he leapt to his feet. 'Stefan, my beloved lieutenant! Can it really be you?' He embraced me in a tight hug and kissed me on both cheeks, tears streaming down his face. 'My dearest Stefko, you're alive! We were told you were dead.'

My heart warmed to him but I was not ready to lower my guard until I had heard more about him and how he came to be there. I was also anxious to know what had become of the rest of my men. Hrehor had been one of my four platoon commanders so he, if anyone, could tell me. Since my return to Voitsberg, I had been worrying a lot about what had happened to them after my defection. It was a matter very close to my heart.

'You can't be alive!' he protested again, laughing with astonishment. 'We were told you were caught deserting the Red Army and had been court-martialled and executed on the spot! But they left us wondering what had become of you for five days before they told us anything. Then a Russian officer took your place at an indoctrination session and was forced to explain. He said you hadn't got far, and let that be a lesson to the rest of us!'

I shuddered but it was what I would have expected. Then I asked about his own escape. He said that a great many of the men had succumbed to the constant barrage of propaganda and become convinced by what the Russian officers told them. Then, when it was reckoned they had had sufficient training and were politically reliable, all the men and some of the younger women were assembled into columns and marched off to the east, heading, they surmised, for the Black Sea port of Odessa. They were told they would be collected by army transport on the way and would eventually sail for the Far East. The column was closely patrolled by Russian officers on bicycles, motorbikes and in cars. Many of the men were frightened of what might happen to them in Japan, and desolated at the thought that they might never reach home, but no one dared contemplate trying to escape. 'Look at what happened to Stefan,' they said.

My old friend Fedir, who had left home with me in 1942, and had later brought me the news of my mother's death, was among those who were on that march, so I can confirm that they did actually go to the Soviet Far East. Many years later I heard that he eventually returned home to Antoniwka but was executed by the NKVD. By that time he had matured into a man with too much knowledge of the world to accept the lies with which the populace was fed, and was too outspoken.

Hrehor said he had made up his mind from the beginning never to serve on active duty in the Red Army. He resolved to desert at the first opportunity. Each day, when the column stopped to rest, the men would sit down in whatever shade they could find, or go to drink and cool themselves in nearby streams or rivers. Hrehor managed to drop back to the rear of the column. One day, during a rest period, he sat down, hidden by the branches of a weeping willow tree, on the bank of a river, and just stayed there. Motionless, he held his breath until the order was given to move on and he heard the column tramp away. That was all there was to it!

Of course, I was not satisfied until I had heard every detail of his escape, and I pressed him hard on his exact route. Like Ivan and me, he had headed for Graz, and told me he had asked his way only from old people who, as a rule, were more hostile to the Russian occupation than younger Austrians. He described the hills, valleys, river courses, farms and villages he had passed on his way, and the towns he had been obliged to bypass. His route was not very different from the one we had taken. When he finished, I embraced him without reserve, saying, 'I believe you now, Hrehor. Your story is so like mine. But I couldn't help being suspicious of you at first. You speak Russian and were brought up to think of yourself as Russian. You could have been sent here as a spy. And you know what the people in these camps do to anyone who betrays them!'

'Indeed I do,' he said gravely, with tears in his eyes, 'and they get what they deserve.' Death was what they deserved.

I signalled to my friends. 'Come and meet Hrehor, who was one of my platoon commanders in the Red Army,' I said. They gathered round, astonished.

'I never really believed all that about you being a Red Army officer before,' one of them remarked.

Any doubts they might have harboured as to the truth of my story were now well and truly banished by what Hrehor told them. He and I could not stop comparing notes on the people we had known and the places we had visited while on the run. So then of course there was a mammoth celebration, with much laughter and toasts all round, and reminiscing and singing and dancing that went on into the early hours of the following morning. Just as well I was not on duty that day!

Chapter 16

1947
Cooking for Tommy

T he year 1947 started well. Following a long, frustrating search, I found a place to live. An elderly couple named Weisser were willing to offer me a bed. They lived on the ground floor of a modern block of flats in Heimat Land, on a hillside on the edge of Villach, within easy walking distance of the El Alamein and Magdalein camps. Admittedly, the bed was in a corner of their bedroom, since there was no other. The flat had only a kitchen, toilet, living room and the bedroom, which had one double and one single bed. There was no bathroom – they washed in the kitchen – but there was a flush toilet, something I had never experienced before.

I wasn't even shaving yet and felt embarrassed at the thought of sharing the bedroom of two old people. It seemed like an invasion of privacy (both ways), but half the time I would be sleeping by day and the Weissers didn't seem to mind. Warm-hearted folk that they were, their desire to help was genuine. 'We have no children,' they said, 'so you can be our son.'

The apartment was shining clean and light, with windows in every room, romantic music playing on the radio, and an air of utter peace. It smelt astonishingly fresh after the camp, and the bed they showed me was furnished with snowy white sheets, feather pillows, and the sort of huge eiderdown we called a *peryna* in Ukraine. The view from the bedroom window was breathtaking, embracing the whole town and a range of mountains beyond, the nearest of which called Twelve O'clock Mountain. This was to be my home! If it had been a castle on the Blue Danube I couldn't have fallen more in love with it or with the lovely couple who lived there and were ready to adopt me as their own.

Frau Weisser was a cheerful, bouncy woman; short and plump, with grey hair pulled back into a bun, like the farmer's wife in children's fairy tales. She wore soft colours, not black as so many of the old women did, and it may be she was not as old as she seemed to me then. She certainly went about her domestic tasks with energy, and announced at once that she would wash my clothes and cook for me whatever she could afford.

'I am sure my husband and I will be able to make you very happy here, Stefan. Treat it as your home. You can have a key and come and go whenever you like. Don't worry about disturbing us if you come in at midnight or after. We are heavy sleepers and shan't mind.'

'But how much shall I pay you for all that?' I asked, beginning to wonder if it would be within my means.

'Just give us what you can afford. That'll be all right with us,' she answered, as though that settled the matter, and both she and her husband offered to shake hands. 'Of course, if you can ever obtain a little soap, or a few decagrams of coffee or sugar, or margarine, or a cigarette or two for my husband, we'd be living in the lap of luxury!'

I assured her I could keep our household supplied with some, at least, of these commodities, and felt deeply touched as I realized how precious, and out of reach, things I had begun to take for granted still were to most people. 'Of course I shall pay something as well,' I added.

Within the hour, I was collecting my belongings from Camp Magdalein. I promised my friends there that I would still look after them, since they counted heavily on the good things I had been able to bring back to the camp. When I said I was moving into a castle, they did not even query the fact. To them, as to me, to sleep anywhere outside the camp was to live like a king. That night, as I snuggled down between white sheets, with their scent of dried roses, and the enormous eiderdown, I thanked God once again for his care of me. Herr Weisser had placed the radio by my bed, promising to turn it off when I fell asleep, and I wondered if even Sergeant Major Tiger was lying down that night in such delicious, peaceful, perfumed comfort, lulled by soft strains of sweet music.

That spring, I really came alive. For the first time in my life, I was free to live like an ordinary adult human being. I had spent five years in Austria and met a number of people who were stiff-necked and contemptuous of foreigners, considering themselves a superior race, but many more who were generous, helpful and compassionate. Now I lived among them as an equal and, though I never for a moment forgot my own dear parents, had a surrogate mother and father to make much of me. Frau Weisser was an excellent cook. She made the best noodle soup I have ever eaten, and it became even tastier if I brought home a little meat to give it extra flavour.

Living nearer El Alamein camp made my walk to work much easier. Being in the town, and going dancing whenever I had free time, I began to make Austrian friends and dress in the Austrian fashion. I got some dark material cheap on the black market and had it made into a suit actually tailored to my measurements! Pete gave me some shorts and a short-sleeved shirt he no longer needed, and Frau Weisser knitted me a pair of knee-length socks. When I acquired my first pair of real leather shoes, I felt well turned out at last and extremely happy.

I began working in the bakery. This broadened my catering experience, since the work was quite different. The bakery was smaller than the cookhouse and had fewer people working there. It occupied a Nissen hut, with a field oven fuelled from outside with coal and wood, and was divided into three parts – the bakery itself, the store room and the patisserie, where one solitary Austrian pastry chef plied his trade. The staff consisted of three or four Austrians, a Romanian ex-army officer, some British soldiers, and me. Of the Britons, there were Maxy, who was Jewish, another Englishman called Tommy, a Welshman known as Taffy, a Scotsman called Jock, and Paddy, who was Irish. At first, I thought of them all as English, but I was soon made sharply aware that even Great Britain had nationality problems.

The bakers quickly got to know one another. Maxy was a happy-go-lucky sort who enjoyed talking politics. Since we were both, in a way, outsiders, we found plenty to talk about. Maxy was very touchy about his Jewishness, however. He could not abide it when jokes were made about people's origins, as they frequently were, and he got his leg pulled. On any other subject he had a great sense of humour.

Tommy was a fly-by-night sort, tall, slim and good-looking – a womanizer with a foul tongue, who was always in pursuit of any creature in skirts. The others frequently warned us to watch out; the English words we were learning from Tommy were not to be repeated when speaking to just any English-speaking person, particularly not if it was a woman! Then Tommy went home on leave and was gone, without explanation, for a very long time. When he returned, he looked haggard and drawn and was very subdued. He shocked me by continually running down his own country. He seemed to have a grudge against England. Nothing was good about it, not even the beer! Having been brought up to be a fervent patriot, I could not understand such talk. Then we learned from Sergeant Major Tiger that Tommy had spent most of his time away in prison, having been caught trying to smuggle a stolen Rolls Royce onto a channel ferry, with the intention of driving it back to Villach. We teased him about this for a while, before he settled down and we got to like him better.

Jock was ginger-haired and freckled. He was amiable enough but spoke hardly any German, having no German-speaking girlfriend to make it worth his while. He could therefore take little part in the general banter.

168

His choice of drink – whisky washed down with beer – astonished the rest of us, who assumed it was a Scottish habit. When we could find another soldier to interpret for us, we would ask him about Scotland, which was the one topic on which he was ready to talk. He even spoke to us in Gaelic, a strange language which he insisted was still spoken in Scotland. We got him to explain about a regimental band we had seen wearing kilts, which amazed us. In fact, we teased him unmercifully until he produced a family photograph showing all the men in kilts. This persuaded us that it was a genuine national costume, and we had to admit that they looked very fine.

Paddy was a small, simpleminded fellow with a passion for clocks and watches. He spent all the proceeds of his black market operations collecting them. I thought perhaps he was planning to set up a repair business on his return to Ireland, but he said he didn't understand how clocks worked, he just liked them. He was also in love with a girl called Maria, who did his laundry for him, and washed and pressed his clothes so beautifully that, if you met him outside the bakery, he was always immaculately dressed.

Taffy, the Welshman, was seriously in love with a beautiful Austrian girl from a good family, and was hoping to marry her. He had an excellent command of German and had done so well selling the bakery surplus on the black market that he had rented and furnished a luxurious flat in the town. Smuggling food out in the quantities that he was, we thought he was taking absurd risks, but he excused himself by saying his intentions were honourable and that, as soon as he got out of the army, he would take his girlfriend home to Wales. We infuriated him by forgetting and saying England, not knowing the difference. 'I am not effing *English*!' he would splutter, but without abbreviating the expletive. 'I am *Welsh*.'

The Austrians, the Romanian and I learned a lot about Wales. Our impressions of Ireland and Scotland were vague and we had always thought of the rest of Great Britain as England. In the bakery, however, we were put straight. The soldiers got very worked up about it when they were wrongly labelled English. Taffy confused us, however, by refusing to speak Welsh. I was the first to tackle him about it. 'Look,' I said, 'I am a Ukrainian and I speak Ukrainian. Jakob is Romanian and speaks Romanian. Jock speaks Scottish. Paddy speaks Irish. Why don't you speak Welsh?'

Reluctantly he admitted that most Welsh people couldn't speak the language. For me, whose national pride was closely bound up with my language and traditions, this was a conundrum. It seemed to me so unpatriotic, so neglectful of his heritage, that I persisted in saying that, if he didn't speak the language, he couldn't be Welsh. At which Taffy became seriously annoyed! Some of the others then backed me up, and the atmosphere in the bakery grew so uncomfortable that he apparently considered asking for a transfer. Then the NCO came to his defence, assuring us that Taffy was telling the truth, and that only some Welsh people actually spoke Welsh, after which the furore died down.

Even now, when life was so agreeable, I was subject to terrible attacks of homesickness and panic, when I felt that everyone but myself had families they could go home to, or at least write to, whereas I would be shot on sight were I to go home, and anyone receiving a message from me would be in deep trouble. Occasionally I had nightmares of being pursued and caught, and shouted out in my sleep (as, indeed, I do to this day).

These feelings were assuaged somewhat when I met a family who reminded me very much of my own. The father had owned a butcher's shop in a town near Kyiv, where he made a decent living for his wife, son and daughter. Both he and his wife were intelligent, cultivated people, and the children, Taras and Olha had received a good education.

Like thousands of others, they had fled to the west when the Germans retreated, dreading a repetition of the godless Stalinist repression under which they had lived earlier, and unwilling to bring up their children in such a climate of fear. Mostly on foot, sometimes begging a lift, they made their way through Poland, Czechoslovakia and Hungary to Austria, eventually arriving in Villach. They confided in me that they had brought with them two kilograms' weight of gold bars. A Russian who was staying behind had given it to them in return for a secret store of cured meat, salted bacon, salami, and some sacks of wheat and barley, which neither the German soldiers nor the Russians had ever managed to find. This hoard was in a cellar beneath the garden of their house, from which they would sell to valued customers or those in desperate need, but even the children had not known of its existence. In truth, the Russian had bought his home and everything he owned with that two kilograms of gold but with it my friend hoped to secure some kind of future for his family or, at the very least, be able to buy their way out of trouble. Since they had travelled most of the way from Kyiv in company, in large groups, it was my impression that he had it still.

I got on well with this family and fell more than a little in love with Olha, a slim, fair-haired girl, with a sweet, round, baby face and smiling, china-blue eyes. She often wore a flower in her hair. She was adorable, unsophisticated and unspoilt but clever, with a gift for writing poetry. As I wrote poetry myself – I had continued to do so even through some of the worst times since leaving home – I recognized a soul-mate.

Our youthful love affair was innocent and deeply romantic, going no further than a tender kiss and a loving embrace. We were both high-minded and idealistic and, young as she was, I would not have dreamed of taking advantage of her. Sometimes we wove fantasies of marrying and emigrating to some foreign country together but it was only make-believe. Our future lay in the lap of the gods, and we both knew that I had much to accomplish before I could think of marriage. We vowed to keep in touch, however, when her father decided to seek admission for his family to France. He believed that a war would soon break out again between East and West, in which Stalin would be defeated, and that he would then be able to return home with his family. I was not tempted to follow them, feeling more drawn at that time to North or South America.

They eventually settled near Strasbourg, where they found work on a farm. We corresponded for a time, but farming was not for me. Although the years were passing, I still dreamed of completing an academic education. Even as I worked in the cookhouse and bakery I was cultivating a high degree of political awareness. My childhood had been happy in many ways, but I was not willing to return to a life where the children ran barefoot, where hardly anyone had good shoes or enough warm clothes, or possessed a radio or bicycle. In Ukraine I had experienced feudalism, Marxism, fascism, all unjust totalitarian regimes in which people lived in daily dread of torture or imprisonment, of having their houses burnt down or their crops confiscated. I was determined to fight such injustice and do all in my power to bring about change.

One day, without being given any reason for the change, I was transferred again, this time to work in the NAAFI. I welcomed every opportunity to gain more experience, always hoping to graduate eventually to a desk job – to be put in charge of something, but moving to the NAAFI felt like a retrograde step. I worked alongside a few Britons and several Austrians, mainly shifting cases of beer and whisky, and boxes of chocolate, biscuits, tea, sugar and sacks of monkey nuts from the NAAFI stores to the canteen or bar. We were under the eagle eye of a female sergeant major, a humourless woman much stricter and more conscientious than Sergeant Major Tiger. Seeing how closely she watched us, I marvelled that anything found its way onto the black market, though it did, and no one was dismissed or arrested for it, at least not as far as I ever heard.

Night duty was marginally more fun, when I worked in the bar, serving drinks to British and American servicemen, and things often got rowdy. The Americans used El Alamein camp whenever they were in transit through the British sector and when men from both countries were drinking in the bar at the same time, we could expect trouble. Fights often broke out late at night between the Yanks and Tommies (or Limeys as the Americans called them) when they had had a lot to drink. Chairs, tables, bottles and glasses would fly in all directions. There was always a certain amount of difficulties because the Americans had more money to spend and liked to splash it about, provoking the British soldiers if they could.

The British were only allowed to spend coupons specially issued for use in the NAAFI. The Tommies would settle down with a drink and a bag of monkey nuts each, then the Yanks would come in, go up to the bar, and order a whole barrel of beer and a sackful of monkey nuts. Next they would push a few tables together and stand around, smoking their American cigarettes and trading good-natured insults with their Allies in the attempt to stir up a little excitement. They were soon taunting one another from both sides, with tempers flaring ominously. The Yanks generally started it.

It was a marvel to me that no one was killed or seriously injured in those fights, at least while I was there. Those of us serving drinks would duck out of the way while someone called the military police. The MPs would encircle the place and come in blowing their whistles to calm things down. Then they would collect up those who were hurt or bleeding, or simply unconscious, and cart them off to the cooler in jeeps or vans. There they could sober up for a few days. Some men spent as much as fourteen days in jug after a free-for-all of that kind, depending on how active a part they had played in it.

My main preoccupation, once the men were gone, was to collect any cigarettes left on the tables. On a good night there might be a tin or packet almost full and the cigarette ends scattered on the floor. I sometimes stuffed 200 or 300 stubs into my well-prepared pockets, with remains of pipe tobacco and unused matches. All were like gold dust on the black market. Back at the flat I opened out the cigarette papers, separated the burned tobacco from the rest, and divided the evening's haul into measures suitable for sale. Though we had come to an equitable arrangement, my pay was barely enough to cover the cost of accommodation with the Weissers, so this leftover tobacco was my only source of income.

I wasn't learning anything useful, just carrying out the same menial tasks, witnessing the same fights, answering the MP's questions as to who started what, and living on next to nothing. Clearly I had to think more seriously about emigrating. I discussed the matter with friends in the camps around Villach. All of us had been holding on, waiting for the international situation to become clearer and hoping for news from home, but they agreed with me that it was time to make a decision.

Not everyone had such a choice. It was difficult for older people, anyone in poor health, or those with large families, to find countries willing to accept them. Some were destined never to leave the camps. But for young, single men in good health, it was largely a matter of deciding where we wanted to go. America, Canada, England, France, Venezuela, Chile, Argentina or Australia? We could apply to any of these countries if we wished to. Then we would have to undergo medical examinations and enquiries into our personal histories. Questions would be asked about the standard of education we had achieved and about the political inclinations – not only of ourselves but of our families.

Neither my friends nor I really wanted to stay in Europe. France was the only continental country offering to take immigrants, and then only a limited number, and we hadn't much respect for the part the French had played in the war. Great Britain offered places to people of working age but, though I had many British friends, I had been put off going to England by the things that Tommy, in the cookhouse, had reported. Rumour and hearsay were the basis of most of our impressions of foreign countries. America, Canada, and Australia were generous in their acceptance of immigrants, and associated in our minds with freedom and wide open spaces, but they were very, very far away. Patriotic spirits among us insisted that they wanted to be near enough to their homelands to be able to fight for them if a new war broke out. We all cherished the hope of going home.

By the summer of 1947, however, people in the camps were growing despondent. Those who had expected a renewed war to drive Russia back out of Eastern Europe and liberate their homelands realized they might never see their loved ones again. Even those prepared to emigrate often faced the break-up of their families, since countries willing to receive their young and vigorous sons and daughters – most countries were short of workers – would not always take on the burden of ageing parents. Such people were in a tragic dilemma. Britain would not even accept husbands and wives together. They had to apply separately, as individuals, as single people, and hope to meet up again in their new homeland.

For us young men, only the choice was difficult. We had no particular reason to prefer one country over another, yet a decision must be made. One evening, when we had been drinking schnapps together, some of us decided to emigrate to Chile. It appeared to be quite simple. We only had to board a special train, which would take us to a camp where we would have medical checks and go through the emigration procedure, to find ourselves transported to Chile! We could not even imagine how we would travel. None of us had been close to a plane or ocean-going ship in our whole lives.

I handed in my notice at the Catering Corps and bade the Weissers a sad farewell. They seemed anxious on my behalf as well as sorry to see me go, but wished me well and said they were sure I would prosper. I packed my belongings and was on my way. Only while actually walking to the station was I assailed by serious misgivings. Suddenly the step I was taking felt like a betrayal of everything I held dear. Would I not be letting down my father and sister, uncles, aunts and cousins, all of whom might be in Siberia for all I knew, unless I stayed as near home as I possibly could? Had I the right to take off for another country, another hemisphere, so far away that I was unlikely ever to return, when I still did not know what had become of my family? Was I so indifferent to the fate of my beloved Ukraine? It was as if God himself spoke to me and shouted, 'NO'!

'I'm not going,' I told my friends. 'I'm not going to emigrate to Chile. I need more time to consider. It's too important a decision to make on the spur of the moment. I can't do it. I'd rather stay closer to Europe.'

Once it was said, an enormous wave of relief washed over me. I hated parting with my friends, especially when I had no job and no place to live, but when I returned to tell the Weissers what I had done, they strongly endorsed my decision and promptly took me in again, behaving exactly like loving parents.

'Don't worry. You'll get another job. If not, we'll have to manage as best we can. I've got some of the stores tucked away that you brought home when you were working in the bakery,' Frau Weisser assured me with her kindly, encouraging smile. Herr Weisser pointed out, in his solid, sensible way, 'You are right to give it more thought. If you went to France or England, you could still go on to Chile, or even Canada or Australia, if you didn't like it there. It wouldn't have been so easy from Chile! Though it was up to you, of course, Stefan. We didn't want to influence you.'

I decided to wait a while before making another application to emigrate. Perhaps it was in my nature that I could not be so easily uprooted as my friends who had gone. Yet I still wanted to go with people I knew. I didn't want to set off all on my own.

In the weeks that followed, I grew bored and listless; I hung about in the flat, lending a hand with the housework, unable to pay my way, or I visited friends. One day, when I was really down-in-the-dumps, an Austrian friend named Rudolf told me that his sister Lisa was getting married and invited me to go with him to the wedding. My spirits rose instantly! In all my years in the country, I had never attended an Austrian wedding. However, I was penniless and my clothes were no longer in very good shape.

'I'd love to,' I said, 'and feel extremely honoured to be asked, but look at me! I have no job, no money for a wedding present, and no clothes but these. I couldn't possibly accept.'

Rudolf brushed all that aside. 'It's not what you have, or what you wear, or what you bring that matters. You're my friend and I want you to come with me to my sister's wedding.'

I was thinking furiously, considering ways and means. I had nothing to sell on the black market, but if Sergeant Major Tiger would take me back, even for a few weeks, I could remedy that. Some chocolate or dried fruit or cigarettes would make an acceptable wedding present.

'But everyone will be dressed in their finest clothes, making me look little more than a beggar!' I protested.

174

Rudolf knew me extremely well. 'I could find you something suitable. Anyway, you'd be welcome, whatever you wore.'

'That's wonderful, then!' I said, glad to be persuaded. 'I'd love to come. When and where's it going to be?'

He told me the date and then eyed me with sudden doubt. 'The bridegroom's a forestry commissioner, in charge of large tracts of forest in the British zone, but his family live near Vienna, in the Russian zone, and I'm afraid that's where the wedding's to be.' I could see he had only just realized what problems that would pose for me.

'*Himmel Gott*! You're not suggesting I should go into the Russian zone, are you?' I cried. 'Not on your life! I escaped once, and that was enough. Let me just drink to your sister's health and happiness on the day. I'll find some schnapps or cognac and that will have to do.' Though I was absolutely adamant, my voice was full of regret. I was a sociable fellow, and to be included in a family wedding party warmed my heart. Accustomed as he was to moving freely from one sector to the other, Rudolf could not see that there was any real problem, but we left it at that for the moment.

Sergeant Major Tiger took me back into the Catering Corps, but said the job might not last long, as he was due to go on leave soon and the appointment of local staff would be up to his successor. Meanwhile, however, I got good meals, could make some recompense to the Weissers for their kindness, and had access to good things unobtainable outside. So, though it was probably the craziest, most foolhardy act of my entire life, I decided, after all, to go with Rudolf to his sister's wedding.

No one in his right mind would have done so. I went without a passport or documents of any kind. Courting danger in this way may have been an act of desperation, brought on by the sense that I was at some kind of crossroads in my life where only God could decide the turning, but it was also an act of youthful derring-do. By defying all regulations and crossing into their sector for a joyful spree, I'd be cocking a snook at the Russians, who thought they were so clever! If my friends in the camps had known, however, they would have tied me up and kept me in Villach by force.

At the border between the British and Russian zones, we left our carriage and were able, thanks to my temporary job, to bribe the engine driver with chocolate and cigarettes to hide us in his engine. We had hoped to pose as his stokers, but he already had two of them and we had to bribe them too. We crawled in among planks and shovels and old iron, while the driver blocked up the opening. In this way we avoided having to show any papers.

Our clean faces and clothes were badly soiled when we emerged and were made worse when the driver and his assistants tried to wipe off the soot with their greasy hands, but all five of us were cock-a-hoop at the success of this ruse. Rudolf and I had the wedding to look forward to and they had a store of provisions of a kind they rarely enjoyed.

Whatever we looked like, Rudolf and I took our full part in the wedding celebrations. It was a glorious occasion, with everyone in the wedding party handsome in traditional Austrian dress. An orchestra played all kinds of music, from Viennese waltzes to foxtrots, folk music and polkas; we only left the floor to sample the delights of traditional Austrian dishes, prepared by master chefs. Local wine, cider, and schnapps flowed as freely as the River Danube. I was astonished by the number of meat dishes served until I remembered that, as a forestry commissioner, the groom undoubtedly had access to supplies of venison.

Once the time approached for me and Rudolf to return to Villach, I became very concerned as to how to make the journey back. The driver of the locomotive might not be the same man who smuggled us over the border the first time, and the new driver might not want to risk his job or the possibility of spending the rest of his life in a Siberian labour camp. However, Rudolf 's new brother-in-law insisted on lending me his passport for our return journey. The picture in it showed a man with a big, black moustache, so it would not have fooled anyone, but he also sent his sister, with whom I had begun a mild flirtation, to make sure I got through safely. On her instructions, I hid in the toilet as we slowed down at the border. The British inspection was short and cursory, but the Russians went through the train examining every single person's papers, though they omitted to search the toilets, so I was more than a little lucky to get back to Villach safely.

During the train journey we saw many hundreds of prisoners of war – Austrians who had returned from the eastern front – being met on station platforms. It was a pitiful, painful sight. Wounded, blinded, on crutches, carried by friends or on stretchers, with faces scarred by suffering, they were embraced with tears of anguish by relatives who had had to wait more than two years for their homecoming. We could hardly bear to watch, appalled at the scale of the continuing tragedy of war.

The Weissers, always protective of me, were greatly relieved to see me back, and scolded me for my folly. It was apparent that I had given them a bad fright by going.

For the next few months, I lived in a kind of limbo, aware that I needed to consider my future but unable to make up my mind to emigrate.

One problem that faced every political displaced person who embarked on the emigration process was that of defining his or her nationality. We had been told that at Yalta in 1945, Churchill, Roosevelt and Stalin had reached an agreement about the repatriation of their respective nationals which stipulated that each person should be returned to his country of origin, whether he wished to go there or not. Since the peace treaties had redrawn national boundaries and spheres of influence, people's home countries might now be quite unsafe for them. This was why we were so frightened by Russian soldiers driving into camps to take people away.

People said that the ruling only applied to those who had been Russian citizens before the war, and not to the people of western Ukraine, which had been under Polish control. The Russians, however, claimed that when the Red Army invaded Poland in 1939, they had simply reunited the two parts of Ukraine, which had always wanted to be one.

It was music to our ears when we heard that the British government considered anyone who had been living outside the Soviet Union before September 1939 could not be forcibly repatriated. However, another rumour circulated that Tito's partisans, who were communists, might invade Klagenfurt and Villach, which were close to the Yugoslav border, in order to keep in good standing with the Russians. In that event, they could send 'home' those they considered Russian nationals. The situation remained nerve-racking. By working in El Alamein camp and living in private accommodation, I was reasonably safe, but many people lived in terror and declared they would rather commit suicide than go back.

The only solution was to emigrate, but to apply for emigration meant settling the nationality question once and for all, perhaps not to one's liking. Suppose it were decided that my brief service as a lieutenant in the Red Army had made me irrevocably a Russian citizen! Or, almost as bad, suppose I were declared stateless. That was like being told that you were nobody, born nowhere, with no parents or grandparents, no national identity of any kind. Once declared stateless, you were assumed to have no allegiance, no roots, no claim on the hospitality of any particular country. You would wander the world like the Flying Dutchman, a wraith, belonging nowhere.

Then, in December, Sergeant Major Tiger went on leave and I lost my job, as he had warned me I might. Not having expected anything else, I was not unduly upset, and had the sense to go to the officer in charge and ask him for a character reference. 'If you could kindly say that I have been employed by the British Army, am of good character, adhered strictly to the rules and discipline of the camp, and so on, it might help me get work if I emigrate to England,' I told him. 'I'd appreciate it very much. Just write anything so long as it is good, and please sign it and put a large military stamp on it. Then people will know that it is valid.'

He smiled and promised to do his best, saying that he had heard good reports of my conduct. The reference that resulted was all I could have asked for and gave a great boost to my morale. Strange to say, it was only really then – when I felt that I held at least one strong card in my hand – that I finally made up my mind to emigrate to England. I started making urgent enquiries and sought out friends who might be prepared to go with me.

Chapter 17

1948
Mass Migration

Friends who had applied to emigrate to England told me it was harder than it sounded. Officials at the British Emigration Office asked extremely probing questions. They put everyone through a series of rigorous medical examinations and the slightest sign of illness or disablement – even a finger or toe missing – was thoroughly investigated. Medical staff took blood tests and asked about your appetite – what you ate, how much schnapps you drank, how many cigarettes you smoked. Those questions struck us as ludicrous. Our customary state being that of hunger, we of course ate whatever we could get, and drank and smoked only if we were lucky! The fact remained: would-be emigrants had to be strong, able-bodied, in perfect health, and without any obvious vices.

For many, the biggest drawback was that England would not accept married couples, families, or old people. You had to be over eighteen, single, and exceedingly fit. Children, old people, or those with a chronic illness were ruled out systematically. Though my friends and I expected to pass muster, we were saddened by this. Life in the camps had welded us into one great family. So we took the trouble to find out what other options might be available for the less fortunate. Luckily, countries such as France, Canada, Australia, and America proved far less restrictive. There were tears of happiness when this information circulated round the camps.

Towards the end of 1947, together with three friends, I presented myself to the British Office of Emigration in Villach. An Englishman ensconced behind an impressive mahogany desk asked us about ourselves through an interpreter and then brought out a pile of black-

and-white photographs of England and its people. Most of the pictures were of farmers ploughing fields and harvesting their crops and he asked if this kind of work appealed to us. We shook our heads. As forced labourers under the Nazis, we had done enough farm work to last a lifetime.

Next he showed us pictures of coal miners, their faces as black as the coal itself. They wore helmets with lamps on them and were often bent double as they hacked at the coal with their picks. They were not prisoners of war like the miners we knew and there was something heroic about them. The Emigration Officer explained how the conditions of life for farm workers and miners in Britain differed. Life at the coal face involved a degree of danger but wages were higher in the mines than on the farms or in factories. Some of my friends were fascinated by the collieries, with their complicated machinery and tiny underground trains, and said they wouldn't mind becoming miners. However, life underground did not appeal to me.

I asked if he had any photographs of people at work in hotels and restaurants, or serving in shops, or working as officials or administrators. What about engineering work in factories, building cars or motorcycles? I wanted to know how wide a choice we had. I imagined myself doing whatever job I started for the rest of my life, so it was important to find work that would interest me. What about the banks and offices? I knew I would be happier using my brain, doing a desk job, as my grandfather, secretary to the Austro-Hungarian Governor in Halyczyna, had done, though not with his goose-quill pen! I had not forgotten my early ambition to become a scholar, but the notion of going into catering (and thereby eating on a regular basis) was also very much on my mind. The official obliged with pictures of hotels and factories, and men on building projects, but gently pointed out that for office work it would be necessary to be able to read and write, as well as speak, English. Unfortunately, none of us could do that yet.

I asked to see pictures of the King and Queen, and of Mr Churchill and his cigar. I pored over views of London and thought that such a very small island must be quite different from anything on the continent of Europe. I enquired whether there were mountains, forests, and small villages, as there were in Austria. The man kept a benign but careful eye on us, and he may have thought we were just amusing ourselves! We were eager to see every photograph he could lay his hands on that might begin to make England real for us. After all, it was there that we were thinking of spending the rest of our lives. Eventually, the Emigration Officer stood up and told us that, if we still wanted to emigrate to England, we should go to the office in Klagenfurt, where we could register as voluntary emigrants.

'But we are political emigrants!' we declared in unison, anxious to make the point that we were not just trying to improve our lot in life but were registering an extremely strong protest against political tyranny.

'Yes, yes, by all means. Register as political emigrants.' And off we went.

In Klagenfurt, we were told that we would be allowed to emigrate provided we could answer the questions put to us satisfactorily, and pass their stringent medical examination. If accepted, we could expect to arrive in England by the following summer. Things were moving! I became so excited my imagination began to run away with me. I saw myself in a bowler hat in London, strolling past the Houses of Parliament swinging my rolled umbrella, or posed among my dogs in tartan kilt and tweed jacket before a turreted castle in Scotland! So much for coal mines and hotel kitchens!

Having suffered all my life from a horror of government officials – the Poles, Russians, and Germans had all treated ordinary citizens in a cruel and arbitrary way – I was elated by the success of these two interviews. In the weeks that followed, I was subjected to examinations by an Austrian civilian doctor and a British army doctor in Klagenfurt, and repeatedly tested for every conceivable ailment. My forms came back marked A1 – which I was told signified 'perfect' – a fact with which I have tried to impress my family ever since! I was officially a desirable immigrant! Finally, we were sent to the Emigration Office in Villach to be fingerprinted and told the conditions under which we would be admitted into Britain:

First, on our arrival in England, a job would be found for us which we could not refuse and which we must not leave for at least three years, and only then with the permission of our employer and with the certainty of another job.

Secondly, we would be given accommodation, which we must accept, in barracks that would accommodate ten to twenty people. If, for any reason, we wanted to travel away from the camp, we would have to report to the police, stating where we were going and when we would return.

Thirdly, if, at the end of three years, we were not happy in Britain and wanted to emigrate to another country of our choice, we would be permitted to do so. We had no qualms about signing the forms.

Two days before our departure date in March 1948, we reported to Camp Kellerberg, a few kilometres from Villach, for the final medical check. There we were issued with all the necessary documents, and given large, brown cardboard labels with our names printed on them in huge letters, so that we could be clearly identified. I was the only Terlezki, but many people shared surnames, which caused some confusion. However, it was of benefit to some. For example, Svetlana – a close friend of my girlfriend Olha – was travelling with her mother and brother but, in order to be accepted, they had had to register as single people. Fortunately, their name was common enough so that their relationship was not discovered. The family was already fragmented, for the father had insisted on emigrating to France, saying there were fewer restrictions there, and he did not want all that deep water separating him from the continent of Europe!

I was ready to go when suddenly Svetlana appeared at my elbow and begged me to undergo a second medical on behalf of her brother Andrij, who had a sore throat and was running a temperature. He had already lied about his age (he was not quite eighteen) and Svetlana and her mother were afraid the authorities might investigate more closely and refuse to let him travel. That would either split the family further or oblige them all to stay behind, just as they were on the brink of departure.

They came to me in tears, and assured me Andrij's complaint was nothing serious. He was a healthy young man and would certainly be fit as a flea in a day or two. All they asked was that I should present myself to the doctors in his place, giving Andrij's name, so that he could show a clean bill of health.

As they were friends of mine, I could not find it in my heart to refuse. Yet I knew that, if I were found out, I could lose the chance of emigrating to Britain and be marked as someone not be trusted. It didn't strike me then that, by my action, I could also be responsible for exporting an epidemic into the country I had chosen for my future home! I simply prayed to God I would not be penalized for doing my friends a favour.

Approaching the doctors in fear and trembling, I gave Andrij's name, and had my pulse and blood pressure tested, eyes, ears and throat examined, while struggling without success to keep calm. Luckily for me, my agitation did not affect the result. I – or rather Andrij – passed with flying colours. Thanking the doctors, I pulled on my shirt and escaped from their presence as speedily as possible, a broad smile on my face. Svetlana, Andrij, and their mother, who were waiting outside, saw at once that their problem was solved. They kissed and embraced me fervently.

After two or three days of waiting, I was restless and wanted to make myself useful, so I approached the Chief Emigration Officer with a genuine offer of help. Judging by previous occasions when I had travelled with thousands of others, some assistance would be needed to maintain order and discipline. 'I served with the British Army Catering Corps at the El Alamein in Villach,' I told him, 'and I speak Ukrainian, Russian, Polish, and German, so I could communicate with most of the people travelling.'

Without hesitation, he appointed me a *Hundertschaftführer*, which had an intimidating militaristic sound, but only meant that I should be put in charge of 100 people, to be their leader, speak for them, and be responsible for their welfare until we reached England. As in similar situations in the past, I was to answer questions, explain things to those who did not understand, read and fill in forms for those who could not write, and report illnesses or other problems that might arise. A number of emigration officers were travelling with us and I would be responsible to one of them throughout the journey.

The day we left – let me say it again, for the promised land – I was handed a list of 100 names and told to make sure everyone on it boarded the train.

The platform was swarming with friends of those departing and there were endless tearful farewells. I had received the heartfelt blessing of the Weissers before leaving Villach, but I still felt sad leaving behind many people I cared for deeply. The worst wrench was saying goodbye to my lovely Olha and her family, who were shortly to leave for France. Olha was not only gentle and thoughtful: she was greatly gifted as a poet and would turn whatever we talked about – our childhood, the war, our present situation, or the future we faced – into verse. She set her verses to music, too, choosing a melody we both knew so we could sing together. Before we parted, she gave me a thick book of her poems as a present to remember her by. I promised to read them on the train, and to think of her. Both promises were kept, but the first one was not kept for long.

My group was assigned to two railway carriages. Everyone wanted a window seat, or at least a window out of which to wave goodbye to their friends, and they pushed and jostled one another like children, at the same time wiping away tears on their sleeves and kerchiefs. We were packed so tight in our compartments we could barely shift or stretch, but most of us were mentally comparing these carriages with the cattle trucks in which we had travelled in the past There were no complaints. On this journey no one would go hungry; each of us had been given a packet of provisions and we carried water bottles from which to slake our thirst. Everyone was chattering in excited anticipation. We couldn't stop talking about England – Britain – Britannia. Everyone pictured it differently. Some imagined the Channel much wider than it is and said it would take us a week to reach England from the Hook of Holland, or even longer. No one cared. We were going, with no question of turning back.

Almost the whole of Eastern Europe was represented on that train; Poles, Czechs, Hungarians, Romanians, Russians, Georgians, Ukrainians, Byelorussians, Moldavians, Lithuanians, Latvians, Estonians. I could hear them singing in a dozen different languages. I wore the arm band of a *Hundertschaftführer* – a legitimate arm band this time – which entitled me to walk the length of the train and I picked up scraps of conversation along the way. It seemed as if pages from the recent history of Europe had been spread out for me to study.

Some of the songs evoked painful memories, but I maintained a cheerful, confident manner, since I could not look after 100 people with tears in my eyes. Even my closest friends did not suspect how desolate I felt at the thought of leaving Europe and abandoning, perhaps forever, all hope of going home to Ukraine. I was leaving both the joys and the miseries of my disrupted youth. In the years since 1939 I'd been so many things – a schoolboy, slave labourer, Red Army officer, wanted man, displaced person, salaried employee of the British Army – then an apprentice cook, baker, pastry chef, barman and storekeeper. I had been a folk dancer, played football, produced plays; and I had also been a black marketeer. And I was still only twenty.

After getting my group comfortably settled, I sat down with Olha's poems and began to read them to myself, conjuring up not only her image but that of her family, which had so much resembled my own. Reading her verses, humming her little songs, filled me with longing for her, but gave me reassurance and renewed courage.

Before long I was called to another compartment to settle some minor dispute and left the book of poems lying on my seat. When I returned, it was gone. I began to question everyone within sight, feeling utterly distraught. Had anyone seen a blue notebook with a hand-lettered, delicately painted cover, filled with poems and drawings? It had been lying on my seat. Had anyone seen it? Had anyone taken it? Had anyone picked it up to look at or pass round? Had anyone come into the compartment and borrowed it while I was away? Was anyone *sitting* on it? Had it slipped down between anyone's bags or bundles or into their baskets?

And I drew a complete blank. They all shook their heads. Everyone seemed astonished, but no one appeared to have any idea what could have happened to Olha's poems. Peering closely into the faces of each of my fellow travellers, I tried to see if they were fooling around, or playing a trick on me – a prank, to embarrass a young lover, or the kind of mischievous practical joke that people play on someone set in authority over them. Yet surely they could see how totally devastated I was! I couldn't believe they would lie to me, or rob me of anything so personal and precious. How could they not have noticed someone picking it up and going off with it? Every single person expressed sympathy, but I got no satisfactory answer.

I enquired up and down the train but it had vanished into thin air. I returned to my seat and sat down, head spinning. Imagining that the others must be hiding something from me, jeering at me behind my back, I felt totally isolated. Could anyone – would anyone – have tossed the book out of the window? It could only have been done with the complicity of everyone in the compartment. But why? I had tried to be helpful and friendly to my group, respecting them and listening to their difficulties. Could I have incurred their spite somehow? Angry and heartbroken, I sat wishing the earth would open and swallow me up.

Alienated from those around me, I stared sullenly out of the window, bidding a silent, sorrowful farewell to the breathtakingly beautiful hills, fields, and farmsteads of Austria. They had become so familiar over the past six years. I thought of the kindnesses I had been shown, which had largely wiped out most of the brutality. Should I ever see Gretel again, or the Weissers, or Rudolf? Or was all my past life to disappear without trace, like Olha's book of poems?

Our train climbed slowly through Spittal-an-der-Drau, bringing dreadful memories of barbed wire and watch towers, Nazi guards and Russian prisoners, hunger, cold, fleas and lice. I sank into a melancholy reverie until we reached Salzburg. There, on the platform, more tearful refugees were bidding goodbye to friends and loved ones before boarding our train.

Then the scene was repeated in Munich. We took on extra coaches and a second locomotive to push us from behind. The passengers who joined us were the usual mix from Eastern Europe, no threat, but there was a palpable sense of unease and anger throughout the train because we were in Germany. The countryside was still beautiful, with the trees in bud on the hillsides, but the people we saw there had been Hitler's people, and there were mutterings in the compartment of words like *Schweinhund* and *Himmelsakrament*. The German curses we had had directed at us were being turned back against the German people.

'What's to stop the Germans from blowing up our train and killing us all, even now?' asked one of the older men. 'We're no use to them, and they've done everything else to destroy our lives.'

A torrent of bitterness poured out as we crossed Germany. All the deaths and atrocities, the loss of homes and families, the years of hunger and humiliation, imprisonment and torture – everything that could be laid at Hitler's door – was rehearsed; reanimated yet again. Younger travellers exchanged glances, wanting to say: 'Let it rest, can't you?'

Our journey took several days and seemed endless. The engines were old and the railway lines in poor repair, so there were constant stops and starts and unexpected detours. Luckily, there were no children or babies among us and the rest of us were used to weariness and discomfort.

When we pulled into the enormous station at Frankfurt it was late. Trains were steaming all over the place on the vast network of tracks: a sulphurous fog hung over the ruined city. Frankfurt seemed a huge city, the biggest most of us had ever seen. There were plenty of bitter remarks like, 'Build it yourselves, Germans! You won't catch us doing your dirty work again!'

Rather nervously we got out to stretch our legs, apprehensive in the vicinity of German uniforms, even if they were only those of porters or ticket collectors, and mentally preparing ourselves to fight back if anyone laid a hand on us. We knew it was absurd – we were under British protection and were on our way to England – but the anxiety was real. Still, it was useful for those of us who had been slaves of the Nazis to travel through the vanquished German Reich as free and independent human beings and see that the Gestapo no longer reigned supreme. No one shouted *Heil Hitler*! any more. We truly had nothing to fear.

All the same, as the train pulled out of Frankfurt station, it was as if the whole train heaved a deep collective sigh of relief at putting Germany and all it represented in our lives behind us.

Next stop, the Hook of Holland – or so we imagined! Everyone burst into song again – national anthems, folk songs, marching songs, waltzes, songs from films. Walking through the train I was aware of how drastically the mood had changed. There was a sense of festivity in the brightly lit carriages. The front of the train, with its twinkling lights, snaked around bends ahead of us, and we could hear the people up there singing whenever our own singing stopped. And as the stars faded from the sky, the train slowed and people scrambled for a place by the windows, expecting a sight of the North Sea and the ocean-going ships that most of us had heard about but never actually seen.

It was daybreak when the train finally stopped. But to our horror the station sign read 'Münster'. The sea was nowhere in sight. I had to field a series of anxious questions. 'What place is this? Where is Münster? Surely we are not still in Germany! Perhaps we're at the border. Are we crossing into Holland?' Beneath it all was the unspoken question: 'Is it possible we could have been tricked and betrayed yet again?'

185

I had been told nothing and had little to say. Then came an announcement over the loudspeaker telling us to collect up our belongings and leave the train. Each *Hundertschaftführer* was to gather his group together.

I went in search of the emigration officers, who had a special carriage all to themselves, but now they were nowhere to be found. I grew panicky, remembering my journey with the Russians three years earlier, when every familiar Russian face suddenly disappeared and others less friendly took their place. Who would give me answers to the questions everyone was asking?

Eventually each *Hundertschaftführer* was called by name to report to the emigration section that had been set up inside the station. We were instructed to inform our respective groups that transport was being organized to take us to a transit camp nearby, not far from the border with Holland. Damn it! We were still in Germany!

The faces of my group dropped when they heard this and they became very subdued. We knew now what was going to happen to us, but no one had troubled to say why. Why were we being taken to another camp when we thought our next camps would be in England? Why were we in Germany and not Holland? The logistical difficulties of moving thousands of people from country to country meant nothing to people like us. Experience had made us mistrustful, and no one took the trouble to give us an adequate explanation. Nothing had been said about dumping us in a transit camp on the way, especially not in Germany! Perhaps they thought, since the responsibility was theirs, it did not concern us.

'Are we near the Russian zone of occupation?' asked one traveller after another. 'Are the British still protecting us? God forbid that something has gone wrong, and that the Dutch, or the British, are refusing to have us! We could still be handed over to the Russians!' In the course of the next few hours, we were conveyed in coaches and open lorries to a huge camp on the River Rhine. That, at least, was a landmark we had heard of! The convoy rumbled through cobbled streets full of potholes. We were tossed from side to side like sacks of potatoes and enveloped in choking clouds of dust. Frightened as we were, we must have looked a pathetic sight.

On our arrival at the camp we were marshalled by guards who shouted at us in German but with a strange accent that increased our fear that we were no longer in British hands. 'Maybe they're Russians,' muttered one pessimist. 'They didn't get us in Austria, so they've set up a new trap for us here – with the connivance of the British, no doubt! This way, they can get hold of a few thousand of us all at once, solving everyone's problems! All that travel just to arrive at another hell-on-earth!' In the face of such remarks it was not easy to sustain people's morale.

The camp looked pleasant enough, however. It was made up of a collection of large brick buildings spread over a wide area beside the Rhine. It was well-kept, with tidy lawns between the buildings. Each *Hundertschaftführer* was given a block and room numbers, told on what floor his group's quarters were located, and ordered to get moving. Once settled in, we should await further instructions. My group never ceased pestering me with questions, especially as to the nationality of the camp guards. When it emerged that they were Latvians wearing American army uniforms, they were not greatly reassured! Alarmed and mystified as the rest, I was equally afraid that we might have been sold down the river, as the Americans say – in this case the River Rhine.

One man said dismally, 'Do you realize that every one of us is between the ages of eighteen and forty and has been carefully checked for physical fitness? We would make an ideal labour force for the Siberian coal mines, wouldn't we? Suppose the British and Russians have made a deal.' The rest of us protested vehemently, in shocked tones, but we knew it was not beyond the realms of possibility. We resolved to take suitable precautions and organized ourselves into groups to mount a watch in case the Russians came into the camp by day or night. Meanwhile, we had to rely on God to keep us safe.

Before long, British officials reappeared and explained that this was only a temporary stop, until cross-channel ships could be found large enough to transport us all. They were working on it! We learned that we should be leaving in two batches, one before the long Easter weekend and the other after it. We were also assured that the Latvian guards, who appeared so ominous, were under British command and constituted no threat. It was just unfortunate that they spoke no English. Some people still suspected a double-cross.

Such suspicions were not foolish or without foundation. Men from a camp in Augsburg said that a group of would-be emigrants from there had been brought to Münster a few months back. They had heard that one day, when most of the occupants of the camp were out of doors, a fleet of Russian lorries had raced into the camp as if mounting a blitzkrieg and fanned out in all directions. There was no camp guard to whom they could appeal, nor any British soldier to be seen – not anyone who might come to their rescue – so it was the same nightmare scenario we had lived with ever since the war's end. Panic-stricken, people began yelling and screaming, 'Run! The Russians are here! They have come to get us! Run to your barracks! Hide!'

Hundreds of people rushed into the accommodation blocks to seek safety, but shortly afterwards there were cries of, 'Don't jump! Don't jump!' Some of them were leaping to their death from the upper storeys rather than be caught and forced into the Russian lorries. Quite a few people committed suicide that day but others, remembering times in Austria when people set fire to Russian lorries, dragged the lorry drivers from their cabs and smashed the control panel or wrenched away the steering wheel with their bare hands.

No one could say how many people went with the Russians. The soldiers eventually drove off, leaving behind some vehicles damaged beyond repair. But, in spite of bitter protests, no satisfactory answer was ever obtained from the British commandant or his staff as to how they could have been allowed to invade his camp and hound innocent people to their death in the first place. I saw where they were buried in the camp cemetery – many people spent their last few coins on flowers to lay on the graves.

I spent the days walking and talking, and some people told shocking stories of recent atrocities inflicted on our people who were refugees. The worst tales came from people who had been in camps near Munich and Augsburg, in the American occupied zone. One young woman said she had been in a camp of 3 or 4,000 people when the Americans dispatched about 600 of them to a Russian assembly point and handed them over in spite of their protests. Some escaped on the way and returned to tell the story; others died trying to escape; but at least 500 ended up in Russian hands.

There was an incident in a church, during Mass on a Sunday morning on an upper floor, when American soldiers drove their lorries straight up to the church door. Soldiers entered the church and began to lead people out to the lorries, even those who implored them on their knees not to take them away. People swore on the sign of the cross that they knew what awaited them at the hands of the Russians – that they would be killed – and begged for mercy. At last the Americans seemed to take pity and drove away but, half an hour later, before the service ended, they were back again with a contingent of Russian soldiers, who dragged people out of the church by brute force, pulling women by their hair and twisting their arms behind their backs. Men and women were herded through the church doors at gunpoint. Some tried to escape by jumping out of the upstairs windows and died; some were severely injured.

Then – showing the confusion that reigned in the occupied zones at that time – an American officer arrived on the scene and ordered his men to stop, declaring that no one must be handed over to the Russians by force. He sent the people in the church back to their camps, but by then it was too late for some. The dead were lost and the injured still suffered.

Just before Easter, about half of our people departed for the Hook of Holland and England. They moved, it seemed, like iron filings to a magnet, an indistinguishable mass to me, such was my sorrow at not being among them. Like them, as they swarmed away, I had hoped to experience a first Easter in my new homeland, and the separation meant saying goodbye to two of the friends with whom I had begun the emigration process in Villach. I knew the rest of us would be following them soon but I remained uneasy until, not many days later, we were dispatched. When that day came, my 100 people and I walked to the railway station and boarded our train in high spirits.

We arrived at the Hook of Holland around midnight, when it was too dark to get a glimpse of the sea, and there was a delay before we were allowed off the train. Once we were allowed to leave the carriages, we were taken to a huge warehouse to wait for the order to board our ship. We were all served with bowls of hot porridge and cups of tea. There were about 1,000 of us. We thought that the efficiency with which we were given breakfast was a good sign that there would be no more difficulties in getting to England.

Dawn was breaking as we were led out in excited groups towards a monstrous vessel, flying a flag with what I had already learned was the Union Jack in one corner. The ship was many storeys high, with little round windows in its sides. The name MARKSMAN was painted on its side, along with the name of its home port and the date of its launch: 1915. Was this actually our ship? Since none of us had ever entrusted ourselves to the water in anything larger than a rowing boat, we were jittery at the thought of crossing the sea.

'Well,' I said, to encourage my crowd, 'this must be an extremely good ship if it's lasted through two world wars and is still going strong!'

The six or eight large boats, not unlike those used by fishermen on the River Dniester, which were suspended on the top deck, aroused great curiosity. What was the point of boats hanging in the air? When we learned that they were lifeboats, for use if our ship sank in the North Sea, our apprehensions increased. Could such an enormous vessel sink?

We were laughing excitedly to disguise our fear as we followed one another up the gangway. It did not seem possible that anything so large – so much more like a huge building than a boat – could possibly float on water!

The interior was a disappointment – just a large open space filled with benches, instead of those gorgeous saloons we had seen in films – but we were reminded that this was a troop transport, adapted to carry the maximum number of people, not a luxury liner. Setting down our bags to reserve places, we rushed back onto the deck to see what would happen next.

In the early morning light of a perfect spring day, the wharves were abuzz with activity. As the gangplank was drawn up and the chains that bound us to the shore were loosed from their bollards and thrown aboard, a wave of emotion swept over the ship. Cries of joy, laughter and lamentation could be heard. The decks were packed as we jostled one another for a place from which to bid farewell to continental Europe. Everyone was talking, waving handkerchiefs and shouting goodbye to anyone they could see on shore, in a dozen different languages.

Before embarking we had been promised two large boxes of sausage rolls, to sustain us during the crossing to Harwich. Considering this a very generous gesture, everyone sighed contentedly. As usual we were very hungry! After standing in line on the dockside for a considerable time the boxes arrived. The men with me could not wait to see what was inside and raised the lids. The sausage rolls looked mouth-wateringly fresh! One fellow did a quick count and calculated that there were more than two each.

Those of us who were greedy got our come-uppance soon after we left port. No sooner were we out in the open sea than the ship began to buck like an unbroken colt, the prow rising heavenward one moment and the stern the next, while the body of the ship twisted and shuddered in between. Those wonderfully satisfying sausage rolls did us no good at all.

Having no experience on which to base our claims, we had all boasted that we did not suffer from seasickness. Now our words rose from the bottoms of our stomachs to reproach us, along with the sausage rolls! The ship was desperately crowded. If we went inside for shelter, the stench was so terrible we thought we should die! Out on deck in the wind, however, we were afraid of pitching overboard.

As *Marksman* moved further out, those who were well enough strolled about the ship and explored its different levels, exclaiming at everything they found, pushing and shoving to make their way past hordes of others doing the same. By now we were expecting to find ourselves well out at sea, but suddenly saw that we were approaching land. Surely that was impossible! We were expecting the passage to take six or seven hours.

'Is that England?' I asked one of the ship's stewards.

He laughed, rather wearily. 'No, *mein Herr*. I'm sorry. It's only the Hook of Holland; we've had to turn back.'

An anticlimax indeed! Frustration knotted in my stomach. But at least we would be spared further seasickness.

Consternation reigned until there was an announcement over the ship's loudspeakers, in English and German, which group leaders were asked to translate and pass on to the people in their charge. The ship had developed a hole in its side, which would quickly be repaired. Passengers were requested to remain calm, and stay aboard the ship on our return to harbour.

Eventually, after some hours, the ship was ready to sail again and we were off! I now began to think of England with eager anticipation. Ukraine would never lose its place in my heart, but I had no hesitation in holding out my arms to my new country unreservedly and offering it my love and loyalty. It was the land where I would henceforth live and grow and have my being, and which I would serve to the very best of my ability under a new flag, my fourth: the flag of freedom.

Chapter 18

1948
A New Life Begins

We arrived at Harwich late in the afternoon and, as we approached the harbour, I joined some of the other boys on deck, looking into the distance where we could see high chimneys and buildings. This was England, our new home. Suddenly we could hear the bells on the harbour buoys ringing, and a priest who was standing near us immediately called upon us to cross ourselves and to thank God for our safe voyage and arrival in a land where we would be free from further persecution.

As we disembarked, ladies with friendly faces offered cups of tea and sandwiches in the landing hall. It didn't seem right to respond to such a welcome in a foreign language, so I struggled to remember the word I had heard so often in my Catering Corps days, a word which seemed to serve for almost any occasion. Oddly enough, it was the same as the one for certain armoured vehicles. I therefore bowed low to the lady who served me and said, very feelingly, 'Tanks', which she acknowledged with a gentle smile. It worked! I had surmounted my last hurdle and was already speaking English.

The immigration procedures took a long time but, with the help of interpreters, officials dealt courteously and patiently with each transaction. We presented our papers, had new ones issued to us, asked innumerable questions, and changed whatever money we possessed into pounds sterling. My forty Austrian schillings were converted into one large English pound note, on which I recognized the head of King George the Sixth, our king, and there I was, a free man in a free land, with money in my pocket. I was twenty.

Once the formalities were over we were taken to a train for the next part of our journey. It was clean and comfortable and ran smoothly, better than any I'd ever travelled on. None of the other passengers spoke any language known to us, so we remained totally ignorant of where we were being taken. But it did not seem to matter.

That night we slept somewhere in London, between clean white sheets, although many of us still felt as if we were swaying up and down on the rolling waves of the North Sea! Next morning we had recovered enough to eat a luxurious breakfast of porridge, bacon and eggs, toast, marmalade and tea, before being loaded on to double-decker buses – the first we had ever seen.

'Half of you go upstairs,' the interpreter told us, 'but no running or jumping, and make sure you don't all sit down on one side of the bus or it will topple over.' We were used to obeying orders, so those of us with enough nerve to go upstairs trod gingerly on tiptoe, and peeled off with precision, one to the right, one to the left, until everyone was in place. We became anxious about having an extra passenger on either side, even for a moment! Once we were all seated, the bus started up, and we were rewarded with a fine view of London. We squealed with delight when we recognized scenes and buildings from the photographs we had pored over months earlier in Villach.

When we reached the depot an interpreter asked us if we had enjoyed the ride. We had, we said, but not until we'd made certain that our weight was evenly distributed to stop the bus from keeling over. This raised guffaws of laughter and we joined in once the joke was explained to us. No doubt it had seen good service many times already.

We continued to laugh as we travelled by coach to Market Drayton in Shropshire, treasuring our first example of English humour, even if the joke was on us. We would not be so gullible next time. Soon we had settled in at a former RAF camp there.

It wasn't long before we grew restless. We drifted into the nearby town of Wellington to see what we could buy. We had each been given a pound note as spending money. But we did not know yet what the real value of this was. Nor did we understand the coupon system. Rationing was still in force, and many things could only be bought if you had coupons as well as money. There was another problem too. In continental Europe bargaining was seen as a right, a part of the culture. We naturally expected to bargain with the shopkeepers here, to make our pounds last as long as possible. I was a skilled bargainer and hugely enjoyed the process when I was buying or selling goods. I'd been well trained by my British Army friends in the Catering Corps in Austria. Out there the buyers did not trust the sellers, or the sellers the buyers. Now that we were in Britain, it was natural to assume that shopkeepers here were just like they were everywhere else. After all, how could they make any money, how could they survive, unless they cheated their customers? I did not mind a little cheating, but I could not help wondering just how much they were taking from us because we were political refugees in a strange land. I felt like a millionaire with my first British pound in my pocket, but I was afraid that if the shopkeepers were raising their prices unscrupulously my money would melt away before I could even touch it.

When we discovered that the shopkeepers wouldn't bargain, there was no one we could go to for help. We spoke no English, and more importantly we did not want to let ourselves down or show our ignorance. I tried to use body language to communicate, and my face, hands, shoulders and even my feet would be working overtime when I needed to explain myself or to ask a question. I must have looked like a one-man band playing music on the street corner, as I tried to illustrate what I wanted to know, or what I wanted to buy or do. And shopping was not the only difficulty that we faced. We would look at the English girls in the town and we were desperate because we could not speak their language. We could have used body language of course, but not on the street in broad daylight!

Our first priority was to find out what our new jobs would be, and where our journey would finally end. We were all furiously playing guessing games about our destination and our employment. We knew there were places called England, Scotland and Wales, and we knew we had a choice of farm work, factory work or coal mining. England, we were told, was a flat country with only a few high mountains, while Scotland which had many mountains, also had a cold climate and frequent rain. Back home we were used to a very cold winter, but this was followed by a beautiful spring, a very hot dry summer and a gorgeous autumn.

Most of us were looking for somewhere with a pleasant climate, with mountains and a coastline. We also hoped for somewhere which, if necessary, would give us a fast route back to Europe. If the West declared war against Stalin's Imperial Russia, then we could even swim to the French coast if necessary, and quickly join the battle to defeat Stalinist Communism and liberate Ukraine. We were all extremely serious about planning our futures. For me farm work was definitely out. I'd had enough of that and even the mention of it made me shudder after my experiences in Nazi Austria. Nor was I sure about factory work or coal mining. I had some reservations about both jobs, especially mining, but I felt I needed to try them out first.

This uncertainty also applied to my choice of destination. A few of us decided to ask if we could go to Wales, mainly because we knew so little about it. Eventually we heard that our request would be accepted. We were not even sure where Wales was, and our curiosity was aroused even further. Because we had learned that there were high mountains there, like the Carpathians in Ukraine, we felt it would be an ideal place to train partisan fighters in the event of war against the Russians. It is difficult to realize now just how likely another war seemed to us. Finally, I suspected that coal mining was not the only work available in Wales. However, before we could put our theories to the test, we were moved on to another former military camp at Full Sutton, north of York.

This camp was much more remote, a long way from the local villages and the city of York. Even the weather was inhospitable, with cold winds blowing from all directions. The contrast with the climate we were used to in Europe was huge, and although the sun tried hard to warm us, it failed. The camp was dreary, unwelcoming. The barrack huts, made of tin sheeting and shaped like half barrels, were cold, smelly and in disrepair. We were being given basic English lessons, but the living quarters were so cold that we had to play football in our spare time to keep ourselves warm. As for the food from the kitchens there were no complaints about the quality, but the small quantities never satisfied our hunger.

This brief time in Yorkshire soon ended. Our seemingly endless wanderings started all over again. We were tired and disorientated and beginning to feel like the nomads who had drifted backwards and forwards across our Eastern European homelands so many centuries before. But at least we felt that we were on the final stage of our journey. Jumping on a train again at Lincoln, bound for Wales, I wondered if I would meet up with Taffy. We were going to the south of the country, somewhere near the sea, travelling through the Severn Tunnel for the first time. Some Welsh officials who were with us said they would pay us £5 if we could spell a Welsh name – Llewellyn, perhaps, or Merthyr or Caerphilly – but no one could do it; their money was safe. The tunnel seemed to go on forever, but then we were through and arrived eventually at Newbridge, where we were transferred to buses and taken for the last few miles to a miners' training camp at Oakdale, near Blackwood.

It was not an encouraging start. As we stepped out of the train onto the platform, the wind and the rain were lashing down; it was cold, and we seemed to be surrounded by mountains on all sides. Not that it mattered – I was used to mountains. On the hillsides there were long buildings punctuated here and there with windows and covered with a single roof. These buildings were curious. I had never seen anything like it and guessed they were continuous barracks or stable blocks of some sort, with strange people walking up and down inside. The interpreter explained,

'They are houses – what we call cottages.'

'What are cottages?' I asked. 'Are there walls inside, kitchens, bedrooms? Is that how people live in this Wales?' It was our first introduction to the terraces of south Wales. We discovered later that those cottages were fantastic little palaces inside.

After that explanation (which many of us still found difficult to accept), I asked if Wales had high mountains, with rivers and lakes. Was it near the sea? We had already been told a little about our new camp, but Newbridge still seemed very strange and puzzling. The interpreter nodded his head and said '*Ja, ja* '. This was music to my ears. For most of my life I had been used to officials who said '*Net, net*', or '*Nein , nein*', or '*Nie, nie* ', and now here at last was one saying 'Yes, yes'. But I had one final question: 'How about the Welsh girls? Are they pretty, loving? Are they good and caring as companions and wives?' When I asked this, I could see that all the boys had stopped talking and were listening intently. The interpreter answered, and I could sense from his body language that he was warning us to leave the girls alone. But what he said aloud was, 'Welsh girls are wonderful, Welsh girls are OK'. That was enough. We were here in *wunderbar* Wales, OK!

Once we had settled in the camp we began to venture further afield. This led to the discovery of Oakdale Miners' Institute, a magnificent Victorian building with a library and a reading room filled with newspapers and magazines. But best of all there was a dance hall on the first floor. We knew we would spend most of the week feverishly anticipating the Saturday night dances there. The boys would have an extra scrub in the shower room with pleasant smelling soap. We had no aftershave in those days, but we expected that the Welsh girls would put on some kind of perfume, which would bewitch us all.

Dance nights became everything to us. When the orchestra struck up we would make a bee-line for a girl we liked the look of and take her onto the floor for a dance. The girls were generally sitting together, sometimes with their boyfriends. If the girl was with a boy I would ask for his permission first. If he nodded in assent I would take the girl by her arm, take her onto the floor and try to sweep her off her feet in the short time available. Once the music had stopped I would thank her, bow my head and take her back to her seat. The girl would invariably be charmed by all this attentiveness but the boyfriend wouldn't always be so enthusiastic about these attempts at gallantry. He would pull faces and make gestures to his friends who in turn would laugh and pull his leg, although it was clear that they were not entirely happy about it either.

Miraculously these little rituals never led to fights and we carried on doing it. The girls seemed to love the old world courtesies of which their own boyfriends seemed incapable. We would dance the evening away as if we were taking part in a Hollywood costume film although we knew that it was, in reality, just a Saturday night hop at the Miners' Institute. Apart from the 'boy meets girl' experiences, I genuinely enjoyed the dancing. I loved to experiment with steps and turns, particularly when I liked the girl and she attempted to follow me. It must have been the Cossack in me! The Institute has since been moved brick by brick and rebuilt in the Museum of Welsh Life at Saint Fagans, with tourists visiting where we had once enjoyed so many magical nights.

We were getting to know a little more about Wales, but the officials were still teasing us to see if we could spell the strange-sounding towns. We were sent to Oakdale to train as miners. We had to be fitted out with helmets, lamps, and boots, and I decided to take my camera – the one I had exchanged in Austria for a box of dried sultanas – down the pit. Life in the pit was all very new to us, and at first I did not realize that there would be so little light down the mine. I knew nothing about flashlight photography either. Down I went with my camera, lined up my friends and took six photographs, using up what was left of the film. However, when we developed the film, all we could see were six completely black spaces! I was puzzled.

'I did everything correctly,' I told my friends, 'how can this have happened?' I began to swear at the German camera and then we all started to laugh, suddenly realizing what had gone wrong. How stupid! I had expected to take perfect photographs underground, where there was no daylight, where I was surrounded by jet black coal and where the only light I had was from a small lamp on my helmet.

I was not afraid of hard work, but after a few weeks I was increasingly apprehensive about the millions of tons of earth on top of me. There was nowhere to run or hide if it collapsed. Apart from that I was permanently black with dust, and there was a constant clanking of chains, clatter of engines and jarring of metal tools. The passages were damp and low, cold winds howled constantly from all directions and I was always bumping into other miners.

We tried to joke about it, asking each other how long it would take us to walk underground to Moscow and place explosives under the Kremlin, or how we could dig through to Australia. But although I tried to hide my fears by being flippant, I knew I didn't want to dig coal for the rest of my life. I had every admiration for the miners who worked so hard, often never seeing daylight during their working hours – even though I didn't always have such warm feelings for some of the union bosses! The thought of spending the next twenty or thirty years of my life as a miner made me shudder.

Before I had a chance to move to another career, my training came to an end and I was sent to Pontypridd, to the Hawthorn Miners' Hostel. It wasn't much by some people's standards, but for a wartime refugee from Ukraine it seemed like heaven! And there was a wage coming in – the sum of two pounds and eight shillings for a forty-eight to fifty hour week. There was a need to be careful about the way the money was spent. As an 'ambassador' for Ukraine I felt I had to be smart and well spoken and not disgrace my country. So I resolved to buy my first suit. People would then say, 'This Ukrainian is well dressed, he looks tidy and pleasant.' It would help to give a good general impression of my birthplace. But to do this sacrifices had to be made. There would be no more smoking, and instead of taking a bus I would walk wherever possible. If, very occasionally, there was enough money for a trip to the cinema, I would watch the film from a cheap seat in the front. I certainly couldn't afford to take a girl to the cinema, and as for the weekly dance I would go by myself and avoid paying for anyone else.

It was a difficult period of adjustment for all of us during those first few years in Britain. We were discovering what our new country was like and how far its people would accept us. Above all it was a time when I could look forward and plan my future. My decision to abandon coal mining as a career could have been very difficult if it hadn't been for the Hawthorn Miners' Hostel. My fellow refugees were staying there so that they could work at various collieries in the area, and of course the hostel provided food and lodgings. The catering requirements, quite unexpectedly, provided me with my escape route from the mines. I already had good references from the British Army Catering Corps, dating back to my spell at the El Alamein camp in Austria. I showed them to the hostel manager, who staggered me by saying, 'You're just the person we need. Can you start straight away?'

And so my catering career was re-launched and I was out of the mines! My hunch that Britain would be a land of opportunity was once again proving to be correct. I started work as a chef pâtissier in the hostel canteen and stayed there for about a year. The highlight was an invitation to cook a traditional Ukrainian Christmas dinner; to prepare and cook twelve different food dishes to represent the twelve Apostles. The dinner was arranged at the local Hawthorn pub. I wanted to recreate the sort of Christmas that I remembered in Ukraine when we would cook *kutia* from wheat mixed with poppy seed, sugar and honey. All the family would sit down at the table, which was laid with a white cloth decorated with traditional Ukrainian embroidery and covered with hay. The display of food would always be magnificently arranged. My father would stand up, and take a wooden spoon and scoop up as much of the *kutia* as he could and throw it on to the ceiling. The more that stuck there, the better the harvest would be next year. The landlord of the pub indulged me and was quite happy to see his ceiling treated in such a manner, as long as we used his premises in a more conventional way as well. So I prepared a traditional Ukrainian feast using *holubtci*, *perohy*, pickled cabbage, sweet beetroot, gherkins, fish, chickens, pork and special pastries for more than 100 fellow Ukrainians, as well as some of our Welsh friends. We drank Welsh beer, Scotch whisky, French cognac and finally Welsh water to clear our heads. It was a huge success.

Encouraged by all this, I suppose, I decided that working in the miners' canteen wasn't really going to fulfil my long-term ambitions. So I found work in a local bakery, despite signing an agreement when I came over as a political refugee that I would stay in the same job for at least three years. My references from the British Army helped me to get over that particular hurdle. Then I found my own accommodation near the hostel. I had a room all to myself – a luxury for somebody with my origins. I was beginning to feel that I had really arrived, in contrast to the rest of my friends. I confess that I was feeling a little smug! But that didn't stop me from visiting them every day.

I was now a confectioner making pastries, Christmas cakes, wedding cakes, chocolate Easter eggs and many other delicacies. My employers, Hopkin Morgan, were well established in the area. They had a contract to provide thousands of pastries every day for Marks and Spencer, and that became my responsibility. My employer was encouraging me to go to

Switzerland at the company's expense and train over there as a Swiss-style delicatessen pâtissier, but I could see that I would be under an obligation to work for them for the rest of my life and that didn't appeal. I wanted to become a businessman in my own right eventually, but in the meantime was prepared to work at the bakery in Pontypridd from seven o'clock in the morning until five at night. In the evenings I would catch the bus and go to the College of Food Technology and Commerce in Cardiff. It was a tough schedule but I wasn't complaining and enjoyed the challenge.

Because of the English lessons I had become aware of the old adage, 'All work and no play makes Jack a dull boy'. I was now beginning to develop an interest in soccer and it seemed amazing that young men were actually paid to play football. I soon became a dedicated Cardiff City fan. They were in the First Division and every Saturday when the team was playing at home I would rush off after work to catch a bus to Cardiff. On the long walk down to Ninian Park it was frequently raining and I would keep myself going with hot coffee and a pasty bought on the way. It would cost sixpence to stand on the 'Bob Bank' where I was surrounded by families who carried stools for the children to stand on. I was to remember all this much later, at a time when hooliganism was already beginning to destroy the idea of football as a family pastime.

After the game I usually made my way to Cardiff City Hall in time for the weekly dance. You had to be in by seven, but I generally managed it and threw myself into the evening's entertainment with enormous gusto. I loved the orchestras with their stiff collars and dickey bows, and I would dance the foxtrot, the tango and the quick-step. I tried to introduce Viennese waltzes but it was hard going. Like Cinderella I had to leave before midnight. In my case to catch the last bus back to Pontypridd.

I was beginning to enjoy life in Wales, and loved the Welsh people in a way which I would have never imagined possible a few years previously. But I was still ambitious. I wanted to achieve the sort of success many people would have thought impossible for someone like me. Being a Ukrainian was undoubtedly a handicap. People knew very little about the country and would ask, 'What is a Ukrainian?' Many of us were thought of as Russians or Poles, which was very hurtful. I still felt I had to be an ambassador for the Ukrainian people and explain who we were. I felt that I could do something for my people by working with my head rather than just with my hands. I also believed that by achieving something with my life I could put behind me the suppression and inhuman treatment I had suffered at the hands of various regimes in my early years.

After Pontypridd I worked for short periods at three of the biggest hotels in Cardiff before moving to the Seabank Hotel in Porthcawl, which was then regarded as one of the smartest hotels on the south Wales coast. It was 1954. The Seabank was patronized by guests from all over the world, including film stars like Bob Hope. When I later became the deputy manager there I had to change my suit twice a day to make sure that I reflected the elegance of the hotel. While I was still a chef pâtissier, I had my own room in the staff quarters. The demands on my time continued. I had to travel to Cardiff in the evenings to continue with my college education. I had very little money, certainly not enough to afford girl friends. Unlike their European counterparts, British girls smoked and expected the boys to pay for their cigarettes and cinema tickets. So I still had to see the films on my own, or with my friends from the hostel. I became particularly fond of Westerns because of the clean-cut romantic image of the heroes: Audie Murphy, Roy Rogers, Randolph Scott, Gary Cooper, John Wayne and others. As well as enjoying them I also learned a great deal from the films and could see how important it was to be orderly, respectful, obedient.

Once I had qualified from the college I decided to move into hotel management, firstly at the Seabank and then at the Mackworth Hotel in Swansea where I was deputy manager. It was at the Mackworth that my past caught up with me very briefly. Having spent so many years avoiding the Russians in Europe after deserting from the Red Army I suddenly came face to face with them again. A diplomatic delegation from the Russian embassy had been booked into the hotel. Normally the British authorities wouldn't have allowed them to travel more than thirty miles from London. But the police knew all about their movements and clearly thought that an encounter between the Russians and myself could prove to be useful. They rang me from the local police headquarters suggesting that because of my background I might learn something from them. When the Russians arrived they asked me to meet them after dinner in one of their bedrooms. Having agreed I entered the room, and was astonished at how full it was. They were all men except for one woman. The obvious thought went through my mind – was she a Mata Hari? They produced numerous bottles of Vodka along with freshly sliced oranges and white bread – an accompaniment which was used to soothe the throat since vodka, traditionally, went down the hatch in one go.

Bottle after bottle was emptied and all the time they were producing maps of the area, which they spread all over the bed. They fired questions at me about local army camps, airports, factories and steel-making plants and they were very curious about the Gower coast. All the time I was laughing to myself, knowing that I was leading these Russian apparatchiks – these political propagandists for the oppressive regime which had done so much damage to so many European countries – well and truly up the garden path. At four o'clock in the morning I was telling them that I was sorry, but I couldn't help. I didn't know the area well. I had only been working at the hotel for a few months and I wasn't Russian as they seemed to think. They were clearly reluctant to believe me, insisting that my Russian was too good. I had to think quickly and told them that I had learned it at

Manchester University. Once they realized they had been tricked they started to grow angry in a way which was typical of *apparatchiks*. They went red in the face, which didn't surprise me, and as their frustration grew their mouths became contorted and I caught glimpses of spiky golden teeth.

The party was over and by seven o'clock I was telling the police what had happened. I don't know what it all led to, but I was very proud to have played a small part in defeating the Russians at their own game.

By now I was married to Mary having met her, naturally, at a dance in Pontypridd one Saturday evening in the early fifties. There were plenty of other girls in the room but as I recalled in a newspaper article years later, 'she shone more brightly than all the rest'. Mary was from Treorchy in the Rhondda Valley and her uncle played a vital part in the next stage of my career. He had read in the *South Wales Echo* that the Central Hotel in Aberystwyth was up for sale. Uncle Marcus, Mary, her father and I all went off to look at it. Uncle Marcus had become a successful businessman in the Valleys after returning from the war, and I regarded him as a man of vision whose example I could perhaps follow. I decided that I wanted to buy the hotel or possibly lease it. It would be an excellent place to launch my career as the first Ukrainian businessman in Great Britain. The hotel was completely empty and I would have to furnish and equip it from top to bottom. My friends in Swansea advised me to go to see a bank manager in Port Talbot who could possibly help me with a loan. I arranged a meeting and within an hour he agreed to lend me £2,500, without guarantees. It was a miracle. I felt I was walking on air as I returned to Swansea.

I soon discovered that running an hotel was exhausting. Friends who visited me in the coming months took one look at me and said, 'Pack up and get out of here. You look like a skeleton.' I had lost two or three stone. I was working from six o'clock in the morning until midnight. But there were consolations. On the very first night I emptied the till in the bar and counted ten pounds. I went up to the bedroom and excitedly told Mary about it. In my working life so far the most I had ever earned was nine guineas a week. I didn't have anywhere to put the money except an in old hat, which I put under the bed for safe keeping. Business was so good that within two years I had repaid the £2,500 to the bank.

Mary and I had two daughters, Helena and Caryl. They were priceless to me and I was the proudest husband and father in Wales. I walked tall and proud. Not only had I assumed full responsibility as a family man but I was also a successful businessman who had come all the way to Welsh-speaking Aberystwyth from the steppes of Ukraine. Soon I felt ready for a bigger venture and Mary and I took on the Cedars Hotel in Cardiff. Still, I owe much to the town where I started both my business career and family life. *Diolch yn fawr*. Thank you very much.

Chapter 19

1968-1977
Cardiff City

My political views were forged by my memories of Polish occupation and Russian tyranny and by the treatment meted out to my father, my family and the rest of the Ukrainian people during the Cold War era. For me the Conservatives represented everything that I'd dreamed about but had never experienced in my early days: private enterprise, freedom of choice, freedom of speech, democratic principles, tolerance and the rule of law. From the moment I arrived in Britain I had an ambition to become a Member of Parliament as part of my crusade to help all those Ukrainians I had left behind under the Communist yoke.

However I knew that I would have to learn to walk before I could run; local government in Cardiff seemed to be the obvious choice. My first break came in 1968, when I stood for a seat on the City Council in the South Ward. It was part of the constituency represented by James Callaghan, who was then Home Secretary in the Labour Government. It was a poor area, close to the docks, with housing, employment and school transport problems and a wide range of ethnic backgrounds. The people were the salt of the earth but it was a challenging starting point for a Ukrainian Conservative. Before I was selected as the prospective candidate I was warned that the ward had been held by Labour for thirty years and my chances of winning were very slight. To whet my appetite the agent promised that if I won, my wife would be given a bucket filled with roses and I would be given a case of vintage champagne. To his surprise I did win. I was now the first Ukrainian-born politician ever to become elected in Britain and, more than thirty years later, I am still waiting for the roses and the champagne!

From the moment I was elected as a councillor I was immersed in all the usual inner-city issues and fought extremely hard for residents who were faced with wholesale re-housing and displacement to other parts of Cardiff. People were having to put up with dreadful squalor.

Despite my best efforts Labour recaptured the seat in 1971. However my absence from the Council chamber was short-lived. The following May I was re-elected to the City Council in Penylan, a rock solid Conservative seat. I won more votes than any other candidate in the nineteen city wards and I could now look forward to serving the people with much more certainty.

Local government gave me something to focus on, my short term adrenaline 'fix' if you like. But I never forgot my long-term crusade against the Communist regime in Russia and in other European countries. I was in regular contact with Ukrainian organizations in this country and I couldn't help thinking about my father, my sister Lywosi, my cousin Wasyl, and my many childhood friends whose lives behind the Iron Curtain had all been affected so deeply, and in many cases so tragically, by Stalin and his successors. In March 1976 some 1,000 British Ukrainians, many of them in national dress, marched through the streets of Cardiff to mark 'Captured Nation Week'. At the Cenotaph, outside the Temple of Peace in the city centre, we laid a wreath to the Unknown Soldier. Inside the building we held a brief conference at which I and other speakers complained about the barbaric treatment which Ukraine, and many other European nations had suffered under Russian 'proletarian' rule. We sent a message of protest to the Soviet Embassy in London and to the United Nations.

I was now fighting for my father to be released from his Soviet Labour camp in Siberia after nearly twenty-five years of captivity. When Boris Ponomarev, a senior figure in the Politburo, came over as a guest of the Labour Party Executive, I drew attention to his role as one of the puppet-masters of the KGB, and when a delegation from the Estonian Supreme Soviet visited Cardiff, I protested to them in Russian about the treatment of innocent people like my father. Their leader told me that my father must have chosen to go and live in Siberia. I found it impossible to deal with such logic, and it only helped to confirm in my own mind that these people were monstrous.

I made a point of working with groups of dissidents in the West who, in turn, kept in contact with groups living in Ukraine and in Russia. As well as sending them literature and encouragement we also tried to discourage local authorities from linking up with cities in the Soviet Empire. I was particularly incensed about Cardiff's formal twinning with Voroshilovgrad, as the Ukrainian city of Luhansk was then known. Some

Labour councillors argued that by continuing with the link, pressure could be put on the regime to improve conditions in the Soviet Union. Others argued that we had no right to interfere with the internal affairs of another country, but I felt that the Conservatives' decision to suspend the arrangement was the right one. It would show our disgust at the Russian regime.

When Labour got back into power in 1979, one of their first policy changes, prompted by their counterparts in Voroshilovgrad, was to reinstate the twinning. I accused Labour of hypocrisy. Only a few weeks before they had cried foul over the South African rugby tour and here they were reacquainting themselves with one of the most imperialistic and brutal states in the world, where freedom and democracy were simply not part of the political vocabulary.

On another occasion a delegation from Voroshilovgrad visited Cardiff on twinning business, and when they came into the council chamber at City Hall the Lord Mayor invited their chairman to speak. As he rose he began speaking in Russian. I saw red in more senses than one and interrupted on a point of order. I could see the whole Voroshilovgrad group looking at me in a state of amazement. I couldn't help thinking that political prisoners in Moscow's Lubyanka prison would have enjoyed the moment. When the Lord Mayor had recovered from his own obvious shock, he asked me what my point was.

'My Lord Mayor,' I said, 'Chairman Ivan Ivanovich has been invited to speak, but he's speaking in Russian and not Ukrainian. If he comes from Ukraine he should speak Ukrainian.' The Labour councillors in the chamber started to become agitated, as I knew they would, although my Conservative colleagues simply smiled quietly to themselves. Then to drive my protest home I grabbed a big walking stick belonging to one of my fellow Conservative councillors and pointed it at the delegation as if it was a Kalashnikov. By now everybody in the Chamber, the councillors and the Ukrainians, saw the funny side of it and were laughing.

However, it was football that made me a well-known personality in Cardiff. It has always been one of my passions and I was a loyal supporter of Cardiff City Football Club from the moment I arrived in Wales as a penniless refugee.

For me, still homesick for Ukraine, the matches were a reminder of church on Sundays. I suppose it was the weekly ritual, the singing and the families getting together. It didn't matter that I would frequently get so soaked that my raincoat would shrink. It was just a highlight in my week that I wouldn't have missed for anything.

As the years went by, however, the golden era began to recede and by the spring of 1974 the club was facing serious problems. I had become a

Cardiff City Football Club shareholder and, at the Annual General Meeting in December 1974, put forward my own ideas for the future, calling for the resignation of David Goldstone, the chairman, and his two fellow directors. My proposals were defeated, but that was not surprising. Out of over 200 hundred shareholders, only twenty attended. Later I told reporters, 'The shareholders should realize that if they have Cardiff City at heart and want to see first-class soccer in the capital, they must attend the annual meeting.'

In February 1975, with City hovering at the bottom of the Third Division, there was a trading loss and no chance of buying new players. By the beginning of July a solution was found, and a syndicate of new shareholders bought out David Goldstone's interest. A new seven-man board was brought together and at the first meeting early in July I was unanimously elected chairman of the Bluebirds club.

By the spring of 1976 the Bluebirds were well on their way back to the Second Division. I had ordered champagne for the coming match against Bury. I promised that we wouldn't just drink the champagne, we'd soak in it if we won. With that victory we would clinch promotion but Cardiff had to keep fighting right up to the final whistle The result was 1–0, Adrian Alston scoring the only goal in the seventeenth minute. If I'd had a tonne of gold I'd have given it to the players, the super subs and the manager, Jimmy Andrews. They were all magnificent and I was the proudest Welsh Ukrainian chairman in the land.

'What a magnificent night for Cardiff and Welsh football!' I told the *Western Mail* after the match. 'Progress is my motto, and I feel confident success will continue to flow in the Second Division next season. We now have a team to be proud of and we aim to go from strength to strength.' We had promised the players a week's holiday in Majorca if they won promotion, and although we were not allowed to give cash rewards, we intended to review their contracts for next season. I was delighted and proud of all the players and staff at the club. In my judgement they each had determination, loyalty, resilience, endurance, guts and self-belief. With such qualities it was never likely that they would let the club down or the loyal Bluebirds' supporters for that matter.

But despite the success there were also problems building up for the future. We knew we would have to spend more money strengthening the team. We were also going to have to pay the former chairman the extra £30,000 on our promotion as agreed when we first took over the club. I fully accepted the obligation as the chairman of the board which signed that agreement, but I had to admit I begrudged every penny. By now I had become a target for humour, and the *South Wales Echo* cartoonist Gren had a particularly fine sketch of me outside David Goldstone's office with a shovel and a pile of coins representing the money that I had begrudged him!

The joy of success was soon to be dampened in other ways. When Wales played Yugoslavia at Ninian Park on 22 May 1976, serious violence broke out. Three policemen were hurt, ten fans were arrested and the referee had to be escorted from the pitch. Some people felt that anyone misbehaving inside the ground should be ejected at once – something with which I fully agreed. Fencing off the entire pitch would be expensive, but it might be unavoidable. We were about to take part in the European Cup Winners' Cup next season, and we wanted to make sure that nothing happened to damage the club's reputation.

We played the Swiss club Servette in the preliminary round of the Cup Winners' Cup. The first leg was at Ninian Park. I had also been to Zurich for the Cup draw, and was disappointed to learn that if we beat Servette we would be playing the Russian cup winners. I could attend the Ninian Park leg of the contest, but I could not accompany Cardiff City to Russia. As I told reporters, 'I have never been to Russia. The first time I met Russians was when they invaded western Ukraine in 1939, and it was a great shock and horror to us all. Because of my political activities in the British Conservative Party, I don't think it would be wise to go now.'

We beat Servette, which meant that our next opponent was the Russian club Tbilisi, which was in fact in Georgia. I felt sorry for the team because they faced a marathon journey for the away leg. 'It's almost as bad as the club's trip to Tashkent in 1968,' I said, 'and it's a terrible draw from a time-consuming point of view.' It also looked like being a very expensive journey. I estimated that it would cost at least £8,000. We queried whether UEFA was right to allow Tbilisi, which I thought was in Asia, not in Europe, to represent Russia. But they replied that all Russian teams, wherever they were based, were eligible because they belonged to the Soviet Football Association which was affiliated to UEFA.

Meanwhile at an away match in September, City fans wrecked a clubhouse at Oldham. Fans on both sides were arrested, and one Cardiff City supporter was injured. I found this new face of football very sad. In the late 1940s, when I first came to South Wales there used to be huge crowds and that was still the case in the 1950s and 60s. But there'd be no need for the police inside or outside the ground. The game was essentially a family occasion with a carnival atmosphere.

Before the home leg of the Tbilisi match I urged our fans to be on their best behaviour and not to set foot on the pitch. 'Let's hear some of the singing for which the Welsh are famous,' I told them. To my relief they responded to my call. Frustratingly the game ended without either side scoring.

Now we began to get ready for the visit to Tbilisi. The Georgian diet was so different from ours that we were advised to take as much of our own food as possible with us, to avoid stomach upsets. Jimmy Andrews, our manager, took the advice and ordered 144 lamb chops, 72 steaks, 180 eggs, 200 pats of butter, 192 packets of breakfast cereal, 400 tea bags, 20 loaves, 7lbs of marmalade, 7lbs of lump sugar, 7lbs of mashed potato, 72 chocolate bars, 4lbs of margarine, 7lbs of peas, oranges and enough powdered milk to make up into 14 gallons! Once again the score was 0-0, and there had to be a play off on neutral ground in Augsburg, Germany. Local football fans were rowdy and hostile towards us, but a huge contingent of British servicemen stationed in Germany also turned up, and with their magnificent support we went on to win 1-0.

Although I did not go to Tbilisi, Georgian officials sent me as a sort of consolation prize two kilos of caviar, several bottles of vodka, fourteen bottles of Georgian wine and two bottles of Georgian brandy. I was subsequently told by a Georgian minister when he visited Cardiff, that Winston Churchill had once visited Georgia and was given some of the brandy which he declared to be the best he had ever drunk. Having tasted it myself, I can only assume that he was being polite!

At a meeting on 25 November UEFA ordered that Wales' home games in the current championship should be played at least 125 miles from Cardiff. Again, I was furious. We had met all the Welsh FA requirements for crowd control and installed £10,000 worth of fencing which we could ill afford.

The threat of crowd violence continued to grow. Local residents in the Ninian Park area wanted to see the ground closed, and we had to find new routes for fans and visitors to follow. Hooliganism and violence frequently occurred on trains and coaches, while mobs wielding flick knives clashed outside the ground. 'They were little better than animals,' I told reporters. 'These hooligans threw coins, stones and drink cans at spectators in the grandstand. Any City fans identified will be banned from Ninian Park for life.'

I tried to organize meetings to discuss ways of combating this rise in thuggery, but although a few individuals supported my efforts, no one else took my campaign seriously and I was even accused of publicity seeking. At the time I strongly advocated the use of the birch as a deterrent, and this launched a fierce public debate in the press. James Callaghan, the Prime Minister, whose constituency included the Ninian Park area, rejected my demands and suggested ways of curbing drinking and keeping hooligans at attendance centres on Saturday afternoons instead. Looking back on it now, I accept that I was perhaps too enthusiastic about corporal punishment as a solution, and he was probably right! But I was also responsible for starting a debate on the use of a new identity card scheme for all supporters under the age of thirteen, a scheme which I'm glad to say has now become fully accepted. In fact when I later became a Member of Parliament I had a private meeting with Prime Minister Margaret Thatcher and we discussed the idea of introducing identity cards in some depth.

But hooliganism was just one of several headaches facing us. The new Safety of Sports Grounds Act, enforced by the County Council of which I was a member, nearly closed us down as a football club. We were told in July 1977 that unless we completed a whole string of structural improvements in time for the new season, we would have to cut the capacity from 46,000 to 10,000. Even getting a 25,000 crowd limit would cost £94,000. We went to see Jim Callaghan, in the hope that the Prime Minister would save his local football club in its darkest hour. Some hope! He said that the local authority had a statutory duty to enforce the safety regulations but he advised us to negotiate. I had already told the *Daily Telegraph*, 'It is ludicrous to cut the capacity to 10,000 at the stroke of a pen. We recognize that improvements are needed, but we must be given breathing space.' After inspecting the ground the County Council agreed to raise the crowd limit to just over 16,000.

Meanwhile relationships in the boardroom were not good. I had felt uneasy for some time about the way some of my co-directors were behaving and I wasn't afraid to say so. In May 1977 I had criticized them for 'washing our dirty linen in public'. The press had been informed about a crisis meeting we'd had with the players, when we warned them about the financial consequences of relegation. I was furious but they were unrepentant. Later, in September, there was another falling out when a member of the board criticized my identity card scheme. The press immediately detected a boardroom split. I tried to play it down but it became increasingly apparent that all was not well. The supporters' club wanted reassurances from the directors that there was no boardroom upheaval but a few days later there was an internal coup. I was voted out of the chair because of my public retaliation against other board members on the identity card issue. I was offered the chance to resign quietly but that wasn't my style. They would need to sack me.

Within a couple of months I was off the board completely. Despite a petition from the supporters, I was voted out at an extraordinary general meeting of shareholders and once again I became the Ukrainian refugee from the early 1950s loyally supporting my Bluebirds from the 'Bob Bank'.

But that wasn't quite the end of the story. I successfully sued the subsequent chairman for libelling me at the height of the ground safety controversy. He claimed that I had no interest in the club and had shown open hostility by threatening to wind it up. In Cardiff Crown Court, Room Number One, a jury of twelve delivered their verdict. His error cost him £4,000, and there was a handsome apology from the *Sunday Times* for printing the allegation! And to prove that my loyalty to the club was as strong as ever I continued to watch them, this time from my beloved 'Bob Bank' rather than the directors' box. In many ways I was grateful for that extra breathing space. I was now fifty and needed time to weigh up my future.

Chapter 20

1973-1983
The Road to Westminster

To win a parliamentary seat was still my ultimate goal. Having witnessed a total dearth of democracy in my early life in Ukraine, I now wanted to exercise my hard-earned rights to the full. And I wanted to be the first boy from the Ukrainian steppes to become a member of the British Parliament. In February 1973 I put my name forward to fight Cardiff South East, which included an area I represented when I was first elected to Cardiff City Council. It was, of course, Jim Callaghan's seat and in my wildest dreams I never imagined I would unseat him. But once I was selected there was a new twist. The International Monetary Fund were looking for a new chairman and Labour's Shadow Foreign Secretary and former Chancellor seemed, to many, to be the perfect man for the job. For a few months there was feverish speculation about a possible by-election in Cardiff.

The by-election never happened. Callaghan stayed on. But the focus of attention on Cardiff South East in the run-up to the general election, which wasn't far away as it turned out, worked to my advantage. My position on the council gave me endless opportunities for publicity. I castigated Labour over council house sales, and over calls by the constituency Labour Party to nationalize Britain's 300 top companies. Callaghan didn't go along with the idea, but until it was debated at their autumn conference the suggestion was something of an albatross around his neck. I challenged him to disown the policy and accused his left wing militant supporters of wanting to stage a political revolution. I warned that even if a more modest proposal by Labour's NEC to nationalize twenty-five companies was adopted it would cost Britain dear, while the full plan would bankrupt the country. 'Cardiff would no longer have a Marks and Spencer,' I warned. 'We'll get a Marx and Mao.'

But if the Labour Party was having its problems so were the Conservatives, as we faced a massive loss of steel jobs in Cardiff. As a local councillor and prospective parliamentary candidate, I felt I had to join other Welsh Conservatives in criticizing our own government. It wasn't easy. There was a deteriorating atmosphere between the government and the unions generally. We had already seen a bitter fight with the miners in 1972 when I accused their leaders of being in the pay of my old enemies, the communists. There were massive demonstrations by steelworkers in the centre of London, and the mood of the country was clearly against us. The mini-budget of December 1973 was brought in because of further industrial action by the miners. On top of the three day week and the power cuts, it did little to lift the gloom. It looked increasingly likely that Ted Heath would have to go to the country early.

In the meantime I was beginning to make my name as an outspoken critic of the Russian hammer and sickle and I included the Labour Party in my attacks because of their own apparatchiks' fondness for flying the red flag. At the Conservative conference in Blackpool in October 1973 I warned the West not to withdraw NATO troops from Europe. I described the life which I and my family had experienced behind the Iron Curtain because I felt that many people, even some of my fellow Conservatives, didn't really believe or understand how grim it was. And I expressed my fears about the way the Russian armed forces appeared to be preparing for Armageddon with their 36,000 tanks, 300 submarines, 335 warships, 3,750,000 men in uniform and another 3,000,000 who could be called up within 90 days. 'I was born into slave labour,' I said, 'I want to die a free man.'

My knockabout style of speaking, which was spontaneous and from the heart, along with my distinctive Ukrainian accent with hints of Welshness, all seemed to go down very well with the party, judging by the standing ovations. The Conservatives have always been the most visibly British of the main political parties, but they've also enjoyed encouraging colourful foreigners like myself as well – as long as there aren't too many of us! I have always been aware of an undercurrent of prejudice towards me as a Ukrainian immigrant in Britain, a country which I nevertheless still love. But the people I worked with in the Conservative Party, at a grass roots level, were almost always genuine and friendly.

Unknown to all of us, 1974 was going to be a very busy year for parliamentary candidates. The miners were still in dispute with the government and the crisis facing Ted Heath forced him to go to the country early. There was a short sharp campaign in February – one of the worst months possible for a general election because of the weather. Polling day was to be on 28 February and on a chilly evening exactly a fortnight beforehand I was adopted as the candidate for Cardiff South East at a meeting in the Roath Conservative Club, a mile or so from the doomed East Moors steel works. I warned in my adoption speech that a Labour victory would lead to thirty local firms being nationalized, including GKN the privately owned steel-makers in Cardiff. A Labour government would soon be rolling out the beer barrels for the trade unions. The sandwiches would follow and Number 10 Downing Street would become a haven for extremists and left-wing militants.

During the campaign I went from meeting to meeting, discussing serious issues with all sorts of people, but also enjoying the jokes and the banter and the endless non-alcoholic beverages and sandwiches. Elections in those days, without the constant presence of television cameras, brought the candidates face to face with the people in a natural and less contrived way. Our main hope of winning this election was to convince the voters that Labour's promises to pay the miners more would only lead us into further difficulties. Inflation and rising prices were a big issue and Jim Callaghan promised that a Labour Government would try to block moves by the EEC to raise the prices on food. I warned people in Cardiff South East that under Labour there would be a fifteen pence increase on petrol, beer and cigarettes.

In reality the election period was too short to have sensible debates – it was all about public confidence in the midst of a crisis and we clearly didn't have the necessary support of the public. Labour won four more UK seats than we did, even though we had a bigger share of the vote, and formed a minority government. In Cardiff South East Jim Callaghan polled 20,641 votes but I was very pleased with my 13,495. I said on election night that, if asked, I would stand again. 'There is so much I would like to do to help safeguard the good things in British life'.

Over the summer it became increasingly obvious that another election was imminent. Harold Wilson's position would become untenable without a clear majority. At least we had a chance to prepare for this one. Jim Callaghan never did take the IMF job and was clearly enjoying his job as Foreign Secretary. So I would be fighting him once again but I didn't mind. It was always useful, in the long run, to have such a high profile politician as your opponent. As I told the newspapers, 'The bigger they are, the harder they fall'. At the same time Jim Callaghan and I were becoming increasingly close and friendly at a personal level. The moment the election was called for 10 October, we sprang into action. Ukrainians living in Britain had sent me warm messages of encouragement in the February election, so I now asked them for continuing practical support. A large coach load of young dancers and musicians from the Ukrainian community in Derby came down to Cardiff under the leadership of Josef Kupranec one weekend to perform in national costume, and in particular to give a concert of Ukrainian singing and dancing in which they excelled themselves. They also canvassed thousands of homes in the constituency by day and danced in a number of Conservative clubs in the evenings. It was exhausting for them, but it was an inspiration for me to have young people with the same origins as my own supporting me in a political campaign in a free and democratic Britain. By way of reward I constantly fed them with the very best Welsh fish and chips and bottles of lemonade. They never seemed to tire of it.

Then, on polling day there was a 4.8 per cent swing to Labour in Cardiff South East. They polled just over 21,000 votes giving Callaghan his biggest majority since 1966. I only managed 10,718. It was, to my mind, a clear illustration of how gullible, irrational and unpredictable voters can be. At one point they were creating mayhem over the closure of the works, and the next moment they appeared to be perfectly happy to see Labour remaining in power despite the prospect of wide scale unemployment. I felt like telling them that it bloody well served them right but I restrained myself. Afterwards I admitted I was disappointed, but added, 'I'll never surrender, I'll get to Westminster one day.'

Harold Wilson returned to No. 10 with the narrowest of majorities – three – but this time there was no sign that Labour would go for another snap election. It looked as if they would slug it out for as long as possible, giving me the chance to concentrate once again on local government.

One visit I very much welcomed was that of Henry Kissinger the American Secretary of State. Jim Callaghan persuaded him to come over in March 1975 to receive the freedom of the city of Cardiff and to help boost Welsh tourism. The Welsh public had been agog earlier in the day because of the style of his arrival at Cardiff airport. His enormous armour-plated limousine was driven out of the Presidential jet onto the tarmac, and wherever he went he was surrounded by hordes of plain clothes bodyguards bristling with barely concealed weapons and radio equipment. I was delighted to meet him at the civic banquet in City Hall that evening, although I couldn't help feeling that I was in the firing line! Jim Callaghan introduced me to 'Herr' Kissinger and despite being completely surrounded by photographers and cameramen we had a long conversation, putting the world to rights, and pulling each other's legs about our respective countries of origin and our foreign accents.

At about this time, the Conservative party was embarking on an historic new path. Edward Heath was clearly finished after that second defeat, and Margaret Thatcher was soon to take over. She came to our Welsh conference in Aberystwyth in the summer of 1975 and took part in a question and answer session in the hall in front of a selected audience. Thatcherism was still in its infancy, and press reports afterwards said she appeared to be sketchy on policy details. I was not necessarily in complete agreement with Heath when it came to Europe, being more concerned about the relationship between NATO and the Iron Curtain countries. Nevertheless, when I was called to speak, I paid tribute to him because of the recent European referendum victory. There was still a lot of sympathy for him at grass roots. My comments were greeted enthusiastically from the floor with a huge amount of applause, but on the platform there was an icy reception. Only one man clapped – William Whitelaw.

There was a big shock in store for Labour and for the country as a whole. Harold Wilson mysteriously resigned and Jim Callaghan took over. For the first time since the Ramsay Macdonald era the British Prime Minister was from a Welsh constituency. One of the first moves I made, apart from congratulating him, was to ask for his help in my campaign to free my father, who had been in a labour camp in Siberia since 1952. It was the beginning of a long battle and Callaghan, along with many other politicians on both sides of the House, gave me considerable support in the years to come.

My interest in international affairs and my support for our continuing membership of the EEC, prompted me to start thinking about the first European Parliamentary elections which were due in 1979. Up till then the parliament was a nominated body and had virtually no influence over the bureaucrats.

My European credentials as a candidate were, to my mind, impeccable and people that I had met all over the country seemed to agree. I could speak five European languages, and my outlook was naturally international. As a local government councillor and former south Wales chairman of the cross-party 'Keep Britain in Europe' campaign, I believed that the European Community could breathe new life into places like Wales where the steel and coal industries were being run down. Above all I believed that a strong Western Europe was badly needed to counterbalance the unstable Eastern bloc. I certainly didn't believe, however, that everything in the European garden was rosy. I was critical of the absurdities of the Common Agricultural Policy where the EEC was paying out £900m a year just to build up butter mountains and wine lakes. What's more they were giving grain away to just about anybody who asked for it, even the Russians. I was also appalled that Labour during its five years in Government had failed to reduce the UK's net contributions to the EEC budget.

The European election was scheduled for 7 June 1979, but we obviously didn't know the date of the general election. I had already decided not to stand against Jim Callaghan in Cardiff South East again. I had told him at our previous contest that if I ever had to fight him for a third time I would 'bloody well shoot him'. With a grin he replied that if I did, one thing was certain; I'd never get to Parliament. We both laughed and the incident showed how British politicians can still get on with each other even when they come from different parties. In Russia I would have disappeared without trace after such a conversation. I always had a high regard for Jim as a good constituency member.

The majority of Westminster seats in the South Wales Euro-constituency were solidly Labour, but I had never let facts like that put me off in the past, and it wasn't going to happen now. They say that a change is as good as a rest.

214

Tackling the butter mountains, the subsidy scandals and the failure by Labour to make good use of our EEC membership was like a breath of fresh air after all the local government issues with which I had become familiar: the litter in the streets, the holes in the road, the housing problems, education, poor public toilets and everything else. Farming, the economy, NATO issues, foreign policy and heavy industry dominated European politics at that time, even more than they do now. In my manifesto I said that membership of the EEC meant that Wales had benefited from loans and grants worth £500m between 1973 and 1979 but I attacked the Common Agricultural Policy saying that any scheme which created unfair competition for our farmers and raised prices for the housewife should be radically reformed.

I felt it was a bit rich when a well known trade unionist in Cardiff defaced one of my election posters by superimposing a picture of Stalin over my own and replaced my own slogan of 'Terlezki for Europe' with 'Terlezki for Russia'. I returned the compliment by sending him a huge pile of my posters to his house by special delivery. 'For most people one message from me is enough,' I told the press, 'but some people need to be told again and again about the evils of the leftist disease.'

We had to accept that much of the political debate was going over the heads of the electorate. Welsh voters had probably had a surfeit of elections that year anyway. There was the referendum on devolution, which Labour lost on 1 March and which helped to drive the final nail into the Socialist coffin. This was followed by the General Election in May, which was another disaster for them. As European candidates, we were concerned about the possibility of a low turnout, with forecasts of between 15 and 30 per cent in the press. The eventual figure of 36 per cent wasn't too bad by modern standards, but it seemed low at the time and showed just how uninterested the public were. It didn't help that commentators were pointing out how little power the European Parliament had. All that one of its most distinguished advocates, Roy Jenkins, could say was that the new elections would at least give the European Parliament a 'moral authority'.

As polling day grew closer it looked as if a low turnout would help our party rather more than our euro-sceptical Labour opponents. We were very confident of winning seats in Wales. When the result was announced we could see that there had been a big swing to the Conservatives in the few weeks since the General Election. I was surprised and delighted to come second, winning 66,852 votes to Labour's 77,784. At the same time I was infuriated that more Conservatives in our strongholds of Cardiff and the Vale of Glamorgan, where so many members of Parliament had been returned over the years, hadn't spared fifteen minutes to turn Labour's comparatively small 11,000 majority into a victory for us. There must have been thousands and thousands of Conservative votes in Cardiff and the Vale which were never cast. Why couldn't they have got off their backsides and gone out to vote for the party which they were supposed to support?

My thoughts turned again to Westminster. This time I was hoping for a winnable constituency. I was selected for Kingswood, near Bristol, but I resigned as candidate. I decided that my future really lay in Wales where I had already served the people to the best of my ability as a local government councillor. I decided to go for Cardiff West, which had been held since 1945 by George Thomas – 'our George' – the Speaker of the House of Commons. Normally, there was an agreement between the main parties not to oppose the Speaker since he was supposed to be 'above party politics'. But there was a question mark over whether he would stand again anyway, so we felt that we should establish an early presence. I found myself on the short list with two other local councillors and was thrilled when I was selected.

The other piece of good news was that the boundaries of Cardiff West were being changed to include the Tory-friendly territory of Radyr and St Fagans, worth 3,000 extra Conservative votes. Unsurprisingly, the Labour councillor who would be my opponent in Cardiff West had objected to this change. To my disgust, he was backed by a Conservative councillor, who had been my agent when I stood against Jim Callaghan. But they had a rotten case and the boundary commissioner gave their arguments a zero rating.

In the meantime there were rumours that George Thomas might leave the Commons early and spark off a by-election. I'd had to put up with that sort of speculation in Cardiff South East of course, with Jim Callaghan, and refused to get too excited about it although I needed more time to raise my profile in the constituency. As it turned out George, with whom I had always enjoyed a warm friendship, decided to carry on until the general election and then resign. I was relieved that he was definitely standing down – it would have been embarrassing and difficult if he had carried on.

Margaret Thatcher's success with her policies, and her victory in the Falklands, meant that the Conservative government was on the crest of a wave. When you're in with a chance it's fascinating to see how the media suddenly become interested in you. The *Daily Telegraph* described me as flamboyant and loquacious; somebody who was either loved or hated by people. They seemed to appreciate my definition of the SDP as 'semi-displaced persons who were wetter than the River Taff'. They also described me as fiercely right wing. Whatever I was, I made my position in the party absolutely clear. On Europe, I was opposed to any talk of coming out because of the potential loss of jobs in Wales. On crime, I called for a big increase in police recruitment. On housing, I fully backed the government's policy on council house sales. And on defence, I criticized Labour's unilateralism. Callaghan took a similar line during the election, saying that his party's policy wasn't a credible one. He was accused of stabbing Michael Foot, his successor as Labour leader, in the back.

At a pre-election meeting of candidates in Hertfordshire in April 1983 I told Margaret Thatcher that my batteries were recharged and I was ready to go. She congratulated me on being chosen to fight George Thomas' old seat, and I assured her that we would win it. During our meeting we were photographed together for my election literature and I couldn't help thinking how charismatic she was, and how relaxing it was to speak to her. Within a few weeks the election was called and I now had to live up to the promise.

My team and I worked from early in the morning until late at night, seven days a week, knocking on doors, attending public meetings and speaking at hustings. At the meetings I would make sure that I put the main point of my speeches across in thirty seconds, even though the speech might last for half an hour. During the speech I would focus on specific groups and give the impression that I was talking to them directly as individuals. The opinion polls and the boundary changes in Cardiff West were all working in my favour, even though it was still a marginal seat in a former Labour stronghold. It was impossible to tell how much of it had been due to George Thomas' personal vote or how much that vote would be distributed in the new constituency. As the *Daily Telegraph* put it, 'there is no one natural and inevitable beneficiary'.

Once the final votes had been cast and the ballot boxes had been delivered to the count, the tension in the hall began to mount. Observers from the political parties were anxiously checking the piles of ballot papers, which were being constantly sifted and counted, to see if there was any sign of a clear winner. Finally, after what felt like a lifetime, the returning officer came to the platform with the candidates lined up behind him. I can still clearly remember the words: 'Terlezki, Stefan – Conservative – 15,472 votes.' I was duly elected as the member of Parliament for Cardiff West! It was a shock result for Labour, but I had always felt at the bottom of my heart that I would win. On top of that the Conservatives had been returned with a huge majority to Westminster and I was going to be part of that majority. Still, in Cardiff, at that moment, I could only think of my own victory. It was a sensational feeling and I was elated beyond description. I was lost for words for a moment and felt as light as a feather. Then I told the cheering crowd, 'It's not I who has won this election. It is the people of Cardiff West.' I paid tribute to George Thomas adding,' I believe I have the courage and stamina to continue his work on behalf of everybody.'

I went home with the family in the early hours of the morning without any sense of tiredness. I didn't even notice that for hours I'd had nothing to eat or drink. I was still feeling totally elated and an image of the House of Commons with Big Ben and all the other magnificent buildings in the background kept flashing through my head. The way in which so many people see Big Ben as a symbol of reliability and security suddenly made me acutely conscious of the responsibility of high office which had fallen on my shoulders. And I couldn't help reflect on how far I had come since my penniless arrival in Harwich in 1948.

Chapter 21

1983-1987
From the Ukrainian Steppes
to St Stephen's Entrance

Was it coincidence or divine providence? Fifty-five years before I was elected to Parliament my parents unwittingly decided to name me after the saint who is also the patron saint of Westminster. I like to think it was the latter.

Entering Parliament for the first time, usually through St Stephen's Entrance, is a strange experience for most new MPs, but for somebody with my history it was particularly strange.

I will never forget the sense of history which overwhelmed me when I first went into the Members' Lobby, an inner sanctum which is only open to MPs and lobby correspondents while Parliament is sitting. As I discovered later, it was the nerve centre of the parliamentary village where mail was collected, gossip exchanged and behind-the-scenes deals negotiated. My immediate memory, however, was of being awe-struck by the bronze statues of Lloyd George and Sir Winston Churchill which stood on either side of the lobby. It was said that when similarly mesmerized visitors from all over the world were taken around by the official guides they were advised to touch the feet of the statues for good luck. But the guides' attempts at being politically neutral obviously failed because Churchill's feet shone more brightly and were far more polished than those of Lloyd George. When I was a ten year old boy my father had told me about Mr Churchill and his cigar and walking stick and how great a leader he was. It was like touching a piece of history.

My own personal memories came flooding back too. I found it hard to believe that I had travelled so far. Here I was, the first Ukrainian ever to become a member of the British Parliament and I felt highly privileged, honoured and proud. However, I couldn't help feeling that I was also an outsider – I could have just as easily been one of the tourists who swarmed into the building every day.

MPs who have experienced the public school system always say that being a new member is very similar to being a new boy in a large boarding school; apart from having to find your way around a huge and maze-like series of buildings, you are constantly trying to work out who everybody is. For somebody with my background it was even more difficult. I tried not to show it but my heart was beating and there were butterflies in my stomach. When I was introduced to other members, particularly the senior ones, I got into the habit of giving them a little bow to show my respect to them and to the institution. No doubt they thought this was just a quaint Ukrainian custom, but it was more than that. It was a genuine reaction, a mixture of gratitude and appreciation. The nature of British democracy meant that somebody like me could stand in the members' lobby or eat in one of the dining rooms and be treated by these people as an equal, but I was still asking myself whether I really was a member of Parliament. During the campaign I also shed a few tears because I was thousands of kilometres from my village of Antoniwka and there was no one from my home in Ukraine to embrace and kiss me and wish me well.

George Thomas wrote to me soon after the election, warmly congratulating me and giving me some friendly words of advice. 'You will be a good House of Commons man', he said. 'You have a rich capacity for friendship. The House will love you if you show that you respect and honour its traditions.' As a postscript, not surprisingly, he advised me always to support and obey the Speaker! I was very aware that I had a lot to learn. In the chamber I made sure that I watched the more senior members' behaviour very closely. I noted their styles of delivery and their body movements and I tried to make sure that in some respects I was like them. But in other ways I was determined to remain my own man. I made a point of developing my own style as well, and it seemed to win the respect of my colleagues, or at least most of them!

There are endless rules about behaviour and procedure and it is always important to make sure that the prefects (or Whips as they are known in Parliament) are treated with caution. They can make or break your career but at the same time they don't always go out of their way to help you. They didn't tell me, for example, what I was supposed to do when I first went into the Chamber. It was very different from the council chamber in Cardiff, and I wasn't sure which side to sit on. There seemed to be spare seats on the Speaker's left as I went in, so I made my way in all innocence towards the opposition benches. I hadn't allowed for the fact that the

Government, who sat to the right of the Speaker, had a huge majority and were finding it very difficult to provide enough seats for all their backbenchers. This immediately caused an uproar and there were jokes about me crossing the floor to Labour before I had even taken the Loyal Oath to the Queen!

But none of this spoiled the pleasure and the sense of achievement in becoming an MP. I had finally arrived. It was still taking a long time to sink in. I was really in the Commons and also, in a small way, making history. My new surroundings were not only something which I could look at and admire. They were where I could also participate. I could join the galaxy of politicians before me who had helped to shape the future of Great Britain. I knew there would be special opportunities on the foreign affairs front. Unlike most so called experts, I believed that the Cold War would end, almost certainly in my lifetime – a highly unfashionable view that saw me labelled as an anti-Russian imperialist. In the meantime, the one thing I wanted to do more than anything was expose what was going on behind the Iron Curtain.

 I wanted to tell the real story, and I wanted everybody to hear it loud and clear all the way to Moscow. I wanted the leaders of the whole of the Communist bloc to know what I was saying, along with our own leaders and everybody else in the free world. Above all I wanted to urge the brutal regimes behind the Iron Curtain, particularly the geriatric bunch in the Kremlin represented by Khrushchev, Brezhnev, Andropov and Chernenko that they should let their people go. Ever since the 1950s I had been collecting articles and papers on foreign affairs and was particularly concerned about the Cold War, the role of NATO and the corresponding behaviour of the Russian Empire. But I would also be able to look after the interests of political refugees who had suffered in the way that I had. I could act as a voice for all those who had been left behind, particularly families like my own.

I was building up a reputation in the London press for being what the *Sunday Telegraph* called a 'dry'. Their political staff wrote that Mrs Thatcher's new intake included ' a vigorous injection of members who were committed to trade union reform, law and order, strong defence, free enterprise and living-within-your-means Toryism.' They seemed to pick me out as one of the most obvious examples, and when they asked me about my views on welfare benefits I replied: 'We can only help the less fortunate when the country is wealthy as a whole. And then we can only help those who are in real need.'

Private Eye's New Boys column featured me within a few weeks of taking my seat. Attracting the attention of the country's leading satirical magazine could be a harrowing experience and some of my colleagues dreaded it.

But I was rather flattered to appear so early. Many MPs had to wait for several years before getting the 'warts and all' treatment. As it turned out it wasn't excessively brutal. I first heard about it when I was walking along one of the corridors leading out of the members' gallery. Patrick Jenkin stopped to ask me if I had seen the latest *Private Eye*. I held back for a second and then said that I hadn't.

'You're in it,' he said, 'but I don't think you can sue them. They're not saying anything too bad. Go to the library and have a look at it.'

When I found a copy I saw what he meant. My election in Cardiff West was greeted, according to the anonymous writer, with 'consternation and bemusement by local hacks who had hitherto regarded Terlezki as a parody anti-communist.' They made fun of my accent, my double-breasted waistcoats and gold watch chain, my 'ostentatious overcoat with Astrakhan collar' and my disciplinarian views. I stood not so much for Victorian values, more for Czarist ones. Unlike some MPs I was an untarnished family man, but they promised that I would provide good copy for the sketch writers, and ethnic variety for the sound broadcasters. But I would only be a one-Parliament member. We'd have to see about that!

One other hurdle for new MPs is the maiden speech. It is a very important and sometimes difficult speech to make. Until it happens MPs cannot play a full part in Parliamentary debates. It's the speech by which many MPs will be remembered for a long time, even though controversy is not encouraged. A major part of it, by convention, has to be about the constituency, and there should be praise for previous members. I was able, with complete sincerity, to speak warmly about my old friend George Thomas, or Viscount Tonypandy as he was now known. I made the speech during a Foreign Affairs debate on 3 November 1983, and for a while I thought that it would never happen. The Chamber had been plunged into darkness on several occasions earlier in the evening because of a power failure. Roy Jenkins was in the middle of a speech; at one moment we could see him; then we couldn't. Those members who liked to mock his ponderous style of delivery cheered in the hope that he would sit down but from somewhere in the void he could still be heard making remarks about Sir Edward Grey.

Peering through the gloom it was just possible to see the Deputy Speaker consulting with the whips and the clerks in wigs. Various officials left the chamber and then messengers came back with lamps and handed them out. I now faced the prospect of delivering my first speech in the Chamber with my notes in one hand and a lamp in the other. How was I going to manage? To my relief the power was restored shortly afterwards, the lamps were taken from us and Roy Jenkins carried on with his speech. The respite was short-lived though. Once again he was silenced and the

Stefan Terlezki
Cardiff West

The House Magazine.

messengers came back with the lamps. Then the lights came back on again, and the Deputy Speaker said we should all wait for an engineer's report.

Eventually Jenkins got to his feet again and was improvising with reflections about Lloyd George. I decided to call it a day but just as I was about to the leave the Chamber the lights went off yet again. The Deputy Speaker called the veteran left winger Ian Mikardo, who said he didn't mind at all as he was regarded by the House as one of the Princes of Darkness anyway! He certainly made the most of it and spoke at such length that the Speaker, Bernard Wetherill, who was back in the chair by now, had to persuade him to sit down so that other members could speak. 'Other members' included an increasingly nervous member for Cardiff West. By now I had decided to stay in the Chamber and miraculously I was called immediately. Even more miraculously the lights were restored. There was no going back. My maiden speech had to be delivered!

Apart from one ill-mannered interruption from a Labour MP, my 'maiden' went off well and I was warmly congratulated by a number of my parliamentary colleagues. I was particularly proud of letters from Bernard Weatherill, the new Speaker, and Jim Callaghan. Bernard said mine was an outstanding maiden speech and the House appreciated my tribute to George Thomas. He also noted the attention paid by members in the chamber to my personal experiences. Jim apologized for missing the speech but wrote later that he was sure my experience of Soviet rule would mark me out as an enthusiastic supporter of the democratic way of life. The *South Wales Echo* described the speech as one of the most emotional maiden speeches heard in the Commons for years.

On the international front my old adversaries in Moscow were still worrying and annoying me. In 1983 I accepted an invitation to go the World Congress of Free Ukrainians in Toronto. There were well over 10,000 delegates representing 20 million Ukrainians living outside Ukraine. We were accused by the Communists of being Nazi lackeys and the Canadian Government was asked to boycott the event because we were trying to overthrow the Soviet Government. Would that we could have done so! But one of our main objectives on this occasion was to remind the world about the 7 million Ukrainians who died from starvation as a result of deliberate orders from Stalin in 1932-33. Brian Mulroney, the leader of the opposition in Canada, said the famine was directed from Moscow and enforced by a regime dedicated to creating a new Soviet Order. I was invited to speak, and I urged young Ukrainians everywhere to become involved in politics to make themselves heard.

My own campaign against people who didn't take the Communist threat seriously continued at home, and when I returned from the anti-Soviet rally in Canada there was a letter in the *South Wales Echo* from a CND member accusing me of antics which threatened world peace. The writer, a fellow Catholic, said I should remember the words of Pope John Paul in Coventry in 1982 when he said, 'Mistrust and division between nations begin in the hearts of individuals.' The writer sympathized with my wartime experiences, and the way I had become one of the millions of refugees who had zigzagged across the face of the earth. But she called for forgiveness and reconciliation. I didn't agree with her interpretation of what the Pope had said but in deference to her obvious sincerity I've kept her letter in my files ever since. A few months later, because of the part I played in the Toronto conference, I was invited to take part in a BBC World Service programme, which was in Ukrainian, Russian and Polish. Some of my old school friends and some of my relatives heard it and learned for the first time what had happened to me and what I had achieved.

I was given another chance to speak Russian when Mikhail Gorbachev, who by then was secretary of the Communist Party and a leading member of the Politburo, visited London. I had been watching developments in Moscow for many years, and it was no surprise to me or indeed any other Kremlin watcher in this country that Gorbachev was their rising star. He had more charm and was more outward looking and modern in his approach than any of the other apparatchiks that we had seen. He had lunch in the splendid Tudor surroundings of Hampton Court as a guest of Sir Geoffrey Howe, who pressed him on the human rights issue, touching upon my own father's plight and his many years in exile in Siberia.

Later, I was invited by the Foreign Office to attend a dinner at Claridges Hotel with Gorbachev, along with other members of Parliament. When I was introduced to him I was very surprised by his opinions, by his easy smile and by his comments on issues that I am sure would have been impossible to discuss with Khrushchev and the others. When I told him that I understood the Russian language well, but found it more difficult to speak it, he continued with his charm offensive and immediately said, 'That's nothing – let's speak Ukrainian'. To my huge surprise he started to recite the Testament of Taras Shevchenko, the greatest poet, patriot and national hero in the history of Ukraine. I was so grateful and so appreciative of what he went on to say about Shevchenko – who was also a personal hero to me – that I felt like giving him a big hug.

As I listened to Gorbachev's private views on Russia, spoken in perfect Ukrainian, a frosty shiver ran down my back. I knew that if he were to repeat in the Kremlin what he said to me in London he would never, ever, become the president of the Soviet Empire. Instead it was more likely that he would spend the rest of his life as a manager in a brick factory in some godforsaken part of Siberia! Gorbachev then told me that I must visit my beautiful Ukraine, especially the region where I had been born, the western Ukraine in the Carpathian Region. I told him that I would love to visit my beautiful Ukraine but I was afraid.

'Who are you afraid of?' he asked.

'The KGB,' I replied

'You are now a member of the British Parliament and we will look after you,' he said. And so he did, as I was to discover later.

I met Mr Gorbachev once again during his visit, at a luncheon in the Café Royale. I told him that we in the West had high hopes of him achieving a far greater level of détente than his predecessors, and that our observers had been backing him as a potential leader for some time. He thanked me warmly for telling him and, as he flashed his friendly smile once again, we shook hands as if his appointment was a fait accompli. He then advised me that he wouldn't be able to achieve any reforms without the approval of the old guard who remained very powerful in Moscow. Despite his charm, I was still cautious about him. I warned those who asked me about him that we shouldn't be taken in too much by his smile and his apparent search for peace but he certainly looked like a much more hopeful prospect than any of his predecessors.

A year later, when he met President Reagan at their famous summit in Iceland, I listened carefully to the English and Russian versions of Gorbachev's statement at the subsequent press conference on television. The English version spoke of peace and friendship while the longer and more verbose Russian version was clearly biased in Russia's favour. I had predicted that Gorbachev would be good at singing two tunes at once and it now looked as if I was right. A few years later I too visited Iceland as a member of the Council of Europe's Human Rights Committee. I went to the place where the two leaders had met and paused briefly to reflect on what had happened, and to look forward to what would hopefully be a period of security and peace for mankind. It strengthened my resolve and my determination to work still harder for peace, freedom and democracy for all.

Of course, constituency issues were a very important part of my daily routine as an MP. Perhaps the most rewarding experience of all was when I helped the family of a young sailor, killed more than forty years before, to secure the posthumous medals due to him. Leon Phillips from Cardiff was a steward on a coal ship torpedoed in the Atlantic eight days before Christmas 1944. He was just seventeen and for his family, particularly his mother Emily, it was a harrowing blow. When the war ended she waited patiently for the medals but they never came. She and her surviving children sent countless letters to ministers and civil servants in Whitehall, all to no avail. Finally, after a gap of forty years I took up her cause, and at last the long lost medals arrived. Mrs Phillips, who was now eighty-six, invited me to her home in Rumney, Cardiff along with local newspaper photographers and reporters. We were shown with great pride the 1939-45 Star, the Victory Medal, and the Atlantic Star. Young Leon may have never been able to wear them but at least they were now being given pride of place in his mother's home and providing her, at any rate, with a little comfort. I hugged the old lady who told me what a lovely boy he had been – the baby of the family. As part of the celebrations I invited her and the family to visit me in the House of Commons. As I had already discovered when I was a councillor, being an elected representative was generally a rewarding and worthwhile experience, regardless of party.

Two major highlights in my political career were undoubtedly my meetings with the Pope. I had met him first when he came to Cardiff in 1982 to be given the Freedom of the City. The Greek Catholic Church, the church I grew up in, recognized the Pope as its spiritual leader despite its observance of the Eastern rites. I was naturally very thrilled as a councillor to be introduced to him when he was a guest of honour at a banquet in Cardiff Castle. We spoke in Polish and Ukrainian and I told him all about my background. He was very interested in the fact that I was the first Ukrainian to be elected to a public position in the UK, and apart from speaking my native language it became clear that he knew a lot about my birthplace and the country in general. I wasn't to know that I would meet him again, as an MP, two years later, in 1984, in Rome.

I don't suppose he recognized me at first and he was visibly surprised when I greeted him in Ukrainian saying, ' Glory to Jesus Christ O Holy Father'. It wasn't what he expected from a British MP. Mary my wife, and my daughter Helena were with me and once again our mutual interests in Eastern Europe gave us plenty to talk about. I told him about my family and my own history as a former slave labourer and he listened with great interest and sympathy. He seemed pleased to meet a fellow Slav and told me that he knew Ivano-Frankiwsk which was only a few miles from my birthplace. Under the Poles it had been known as Stanislawiw. He turned to Mary and asked if she was Ukrainian as well. We explained that she was from Wales.

'Ah she's from Veils,' he replied.

'No she's from Wales – Cardiff,' I told him.

'Ah, Cardiff,' he said, remembering his visit in 1982. I went on to tell him that I was now the first Ukrainian ever to become a member of the British Parliament and I could see his eyes light up. He raised his eyebrows and light-heartedly replied that the Ukrainians had definitely stolen a

The Times, Wednesday, 25 March 1987.

march on his own countrymen, since no Pole had so far been elected to the British Parliament. When the audience ended after about an hour and he'd made his way to the door, I called out in Polish, 'Goodbye dowizenia, Holy Father.' He turned back to wave briefly before leaving the room.

Because of my admiration for Sir Winston Churchill, I had for a long time harboured the idea of commemorating him in a special way. Eventually I put it to the test when I tried to replace May Day, with a Sir Winston Churchill National Day with a parliamentary bill of my own.

It would have reached the Statute Book as an Act of Parliament but, when I subsequently lost my seat, my colleagues, to my dismay, decided not to pursue the matter any further. By now I was beginning to take stock of the situation back in Cardiff. I had always hoped that I would be given a second or even a third term in Parliament, but I knew that the 1987 campaign wasn't going to be easy.

In the last few weeks before the election it became obvious that it was going to be a very close finish between myself and my Labour opponent, Rhodri Morgan. An early poll showed that I was about three points ahead, and I felt that my hard work in the constituency over the past four years was going to clinch it. The bookies were also giving me better odds than Labour. Even though the press didn't always give me a fair crack of the whip, they weren't audacious enough to stick their necks above the parapet and predict that I was going to lose, although the gap was rapidly narrowing. I described myself as the second George Thomas, a candidate who could appeal to all voters – regardless of their background. I worked relentlessly, meeting thousands of constituents over the election period. And I constantly predicted that a Labour Government would increase taxes, destroy jobs and create a divided kingdom.

There were days when I felt that I was beginning to make a breakthrough but there were others when I feared the worst. I never conceded that I might lose however, either in public or in private. My agent, Charlotte Mortimer, my constituency chairman, Keith Flynn, my fundraising director, Ron Trigg, and a great many constituency members worked relentlessly and were a source of enormous strength and encouragement to me throughout the campaign. My approach clearly struck a chord with some journalists. One wrote: 'The sheer nerve and verve of the man can be breathtaking but the evidence is that despite his confidence and his claim that he has personally spoken to thousands of electors, he is neck and neck with Rhodri Morgan.' Another said: 'Stefan Terlezki can feel well pleased with himself. He took the seat during a Tory landslide year. It has a strong socialist tradition. Yet he has hung on to his vote and has a good chance of keeping his seat.'

The battle in Cardiff West, as it turned out, hinged on the floating voter.

Tactical voting was still in its infancy at the time but was central to my Labour opponent's tactics. I was one of the early victims of what I regard as a totally negative approach to elections, as former SDP supporters were persuaded to vote Labour. I still feel that if the former European Commissioner, Ivor Richard, had succeeded in his bid to be selected by Labour for Cardiff West I *would* have retained the seat.

When the declaration came, I had increased my vote but Labour had increased theirs by more. As Labour supporters inside and outside the hall cheered wildly, I could do nothing apart from feeling hugely disappointed about the way my triumph of 1983 had turned to defeat. My dreams of carrying on as a Member of Parliament for at least another term had come to nothing. Enoch Powell once wrote that 'All political lives, unless they are cut off in midstream at a happy juncture, end in failure, because that is the nature of politics and of human affairs.' But my own feelings at that moment were not so philosophical as Enoch Powell's. Instead I took my cue from Churchill's immortal words - 'in defeat; defiance'.

Chapter 22

1984
From a Siberian Grave

My life had been transformed by those four years as a Member of Parliament. As an MP I had many wonderful opportunities. But of course by far the most precious had been the chance to be reunited with my father. After many years of trying to get permission from the Soviet authorities for him to visit Britain, my efforts began to meet with some success in the summer of 1984. Sir Geoffrey Howe, the Foreign Secretary, was going to a conference in Moscow. I knew that Geoffrey would be meeting Andrei Gromyko, his Soviet counterpart, and I implored him to speak to Mr Gromyko on my behalf.

'Tell the Russian Foreign Minister,' I said, 'that I have been writing to my father for many years now, asking if he can persuade the commissar in Irkutsk to allow him to visit me, his son, in Britain. If we could have a month or perhaps just a week in Wales, it would be like a gift from Heaven.' I described how I had last seen him in 1942 before being taken away by the Germans into slavery in Austria. Geoffrey was totally understanding and sympathetic and promised me that he would do his best to speak to Mr Gromyko.

'Send me all the details you have about your father,' he said. 'Where he is living, his address and any other documents you may have.'

'I have his address near Lake Baikal, in the province of Irkutsk,' I said. 'Apart from that I only have traumatic memories of our parting in 1942 and I shudder to think of my father and my sister living in Siberia.'

Although I had no documents, I could imagine what my father had suffered. Even the censorship of letters could not hide everything. I knew how he and my sister had been woken up at 3 o'clock one morning and given half an hour to pack their bags. My father had been told to take a spade. This was needed, not only for his work in the labour camps when they got to Siberia, but also to dig graves for those who died of cold and hunger on the long journey there. His letters would mention unpleasant people and tragic events from my childhood as coded references to what was happening to him in Siberia.

As for Siberia itself, that godforsaken open prison, my father wryly summed it up in one of his letters. 'We've got a marvellous climate here,' he said, 'We get twelve months of winter and the rest is summer!' The way the state treated its workers was as unrelenting as the climate. At times there weren't even enough potato peelings to go round and potatoes themselves were a luxury beyond the reach of most.

Geoffrey Howe was as good as his word. Once he reached Moscow he made a personal plea to Mr Gromyko on my behalf. When he got back to London he contacted me.

'Stefan, I passed on everything you wanted me to say to Gromyko but you know Russian bureaucracy better than I do. I hope your father will be allowed to visit you.' Four months later, as I sat at my desk in Parliament, doing some constituency work, the telephone rang. I picked up the receiver and a voice at the other end said, 'Your father is arriving at Heathrow at 9 p.m. tomorrow evening.' At the same time, in far away Siberia, my father also learned of his imminent journey.

He would be arriving at Heathrow Airport on an Aeroflot flight from Moscow at 9 p.m., as promised, on Tuesday, 2 October. When I heard that he was coming, I could not believe it. The tears were streaming down my face and I was crying for joy. The news was as exciting and as miraculous as the landing on the moon. I didn't know at that point what sort of visa my father had been given, or how long it would be valid for. But the main thing was that we would be seeing each other again, for the first time in forty-two years.

Neither of us knew what to expect when we met. My father's last memory of me was as a fourteen year old boy, standing with my friends in a wagon at the back of the train as we left for Austria, desperately clutching at him in a last farewell. I was now a man of fifty-six, with a family of my own, and yet he was still half expecting to see that fourteen year old boy waiting for him. As for me, I knew he was unwell, and I wondered how frail he would be as he came off the plane. In reality it was quite different from anything that either of us had imagined. My wife Mary had come to Heathrow with me, but the news of my father's visit had come so unexpectedly that our daughters Helena and Caryl were still abroad. As I waited for him, the memories came flooding back.

I could see myself at home, growing up with my family. Then my father was being imprisoned in a Polish jail, my uncle Roman was sentenced to hard labour in the Siberian labour camps, my cousin Wasyl, a student at the university, was condemned by Russian commissars to five years of hard labour in the Urals, merely for being a Ukrainian patriot. I remembered the accounts of my mother dying of a broken heart because her only son had been taken away from her, and then I remembered escaping from the Red Army so that I wouldn't have to go to fight Japan for Father Stalin and his glorious motherland.

But my own memories of my mother were the most poignant, especially the moment of separation in 1942. She held me closely and as she stroked my head I could feel her heavy breathing, her emotion and her deep pain as the time approached for me to go. She was devastated. My sister Lywosi was at my mother's side. She put her hand on my shoulder and said tearfully, 'Don't forget to write, *Bratchyku* (my little brother). I'll pray to God to take good care of you and bless you wherever you may be.'

I was almost overcome by the flood of memories, but still I concentrated on the entrance through which my father would come. 'Will he look out for me?' I wondered, 'Will he recognize me, if only a little? Will he be as I remember him, tall, straight, well-built, with a friendly face, or will he look quite different? What clothes will he be wearing? Will he smile when I get close to him, and what will be his first words to me? Are his legs all right? Can he walk just a little? Please God, yes!'

At last an airport official came out and my father was with him in the wheelchair. I wanted to run to him and embrace him, as I used to do when I was a little child at home, so that he would lift me up and say, 'How is my little kozak?' As it was, I moved quickly forward, with the bouquet of flowers in my hand. I was still feeling very shocked, very emotional. I went down on one knee, almost breaking down, so deep were my feelings and sorrow.

'My dearest Father, this is your son Stefan,' I said. 'I thank God that you have arrived. And this is my wife, Mary.'

His first words to me were, '*Oh Synku, mij Synku, Oh mij Bohze*'. (Oh son, my son, oh my God.)

He had a hat on his head, a brown Homburg, a heavy overcoat and a very small case. I noticed at once that he was heavily sedated, possibly drugged, and that he smelt strongly of something like mothballs or iodine. The smell lasted for several days and brought back unpleasant memories of the time when I and my fellow slave labourers had been deloused by the Nazis. At least, by 1984, my father had been released from working in the forests because he was considered to be too old for useful labour. But even those memories of tyranny couldn't spoil our reunion. It was like meeting up in paradise, where the fear of interrogation by the brutal KGB could no longer touch us.

We drove straight back to Cardiff from Heathrow Airport but instead of going to bed we stayed up talking until about half past three in the morning. My father had brought a bottle of vodka with him to celebrate his arrival although we were so busy swapping stories and filling in all the gaps that we never opened it. As my father said, 'Between us we have a total of eighty-four years to talk about, and only a month to do it in ... that is a lot of talking and a lot of catching up to do!'

One of my first tasks was to arrange for my father to see a doctor. He had a stomach problem and had also been prescribed medication for back pain and headaches. On top of that urinating was very painful for him. But he was well enough to go sightseeing and he was also enjoying the novelty of living in a British home – an unimaginable contrast to his one-room shed in Siberia which had previously been used to house a tractor. Our central heating system and flush toilets were a welcome and endless source of fascination for him.

He was puzzled at first when he saw our lounge and kitchen and wanted to know where we slept. I explained that we had bedrooms upstairs, at which he commented, 'Why do you want to be a Member of Parliament as well, when you have a house as nice as this?'

Welsh food was also hugely appreciated and on his first day with us he enjoyed a full cooked breakfast. He grew to love fish and chips, while Welsh soup (*cawl*) and Welsh lamb also became favourites. These everyday features were obviously a novelty to him but I knew that there were other things which would also be totally alien to him. Although he understood the meaning of the words 'freedom' and 'democracy', my father had no personal experience of them in practice. As I told one journalist earlier, 'I'm sure he's unaware of the fact that there are no queues here for bread, for meat or for vegetables'. Soon he made a joke of this, saying that in Wales we had queues of journalists looking for interviews instead of queues of shoppers waiting for food to arrive. There was an atmosphere of mutual fascination between him and the journalists and the *South Wales Echo* cartoonist Gren amused him enormously by drawing a picture of me saying to him, 'I really don't like to bring it up Dad, but all those years – the pocket money.'

During the happy but painfully short period that he was with us I quickly came to learn of his life in Siberia and the hardship which he had suffered. He had been classified as a 'people's leader', and was allocated work in the forest which was one of the hardest jobs in that particular sector. The sides of the hills on which the forests grew were as steep as walls. He used to search for certain trees in the forest which had nutritional properties in their roots so that he could supplement the household rations. The work would involve cutting the trees down into logs which would then be trimmed and thrown into the river so that they floated down to the sawmills.

"I really don't like to bring it up Dad, but all those years . . . the pocket money"

South Wales Echo.

Fifty or more women would be working on the river with axes in their hands. Their feet were generally wrapped in rags as they walked on top of the floating logs and they would steer the logs with their axes so that a raft would build up on the way down to the mills. Many women would fall into the icy water and within a few minutes they would be dead. There were no safety measures and there was no supervision when an accident took place. They just had to fend for themselves and if they died they were regarded as just another statistic and another lorry load of women would be brought in to take their place.

This murderous system was the norm year in, year out. Stalin only had to flick his fingers and thousands of slave labourers, sometimes whole families, would be transported from Ukraine, Poland, Hungary, Estonia, Latvia, Lithuania, Romania and East Germany to satisfy the hunger for human labour in places like Siberia. This cargo of human misery, involving hundreds of thousands of Ukrainians alone, needed constant replenishment because so many disappeared without trace into the frozen rivers or under falling tree trunks. Stalin's purge was at its worst between 1950 and 1952, the time when my father and my sister were first caught up in it.

When they arrived in Siberia, they had to join up to seventy-five other families in long single barrack blocks. There were no toilets, no kitchens, no bathrooms or showers and only one or two cast iron stoves. To relieve themselves they had to go to one end of the building where rows of buckets were shielded by ragged curtains. The slopping out would be done on a rotational basis. Each family would be put into groups to cook soup which generally consisted of little more than potatoes, or dried vegetables such as beans or peas, or sweet corn. There was rarely any meat. The cooking was done in a bucket-like utensil and the soup had to last for several days before more vegetables were found. The only other ingredient in the diet was bread from the camp store. Life expectancy was very low, suicide was common. It was easy to kill yourself, according to my father; all you had to do was sit outside the camp for twenty minutes in the winter and turn into a block of ice. Old people who were no longer able to work but who weren't disposed to kill themselves were often forcibly taken outside the barracks by the camp guards to suffer the same fate.

My father and other people in the camp would watch out for bears during the winter, because they would come into the nearby cemeteries and dig up the corpses with their strong claws and drag them away for food. The graves were very shallow because the ground was frozen at a depth of more than one metre. But the men from the camps would also hunt bears for meat and for the skins. They made excellent coats for the winter, my father said, and the meat had a sweet flavour to it.

My father, not surprisingly, grew tired of living in the barracks and that's why he moved to the tractor shed. He suggested to the camp commandant that there was no reason why he and my sister shouldn't move into the building and after a few months the commandant reluctantly agreed. He became the first house owner or ' capitalist' in the camp! To make the building more habitable he built wooden partitions inside and put windows in.

On one occasion, because my father was the recognized leader of the people in the camp and consequently regarded by the camp commandant and his apparatchiks as an agitator and a trouble-maker, a plot was hatched to get rid of him. They clearly felt that once they had done that they could then persuade the internees in the camp to replace him with someone who was more acceptable and more compliant. A huge *maszyna* or lorry was being prepared to transport fifty men, including my father, up to the forest where they were working. The driver, who was one of the commandant's henchmen, was part of the plot. He was instructed to drive very close to the river's edge, turn the wheel just at the last moment so that the truck was facing the direction of the water, and then jump clear. The lorry would hurtle into the water and all the passengers, including my father, would be trapped under a tarpaulin and left to their fate. Even if they didn't drown the freezing water would kill them in minutes. There would be no survivors. This planned execution was delayed for several days because, despite the cold wind and snowy weather, it still needed to be icy enough to provide the driver with excuses for what was about to happen. The weather just wasn't bad enough yet. It was the delay which saved the men. As the days went by the driver started to turn it all over in his mind. As a family man himself he realized that if he carried out the plan he would live with a guilty conscience for the rest of his life. He was also worried that his secret might escape – that he might blurt out in a drinking session that he had driven fifty men to their death – and he himself would be killed in revenge.

After a day or so the driver arranged to meet my father secretly in the cemetery near the camp. They chose a moment when it was snowing slightly so that their clothes would be indistinguishable and their faces would be disguised under their *kuchma* or hats. People would think they were just workmen tidying up the graves.

The driver then confessed to my father that he had agreed to take part in a plot to drown him and the rest of the men but had now changed his mind because he felt his own family and God would never forgive him for committing such a crime. So when the day came to go to the forest he wanted my father to get the men out of the truck the moment he started to drive along the riverbank. He would drive very slowly to help them jump out and would then turn the steering wheel towards the river, by which time the men would be clear of the lorry. My father crossed himself, hugged the driver and told him that he would have fifty men and their families thanking him from the bottom of their hearts and praying for his soul. He promised him that the men would rather be tortured than tell the authorities what had really happened.

Finally the fateful day arrived and the decision was taken to make the journey. The weather had become bad enough and the snow was so thick that the men could only see a short distance ahead. It all went according to plan and all the men survived the 'accident'. But nobody knew what had happened to the driver. When my father and the men got back to the camp they were asked about him. They revealed that the weather had been so atrocious that they hadn't been able to see anything through the snow. My father, when I asked him, said that they didn't know to this day what had happened to the poor driver. He was one of the best drivers from their point of view and they had got to know him well because of the frequent trips to the forest. They could only assume that he hadn't been able to get out of his cab. My father and the rest of the men prayed for his soul, and although they had escaped themselves, they were nevertheless shocked by the tragedy.

This incident represented only the tip of the iceberg as far as organized brutality and wholesale state sponsored murder by the Communist regime was concerned. The scale and complexity of the labour camp system in the Soviet Union is still not fully appreciated by the vast majority of people in the West. The truth was that the Russian Empire was made up of a string of slave colonies despite the claim that each republic in the USSR was an independent and sovereign country. The Soviet economy relied heavily on free labour and many of the prisoners were genuine criminals. But the system wouldn't have worked without millions of other people in the satellite states being arrested for political reasons on trumped up charges. To this day many of those people still don't know why they were imprisoned or what crimes they were supposed to have committed.

The scale of misery is impossible to describe in a few short paragraphs. Prisoners would be arrested and deported immediately without the slightest chance of telling their families what had happened to them. They would immediately lose all their rights and would be interrogated by the KGB, often in the most brutal and degrading way imaginable. The interrogators would threaten the prisoner's family, or persuade mothers or wives to provide them with the necessary details. They knew how to intimidate prisoners physically and psychologically, threatening them with beatings and making them listen to the terrible sounds which came from other cells. They would be put into solitary confinement, deprived of sleep, or they would be watched constantly through peepholes. Sometimes they would never get round to interrogating the prisoner; over the weeks and months they would break him down until he felt totally abandoned; a worthless object. And all the time he might be waiting for an interrogation which never came. This would be followed by a show trial. The KGB never really had to prove whether a man was guilty or not. As long as they were able to find somebody who was prepared to bring charges against the prisoner, that was enough. All they needed to do was provide some evidence, however spurious, of anti-state sentiments.

Once all that had finished, the next ghastly stage would begin. The prisoner would be sent from the investigation camp to a transportation centre where he would share a communal wooden bed with all sorts of prisoners, possibly for months. The prisoner would have no idea where he was being sent, and this often meant that he had no suitable clothing, particularly if he had been arrested in the summer and was going on to a much colder region. Once he had arrived he would have to rely on clothes from camp stores – clothes which were dirty and ill-fitting and which were frequently taken from the dead bodies of prisoners. Transportation was another source of misery. In some cases forty prisoners would be crushed into closed trucks or *voronki* designed to take no more than twelve passengers. Dangerous or awkward prisoners would be forced into metal boxes where they would sit with their knees up under the chin, gasping for air. Sometimes exhaust fumes would leak into the trucks, turning them into mobile gas chambers and the prisoners would have to be dragged out fainting or unconscious. The trucks displayed signs suggesting that they were carrying bread, meat, or ice cream rather than human cargo; most of the passengers would have given a right arm for such luxuries! As it was they were fed on dried bread and salted herrings, and the single mug of water which they were given twice a day did little to satisfy their inescapable thirst. The toilet facilities were equally unbearable, another form of sheer torture. The prisoners were only allowed to go twice a day and there was no paper or water. They frequently starved themselves deliberately to avoid having to go to the toilet.

There were other forms of transport as well, all of them equally unpleasant. Barges, ships, and trains all had prison holds. Cattle vans had communal wooden beds where prisoners would sit doubled up on planks. They at least had openings in the floor which could be used as toilets. Even aircraft were used.

Male prisoners suffered every imaginable kind of bad treatment; sleep deprivation, beatings, body shaving, starvation, exposure to the cold, deliberate humiliation and the ever-present fear of premature death. With their constant interrogations the KGB had ways of turning prisoners against each other, of isolating them. And they had ways of making prisoners confess to crimes they hadn't committed in the belief that they would be protecting their families and friends. In reality these confessions often led to the KGB convincing the others that they had been betrayed by the prisoner. The women prisoners suffered all of that and a lot more. Guards would be constantly forcing them to have sex, whenever they were alone with them. Criminal prisoners would bribe the guards to allow them to do the same. And even if they weren't subjected to that, the women suffered from constant rudeness and humiliation and the general hardship was much keener for them than it was for the men.

The nomenklatura – the unelected bureaucrats – had a huge range of choices when it came to deciding where to send the prisoners. There was a whole network of slave camps including places like Kuibyshev, Volgograd, Yaroslavi, Tselinograd, Krasnoyarsk, Novosibirsk, Omsk, Irkutsk, Chita and many, many more. Oil was one industry which depended on slave labour and hundreds of prisoners died from overwork and disease every day. The need for oil, which had to be extracted, transported and refined meant that camps were set up all over the Soviet Empire. Prisoners were in danger from the cold in Siberia and from malaria in places like the Lenkaran swamp on the Caspian Sea, where ordinary civilians refused to live. They also worked in nuclear weapons plants and ammunition factories where they were equally at risk from radioactive materials and explosives. The need for minerals meant that prisoners were sent beyond the Arctic Circle where they mined nickel, chromium, diamonds, gold and coal. The camps, for many hundreds of thousands of people, were little more than death camps where their bodies were buried in unmarked graves once they had served their purpose. The Soviet Empire, like the Nazis, managed to create a hell on earth.

Chapter 23

1984-1985
Returning Home

When my father was with me in Cardiff, he could walk with the aid of a stick but it was easier for him to go sightseeing in a wheelchair. I took him to Marks and Spencer in Cardiff to buy some thermal underwear to keep him warm when he returned to Siberia. While we were out he was quickly recognized and greeted by many of the shoppers who had seen the story of our reunion in the newspapers or on television. He shook hands with them, kissing the hands of the ladies, much to their delight. When the shopping was done we returned home and my father asked me if there were more stores like that in this country. I assured him that there were thousands of them, catering for just about every need. I told him that they were all run by private enterprise and not by the state. He was clearly deeply impressed and replied, 'You know *mij synku* – my son – I have been thinking about that store. One can walk into it hungry, bare footed, naked and thirsty, and buy very beautiful clothes, food, footwear and enough wine to get drunk on and walk out a gentleman – all under one roof! It's a miracle!'

Later I took him to the seashore near Cardiff and we also visited Caerphilly Castle, where we bought samples of the famous cheese. When I asked him if he had enjoyed what he had seen, he said simply, 'How can you not like it?'

I also decided to take him to London to visit the Houses of Parliament and this was undoubtedly going to be one of the highlights for him; a very special occasion. He wanted to see where I worked, and to see Churchill's statue – the man he had admired for so many years. The night before we left for London he said, 'Stefan, *synku*, I have seen you and your family, I have seen Cardiff, and tomorrow I will see the Houses of Parliament. Now my life is complete and I don't mind if I die there.'

I teasingly told him that there was no record in the parliamentary archives to show that a Ukrainian who had been a slave labourer in Siberia, had come to visit his son and died in the British Parliament. He looked at me, in a happy and contented way and said, 'Why can't I be the first?' Fortunately our visit had no such outcome. My father had reason to be particularly grateful to at least one member of the House of Commons; without Sir Geoffrey Howe's intervention he could never have left Siberia and nor would I have ever seen my father again. As he told one journalist, 'If the opportunity presents itself, it would be an honour and a privilege to meet Sir Geoffrey to thank him for what he has done. The man is God-sent. He didn't get any medals by helping me and my son. He must have spoken from the heart.'

Not surprisingly the story of our reunion attracted a great deal of media attention from all round the world. I was constantly interpreting for him since he spoke no English. When he first arrived at Heathrow a reporter asked him, through me, how he felt now that he was in England. 'Coming to Britain is like coming from the grave,' my father said. 'If someone offered me the chance to live for another twenty years, I would choose instead to live only one year, if I could only go and see my son.'

Once he had seen something of Britain he began to appreciate the country for its own sake, rather than seeing it merely as the place where his son had found a home and a good life. He sometimes felt that the people of Britain didn't realize how lucky they were. They inhabited a completely different world from the one that he'd known in Siberia.

My father's visit coincided with the miners' strike, and as he watched colour television for the first time, he saw pictures of the riots on the picket lines. As a former trade union activist, he watched with interest as Arthur Scargill addressed the striking miners. He amused me with the comment that the miners' leader's performance had something of the style of Goebbels about it. Then he turned to me and said, 'Stefan, now that you are a member of the British Parliament you can do anything you like.' Sensing a touch of humour in the question, I said cautiously, 'Not quite, father, I can't do what I like just yet. It's a bit too soon! But what's on your mind ?'

'Couldn't you arrange it so that Mr Scargill is sent to take my place in Siberia, and I could take his place in Britain ? Because I would soon get those miners back to work. I would give them a choice – either to go back to work here in Britain, or go to work in Siberia.'

'If I could arrange for Mr Scargill to take your place in Siberia,' I told him, 'I wouldn't wait until tomorrow – I'd do it today.'

The Conservative Party conference that year was being held in Brighton in the second week of October. On that occasion I did not attend the conference, but stayed at home with my father, to make the most of his twenty-eight days of freedom. He watched the television reports from Brighton and was particularly interested in Mrs Thatcher, the Prime Minister. I told him as much as I could about her background, and about her work so far. He listened very attentively to what I was saying, then, after some thought, he said, 'I like that lady and I like what you have told me about her. If she was to come to Siberia, the snow would melt and we would jump for joy, like newly born lambs in the spring.'

That year the conference turned to tragedy when terrorists planted a bomb in the Grand Hotel, killing five people and injuring many others. My father watched the news reports, then turned to me and said, 'The trouble with you British is that you think it could never happen here.' I had to agree with him. Evil can be made to disappear underground, but it is impossible to eradicate.

Sadly the twenty-eight days on my father's exit visa were about to expire and it would be time for him to return to Siberia. He had to board a plane to Moscow and from there he would be flown back to Irkutsk, near Lake Baikal. I was heartbroken that he had to go back, and I wished that things had been different. But my sister and her family were still in Siberia, as were other relatives, and he didn't want to create trouble for them. In fact, knowing how outspoken my father could be on politics and human rights, particularly on democracy and freedom for Ukraine, I took great care during his visit to protect him from any questions which, if answered candidly, might cause serious difficulties for the Terlezkis in the Russian Empire. My father was a man of great honour. The terms of agreement for his visit were that he would come to Britain for just one month, and he had every intention of honouring that agreement. At least his mind was at rest that his son was not only still alive, but had also found freedom and success in his life under the British democratic system. To the journalists who came to see him before he left Cardiff, he said, 'For forty-two years I was longing to see my son Stefan. Now I am happy and satisfied. I have new thoughts, new wonderfully happy memories, and even a new skin on my body!'

He was still in Cardiff on 29 October for my fifty-seventh birthday and, for the first time, I received a birthday card from my father. Then, on 30 October Mary, Helena and I drove him to Heathrow where we had our final hour with him in a departure lounge. When the time came for us to say goodbye and for my father to be taken to the aircraft, the journalists and television crews were waiting. I felt that my insides were being torn apart. That sort of experience must be the most painful and damaging that any human being can be asked to endure.

The mechanical crane was waiting to lift up the wheelchair with my father in it, and drive him to the waiting aircraft. We embraced him for the last time. He lifted up his head and said sadly, '*Mij synku* (my son), my life is complete and if I die tomorrow, it would not worry me.' Even the journalists looked sad for us. They had families and parents too. They asked me if I thought I would see my father again. A lump in my throat was choking me and I could not stop my lips from trembling. Pushing the wheelchair with one hand, with my other hand on my father's head, I replied through quivering lips, I would love to say yes, but I feel in my heart and my bones that it will not be so.'

One reporter asked me what I intended to do next. 'I've written to Mr Gromyko. We are grateful to him for helping us to have this time together. Now I want him to get my father transferred from Siberia, back to our home village in Ukraine. There I hope my father can spend the rest of his life in peace, and die there, and be buried next to my mother. I know he's not well enough physically to come over again, even if he was allowed to do so. I'll also apply for permission to go and visit him in Antoniwka myself. Hopefully, if all goes well, he'll already be there when I arrive.' In fact, when my father reached Moscow the KGB were waiting for him. He was taken straight to Antoniwka and simply ordered out of the car at my uncle's house.

My father's visit had been a time of incredible happiness for both of us – a miracle no less. It had been an experience which I found impossible at the time to describe in words. I could only treasure it privately, deep inside me. I knew how fortunate I was that he had been allowed to come to Wales and I was eternally grateful for that. And I hardly dared hope that I would see him again. I remembered Mikhail Gorbachev's suggestion that I should visit 'Beautiful Ukraine and the Carpathians' as he put it. But I was very wary. I might be allowed into Ukraine but someone would surely check the records and notice that I had once been 'drafted' into the Russian Red army and had become an officer before deserting to the West. Would they allow me to leave after that? They might well decide to regard me as a Soviet citizen and a Western spy. There was also another problem. I had been invited to visit my birthplace in Ukraine as well as Siberia, and I was aware that SS20 missiles were sited not far away from my village, and that other parts of Ukraine were also 'no-go' areas. I put these points to Major General Rogov, who was in charge of security during Gorbachev's visit, but he refused to confirm or deny what I had told him. I considered these matters very carefully and wondered whether it might be prudent to take a journalist or a fellow MP with me for insurance if my family and I did go to Siberia and Ukraine.

In the end I decided, for the time being at any rate, that it would be unwise to go ahead and plan a visit to Antoniwka, where my father was now living once again. Then fate took over. Just before Christmas that year I heard that he was in hospital, but had then recovered. At the beginning of March 1986, just over a year later, there was a telegram from my Aunt Ustyna in Antoniwka, saying that he was seriously ill and was not expected to survive. At once I began to arrange visas so that we - Mary, Helena, Caryl and myself – could all go to my home village for what might well be our last meeting with him. On the following Monday I was on a Parliamentary delegation in Holland where we were gathering evidence about tourism. Another telegram arrived in Cardiff from my aunt to say that my father had died. Mary telephoned me and I left the delegation in a state of distress and flew back to Cardiff immediately. I was comforted by my family and by messages from my parliamentary colleagues. I received a particularly warm letter from Margaret Thatcher.

10 DOWNING STREET

THE PRIME MINISTER

19th March, 1986

Dear Stefan,

I was deeply saddened to learn of your father's death, on the eve of your visit to the Ukraine to see him. I understand that your visit is still going ahead and I am glad at least that you will be able to take part in the family funeral.

Your father certainly attained a ripe old age and caught the imagination of everyone in Britain - as well as more widely - and lifted up our hearts when he was able to visit you here last year.

Please extend my deepest condolences to your family and other relatives, whether at home or in the Ukraine.

Yours ever

Margaret

Stefan Terlezki Esq MP

My priority now was to go out to Ukraine, and to my village, in time for his funeral. I asked my aunt to postpone the funeral for as long as possible. Even if I obtained the visas in time we would have to fly firstly to Moscow where we would have to spend the night, before finally reaching western Ukraine by train. It was now Saturday and knowing how slow the train service was, it meant that we wouldn't be able to get there until the following Wednesday at least. In 1942 I had been prevented by the Nazis from going to my mother's bedside when she was dying of a broken heart because of my enslavement in Austria. I was also denied the right to go to her funeral. Now the process seemed to be repeating itself, as I told our local daily newspaper in Wales, 'I wanted to be by my father's side but I have been unable to be there.' Now I wanted to see my father buried near my mother in the village cemetery but just like the Nazis, the Stalinist KGB made sure that I could not attend my father's funeral.

Eventually, however, the visa came through, and the journey was made. As I feared though, it was too late for the funeral. My relatives welcomed me with overwhelming warmth and love however, and greeted me with 'flowers and tears', as one newspaper put it. I was reunited with two uncles, two aunts, numerous cousins and second cousins, and countless childhood school friends. My relatives were able to show me photographs of my father's funeral and I also visited my parents' graves where the evidence of my father's recent interment, with the bare earth and mountains of flowers, was painfully obvious. My arrival in Antoniwka after forty-two years was inevitably a deeply emotional experience for me. I visited my village school, and the head teacher Marijka composed a song in my honour which the children sang, accompanied by another teacher on the accordion. Their singing was utterly beautiful and I was particularly touched by the way their eyes were constantly focussed on my face.

Home Coming Song

I came home to my village,
The meadows they greeted me
As if summer had never even been,
The grasses were heavy with dew.

Refrain:
I recalled those childhood years
Walking barefoot to school,
And mother's fervent love
Which shall never be forgotten

I stood on my own doorstep
And mother fell into my arms
'You just couldn't forget your home,
I just knew, my son, I just knew.'

Refrain:
I recalled those childhood years...

O village, my dear village,
It's time to say goodbye.
Let fortune be my destiny,
As I bid you goodness and plenty.

I took Mary and the girls to find the house where I grew up but it was in ruins. Now all I could see as I looked around the roofless remains was a knee-deep infestation of weeds. The kitchen garden which was once full of sweetcorn, potatoes, tomatoes, horseradish, onions, garlic, lettuce, carrots, peas, beans, caraway plants and poppies had vanished, along with the orchard and its plum, apple and pear trees. I could no longer smell the beautiful multi-coloured flowers, heavy with scent, which I had so often picked for my mother. The lily of the valley had been – and still is – one of my special favourites. It was a heartbreaking experience. I was dejected and disenchanted to feel that my family home was now just a tragic memory. I tried hard to keep my feelings under control and stay calm, kept telling myself that although such tragic memories can never be erased happiness can still be found and I should consider myself very lucky.

My overriding impression was that the village I left in 1942 was nothing like the present village. Instead of the beautiful and well cared for homes I remembered, everywhere was shabby and neglected. The thatched houses were long gone. The villagers were only allowed bottled gas in the winter months and although there was now electricity in many of the homes it was very low voltage. I noticed that most houses had a radio but I soon discovered they could only be switched between two channels – one for weather forecasts and one for political propaganda. Day and night there was the same monotonous repetition from the government, but my friends and relatives only tuned in briefly in the morning and kept it switched off in the evening. So much for progress and for the workers' paradise, which they were all now supposed to be enjoying!

My village homecoming was a bitter-sweet occasion; desperately sad because of my father's death, but softened by the kindness of my relatives and friends. The official reception by representatives of the Russian empire was both oppressive and at times farcical. We were met at Ivano-Frankiwsk railway station by Halyna Lykhachova, described by the local newspaper as the Deputy Chairperson of the Executive Committee of the Ivano-Frankiwsk Regional Soviet of People's Deputies. The old phraseology was just the same as I remembered it when I was last in Ukraine! As we climbed into his car we had no idea whether our guide was a KGB apparatchik, a Communist administrator, or indeed both.

As soon as we arrived at the Hotel Ukraine in Ivano-Frankiwsk we registered and started to unpack, thinking that we were going to have a quiet hour or so to ourselves. We were wrong. Within a matter of minutes two men burst into our room uninvited and introduced themselves as journalists from Moscow and Kyiv (Kiev). I was furious at their arrogance and audacity but I had withstood Nazi interrogation and I could certainly beat them at their own game. They wanted me to praise Ivano-Frankiwsk's new buildings, the blocks of flats with their communal kitchens and bathrooms. I replied that we had far better facilities in British homes. I was a British Member of Parliament and I defended Queen and Country! Later I had a less combative interview with a local journalist from Ivano-Frankiwsk. He had at least requested it and behaved with some decorum.

We seemed to be under constant supervision; secret agents in the hotel were watching our movements around the clock. In the corridor outside our bedroom an old babushka was sitting at her desk, keeping an eye, no doubt, on everybody who came into our room, and checking the time when they came out. My friends, and friends of my father who had been in Siberia with him, were not allowed into our bedroom. And while Helena and Caryl were in their room they were being constantly telephoned and questioned by journalists. I insisted that I was the only one who would answer questions. I knew that the journalists would have been accredited by the KGB.

They then arranged a press conference for me in the hotel restaurant. As Mary and I walked in the journalists said that they would ask me twenty or thirty questions, and that I only needed to answer by saying 'yes' or 'no'. I immediately objected to this bizarre procedure, but they insisted that was all they needed. I reminded them that I had learnt my politics in Britain, not Moscow, and when they persisted I sent them packing. I told them to get lost, told Mary we were leaving and brought the press conference to an abrupt halt.

But there were good moments as well. We were taken to a number of towns and villages in the region, including Yaremcha, a famous skiing resort in the Carpathians. The mountains were still as romantic and majestic as they were in my boyhood. I was given the opportunity to speak on a number of occasions about international relationships. The only problem was that the government controlled press invariably put their own spin on it. I was portrayed as the prodigal son who had returned home and was now overwhelmingly impressed by the way life and services for the inhabitants of my village, and everywhere else, had been improved by the benevolent Communist government. Would that it had been so; it was a total distortion of the truth.

During the visit the behaviour and attitudes of some of the officials who had been allocated to us became increasingly eccentric. One regional official told me that he knew for a fact that each British soldier carried a nuclear rocket which he could fire at will if he felt it was necessary. I had to explain to him that it was an absurd suggestion and that he was simply a victim of Moscow's deliberate propaganda. No soldier in the West carried nuclear missiles individually, and only the Prime Minister or the President had the power to order a nuclear attack. I described the elaborate security measures under which two keys held by two separate guards had to be used to open the rocket silos.

Throughout our stay the authorities wanted us to travel in two separate chauffeur driven cars – one for Mary and me, the other for our daughters. I will always remember eating in the restaurant *Vekhovyna* in the Carpathians where we were the only diners. No other guests had been allowed in. Another example of stage management was in Ivano-Frankiwsk when a special play was put on for us which described the way in which the peasants had suffered under the landlords – the kulaks – during the First World War. It was a heavy-handed piece of propaganda, deliberately orchestrated for us.

At the end of our visit we made our way back to Moscow, before flying on to London. We spent the night at the Intourist hotel in Moscow and were once again provided with cars to take us to the airport. We were five suitcases lighter than when we had arrived, having left most of the contents as presents in Antoniwka. They were worth a small fortune to my relatives. The big question now was whether my mind would be similarly unburdened while we were still on Russian soil. When we were at the airport and all the red tape formalities had been completed, I was still very uneasy. Even though I'd had reassurances at the highest level that my status as the first Ukrainian born member of the British Parliament would protect me, I still found it difficult to relax. I couldn't help thinking that it was just possible, just conceivable, that a KGB official might suddenly tap me on the shoulder. He would tell me that while my family would be allowed to fly home to Britain, I would have to stay behind and take another flight the following day. I imagined that flight, rather than being destined for London, would take me far away to Siberia. In that godforsaken hell on earth, I would take my father's place in a slave labour camp. Fortunately the Almighty was watching over me and my family.

When our flight was eventually called, Mary made her way towards the tunnel in the direction of our plane. She held her passport in the air and asked the stewardess at the entrance of the plane to reassure her that it was a British aircraft. The stewardess smilingly confirmed that it was. I in turn was relieved because I had never told my family about my own fears for our safety. I was determined to spare them the burden of knowing about my anxieties until we'd reached Wales, the land of beauty and song and wonderful people. I would be able to start my duties again as a member of the Mother of Parliaments, the cradle of democracy. I immediately summoned the head steward and ordered a bottle of champagne to celebrate our safe exit from the evil Russian Empire. He brought a bottle and four large glasses and smiled broadly when he served us, as if to say 'you have nothing to fear now'. We were soon drinking toasts accompanied by cries of 'Rule Britannia', 'London here we come', 'Home to Wales' and so on. The flight and the subsequent landing were the sweetest and softest I had ever experienced in my life.

Chapter 24

1985-2005
Freedom

S adly, there was one relative who had been unable to make the journey from Siberia to Antoniwka, my precious sister, Lywosi. We were not just torn apart by Hitler but kept apart by Stalin and his successors. There was to be no joyous reunion and she died young, not long after my father. She ended her days working as a night watchman at a state garage.

When my daughters were growing up, our happiness as a family used to remind me of my own childhood with Lywosi. I was determined that they would not be denied the life chances that had been snatched away from us. My own education had been cut short by the Nazis but my girls were going to get the best schooling possible. Education is like a treasure and once acquired, it will never leave you. Helena's sporting prowess won her a place at Millfield School in Somerset and Caryl went to Sidcot School in the same county. Unlike the aunt they never met, both Helena and Caryl had the freedom to pursue the careers of their choice wherever they wanted. Helena is now a much admired and sought after art restorer in Boston in the United States; Caryl is an interior designer and architect on the island of St Maarten in the Caribbean.

I am a very proud father, who cheered on Helena when she played netball for Somerset and applauded Caryl when she took a leading role in *Under Milk Wood* at Sidcot. They are *Moyi Zoloti Ruzi* – May's Golden Roses, the two most beautiful and loving daughters in the world. I rejoice at their success but I feel nothing but anger and sorrow at Lywosi's fate. I can only take the coldest of comfort from the fact that the Soviet political system, which so cruelly diminished her life, barely outlasted her.

The evil Russian Empire that was the Soviet Union finally collapsed at the end of 1991, after every single part of Ukraine had voted to leave the USSR. The Russian president, Boris Yeltsin, could hardly believe it when he was told that even largely Russian speaking districts, in the east of the country, wanted to be part of a free Ukraine. Of course, there had never been any doubt that the people of western Ukraine would vote overwhelmingly to rid themselves of Russian rule. But Yeltsin joined President Kravchuk of Ukraine in deciding that Mikhail Gorbachev must be told that the end had come.

Not that Moscow was reconciled to Ukrainian independence and the country's first years of freedom have been difficult ones. President Kravchuk was succeeded by Leonid Kuchma, a corrupt and pro-Russian leader who did much damage to Ukraine's reputation. It was thirteen long years after independence that democracy finally triumphed when Viktor Yushchenko won the Presidential Election on 26 December 2004. His Orange Revolution was a victory for Ukraine and for freedom and democracy. Forty-eight million people were determined to choose their own destiny.

The Russians had tried to divide Ukraine and they distorted the truth by claiming that Crimea had been a gift to Ukraine from Khrushchev. In fact legal documents prove that the transfer to Ukraine was agreed by the highest court in the USSR. Knowing the Communist outlook and methods, I was not at all surprised that President Putin, a KGB operative in East Germany during the Cold War, blatantly interfered in the internal affairs of free and independent Ukraine two days before the election, when he visited Kyiv to influence voters to support his favourite comrade and Presidential candidate, Viktor Yanukovych.

Putin's candidate was prepared to surrender Ukraine into Russia's orbit, so that Putin could recreate a Russian Empire by forging an alliance with Ukraine, Belarus and Kazakhstan. Ultimate power would rest with Moscow.

It is obvious that Moscow has not changed its Stalinist dogma of intrusion and interference in other countries' affairs. Putin failed to grasp the depth of Ukraine's commitment to democracy, to national identity and solidarity and to the God-given right to be free. Ukraine is one of the largest countries in Europe and will now shake off its reputation for authoritarian rule, shady dealings and missed opportunities. It will extend the values of freedom and democracy eastwards, all the way to Vladivostok.

After years of corrupt rule, Ukraine has regained its confidence under Viktor Yushchenko, a former Prime Minster and President of the National Bank. He will set Ukraine free on the path to prosperity and democratic accountability, to membership of the European Union and NATO. Most importantly he will tell President Putin to take his entire Navy out of the Ukrainian Black Sea sooner rather than later.

I became a Yushchenko supporter when we first met in his office in Kyiv. I was impressed not just by his great interest in the European Union, NATO and the World Trade Organization but above all by his overwhelming care, love and concern for Ukraine and its destiny. I realized as I listened to him that he was the man to lead the country.

President Yushchenko's triumph is all the more remarkable because he came so close to being killed. The scandalous attempt to poison him left him disfigured but not disheartened. His opponents' criminal behaviour backfired, uniting millions of Ukrainians in a show of people power in support of his 'Our Ukraine' party.

With icy winds blowing in Independence Square, Viktor Yushchenko told the tens of thousands waving orange banners, 'Our place is in the European Union. We are no longer on the edge of Europe. This was a victory of freedom over tyranny, a victory of law over lawlessness. We have a single aim: a democratic and prosperous Ukraine, not a buffer zone or a testing ground for anyone else.' The Ukrainian people wrote themselves into world history with their peaceful Orange Revolution. There was not a Kalashnikov used in anger; not a shot fired nor a person killed.

It is imperative that the West must now help to consolidate democracy and encourage economic reform in Ukraine. European Union membership should not be postponed and Ukraine should be embraced into the commonwealth of European nations. President Yushchenko deserves that embrace; he held to his heartfelt principles, risked his life and won a popular victory.

I feel deeply that President Yushchenko will establish freedom from oligarchs, freedom from fixed elections, freedom from criminal governments, freedom from corruption and extermination, freedom from external threats, freedom to choose and freedom to live, freedom from unacceptable poverty, and freedom from the dreams of Lenin and Stalin that became nightmares for millions of oppressed people.

Love and respect for one's country is not a crime and I believe that if a nation forgets its past, then it has no future. In 1932-33, 10 million men, women and children starved to death on Stalin's orders. He confiscated farmland and animals and within two years some people had been reduced to cannibalism. This holocaust was the biggest single act of genocide in European history and I ask myself, 'How many world leaders, how many journalists, how many people knew, read or cared about it at that time or since?'

Stalin once said that if one person dies it is a tragedy, if millions die, it is a statistic. When Stalin died, some of his supporters prayed for his soul. I also prayed, to thank God for getting rid of a bloodthirsty monster.

To paraphrase my hero, Churchill, 'Never in the field of human conflict have so many suffered so much for so long'. The Ukrainian people have suffered for centuries but I hope that they will now look to the future with great optimism for economic progress, stability and a better life for themselves, their children and grandchildren.

Today my beloved homeland has its freedom and I visit it as often as I can. I often reflect on the way Ukraine now has a national football team which can take part in the World Cup and which can play against my adopted country of Wales in the Millennium stadium in Cardiff. I can now acknowledge my three flags – the blue and gold representing the sky and cornfields of Ukraine, the Red Dragon of Wales, and the British flag with pride, honour and love.

But despite my many visits, it was 2002 – sixty years after I was taken from my home in 1942 and was sent into slavery in Austria – before I returned to Antoniwka to take part in the special celebrations of Easter, which are the highlight of the Ukrainian religious and social calendar.

The Ukrainian year is made up of one long cycle of holidays, enriched by charming customs and ceremonies, many of them originating from pre-Christian times. Ukrainians have always refused to discard their ancient beliefs and traditions and they have adapted their ancient culture to Christian ideology. A rich blend of pagan and Christian elements has sprung up from all this.

At dawn on Easter Sunday a special Resurrection service is always held with a procession around the church. The most beautiful feature of the service is the joyful heralding of the risen Christ with the singing of the traditional Ukrainian hymn, 'Christ Is Risen'. The whole congregation sings in unison with a growing sense of ecstasy. At the end of the service there are rows and rows of baskets outside the church containing *pysanky* (decorated eggs), *Paska* (special Easter bread) and other delicious home-made delicacies, each covered by richly embroidered tapestries and illuminated by a single candle. The priest blesses each basket in turn and sprinkles holy water liberally in every direction. It's a widely treasured custom and throughout the festivities people greet one another with the words '*Khrystos Voskres*' –'Christ is risen', to which the reply is '*Voistyno Voskres*' – 'He is risen indeed'.

After the service in the church, people return home to an Easter breakfast of boiled eggs, hot and cold meats, salads, roast suckling pig, homemade butter and cheese, salads, fresh horseradish, beetroot relish, bread and delicious pastries. *Horilka* (Ukrainian vodka) helps to wash it all down. I was intrigued to see whether it was still as joyous as it had been in my youth.

I finally got the chance to return at Easter because a camera crew from the television station, HTV Wales, were filming my life story. So it was, with my every move being recorded, that on Easter Sunday morning, with the sun just beginning to rise over the hills around Antoniwka, I was reunited with the people of my village in the church that I had once known so well. To my relief and to my pleasure the ceremonies were unchanged. The choir sang in the way that they had always done, the cheerful young priest carried out his ceremonial duties in the time honoured fashion, the children dressed up in their Sunday best – their Ukrainian national costumes – while their parents brought baskets of food and eggs, decorated in an art style which is unique to Ukraine.

But while these thoughts raced through my head I also remembered that only a few hundred metres away stood a house where I myself had spent a happy boyhood. I recalled so well my parents and my sister Lywosi, carrying the basket full of aromatic, mouth-watering food to the church to be blessed by the priest.

They were idyllic days, but now the house was no more, only a heap of rubble. Curiously, it was the only house in the village to have disappeared in this way. It distressed me that what had been my little world was now so unrecognizable and derelict. Later that day I revisited the site with the television crew, and as I stood and looked around at the desolation I reflected that as well as the missing house, there were no cows or calves, no chickens, ducks or geese, no pigs. The chicken shed and the pigsty had both gone. As I walked into the cowshed, which was at least partly standing, I remembered the cattle and the smell of the farmyard.

Between the site of the house and the dried-up bed of what had once been a sparkling stream I noticed the *jasin* (ash tree) that I had planted at the age of eight or nine. It had then been about one metre high but to me it now seemed more than 100 metres tall. That cheered me immensely. No one could destroy my *jasin* nor had anyone destroyed me. One of my reasons for agreeing to take part in a television programme was to refute the suspicions of people who have refused to believe my story. There are of course plenty of idiots who refuse to accept the brutal truth about Hitler and Stalin, people who refuse accept that Hitler murdered millions of Jews or that Stalin murdered an even greater number of Ukrainians. But some of my lazier political opponents have also found it easy to accuse me of having had some sympathy with the Nazis who, in fact, enslaved me. So in order to put the record straight once and for all, I travelled with the Welsh television crew from Antoniwka to Voitsberg in Austria, where I had been sold as a slave sixty years earlier.

Of course, it was a very different journey. Instead of the misery of the cattle trucks, it was simply a case of changing planes in Frankfurt. A complimentary drink in an airport business lounge is a long way removed from the mouthful of warm water that I had received in Bratislava the last time I had made the journey. Naturally, Voitsberg had changed a lot as well since I had last seen it in 1945 but we found the site of the slave market. I wasn't sorry to find that there was now a shop where the Gestapo headquarters once stood but after all this time, would I be able to find the farm where I had been put to work?

I still had a photograph of Hansel, the farmer who had bought me, in his German Navy uniform. I had taken it with me when I left the farm. I also had a postcard with the address on it. But so much had changed. A new bypass had obliterated the route out of town that I remembered. Still, the farms scattered through the district known as the Kowald had numbers and the postcard told me the number I was looking for.

Television crew in tow, I set out along the new road through the Kowald but at first we could not find the farm. We stopped at a café for coffee and I explained my predicament to the two women who served us. I had no idea how they would react to the idea of an *Ostarbeiter* trying to track down his former owners and in fact they promptly announced that they were calling the police! However, the women quickly explained that there were now fewer farms and they had been completely renumbered when the new road was built; the police would know the farm's new house number.

Once they had the number, the café staff said they would telephone ahead to see if we would be welcome. Within a minute, they told me that Hilde would be delighted to see me. Hilde! Mutti's granddaughter! I remembered her as the girl aged about nine or ten who had at least given me a smile when I was first put to work on the farm. We were there in minutes and with the television crew recording the moment, I rang the doorbell. Hilde had changed of course and so had I. But she said her family had often wondered what had become of me. She was delighted with the photograph of Hansel and grabbed it from me, shouting '*Mein Onkel, Mein Onkel!*' Hilde invited us into the house and although it was much modernized, I soon got my bearings.

Pictures of Mutti and her daughter were proudly displayed in the hallway, as well as Hilde's father, who had spent most of the war with the German Army in Paris. Hansel had survived the war but died in the 1950s and there was even sadder news about his younger brother Toni, who had been kind to me before he was called up into the Army. Hilde showed me into a private room where photographs commemorated Toni's death from the wounds he received on the Eastern Front.

Outside, I looked up at the now glazed window of the attic where I had frozen and I went into the cattle shed to pay my respects to the animals. I had once shared the straw bedding with their predecessors! When I emerged, Hilde produced some *must* – the Austrian cider that I remembered so well. We toasted each other's health, free to be friends at last.

When I look back at all the destruction and all the brutality associated with the Austro-Hungarian, Polish, Russian and Nazi occupations of my homeland, and all the cruelty and sadism inflicted on millions of my people by these ruthless empires, I realize that those tyrants would never have been content until they had destroyed not only the people's homes, towns and cities, but also their human spirit. But successive invaders failed to do that – they were up against an indestructible force possessed by people who were too resilient, too strong to be crushed by evil tyrants. I pray that any attempt to destroy the human spirit will always fail wherever it manifests itself in this God-given world. People must always be granted the right to live and to enjoy freedom.

The individual needs room to think, to speak and act, and to be free to do all these things. Repressive totalitarianism begins by denying all these individual rights and if my life has one central purpose, it is to fight to the last drop of my blood for the right to individual freedom, for you, for me, for every human being everywhere on earth.

Appendix A

Author's Maiden Speech in the House of Commons
3 November 1983

I am grateful to you, Mr Speaker, for allowing me to speak for the first time in the House, with my Anglo-Ukrainian-Welsh accent.

I should like to tell the House something about the constituency of Cardiff, West which I am honoured, proud and privileged to represent. Cardiff, West and its people could perhaps be described as the United Nations on a smaller scale. There are the Welsh, the English, the Scots, the Irish, the Ukrainians, the Poles, the Pakistanis, the Africans, the West Indians, the Indians, the Italians, the Spanish, the Portuguese and people from many other parts of the old and the new Commonwealth. Strong community links have been forged with the ethnic minorities on a very amicable basis, and social, educational and cultural understanding is being promoted. I am proud that Cardiff, West can be looked upon as a model of good relationships between different people, and those people, too, are proud to be British.

I am pleased to say that we have several colleges, high schools, and junior and infant schools, as well as a Church of England school, a Church of Wales school, Roman Catholic schools, nursery schools, and special and private schools. Again, those schools help pupils with different social and religious backgrounds to integrate into society and to be good citizens of Great Britain. There is some light industry in the constituency as well as hospitals, good shopping facilities and Cardiff City football club. Indeed, I was once privileged to be that club's chairman. Of course, there are also rugby clubs and quite a few political and non-political clubs. We also have the BBC and HTV studios in the constituency.

I hope that you will allow me, Mr Speaker, to use two words that have echoed through the House, throughout the land, and over the oceans and hills. They are 'Order, Order'. Those are the words of my predecessor, Mr George Thomas, or 'our George' as he is affectionately known. He is now, of course, Viscount Tonypandy and he certainly deserves that great honour. I have known him for many years, as my wife was born just a few miles up from Tonypandy. He and I have much in common, in relation to not only the Rhondda and Tonypandy, but the broad fabric of the social structure of our society.

Mr Thomas served the people in Cardiff, West exceptionally well for thirty-eight years. Although I have no intention of following in his footsteps to the Speaker's Chair, I should certainly like to follow him in being as good a Member of Parliament for Cardiff, West as he was, and in being as much in touch with the people there as he has been in the past thirty-eight years. He is a great and much-loved man. I greatly respect him, and am very happy to have paid him a great tribute in this great House.

People matter a great deal to me, irrespective of their colour or background. We must all try to help, protect and respect one another, to be good citizens, to respect the law of the land and to be good patriots of this great country. People in many parts of the world have sought for centuries to copy our constitution and laws and so to guarantee their liberties. The antiquity and continuity of our political structure is a marvel to many. As a result of our ancestors' endeavours, our freedom and democracy are now second to none. I was not born with a silver spoon in my mouth, but I have found the silver lining in reaching the Mother of Parliaments, the cradle of freedom and democracy. I am very proud to be here and to speak, knowing very well that I do so in freedom. If my father and my friends in the Ukraine knew that I was standing here and what I was saying, their tears would flow with joy.

The purpose of our foreign policy is to help, as we have done and continue to do, in many parts of the world, materially, culturally, educationally, politically, democratically and in many other ways, when possible. Soviet foreign policy exports Marxist ideology in great quantity – most of the time against the wishes of the people. Its aim is not to introduce freedom and democracy, but to suppress and eradicate them whenever possible. If one looks at where Marxism is preached and practised, one will have no illusion about which foreign policy serves its people best – Soviet or British. I have experienced feudalism, Marxism, Communism, Fascism, Nazism and, at the age of fourteen a slave labour camp. I believe that I can justifiably claim that I know how to appreciate freedom and democracy.

I knew nothing about British foreign policy or Britain's freedom and democracy until we were liberated by the British and Americans in 1945. One may well ask: what about the Russian liberators? They liberated a part of Europe from its freedom, democracy and good living standards and they have put an iron curtain around it. Since 1945 people have been born and lived in open prisons. If people do not believe me, they should write to my friends and my father in Ukraine. If they are allowed to tell us, they will.

British foreign policy protects and defends Britain on all fronts – land, sea and in the air. Let us not be rhetorical and use a sea of words when we talk about defending Britain. Defending Britain means that what our fathers and grandfathers have fought and died for is worth defending and protecting, so that we, our children and our grandchildren will live in freedom without experiencing slavery, tyranny and oppression, as, regrettably, some of us had to.

Communism is not interested in the flourishing of a country, the health and welfare of its people, freedom, political democracy, religion, culture, or its history. Soviet imperialism has oppressed, abused and terrorized nations and has kept many in a political straitjacket in the name of Socialism, Marxism and Leninism.

There are more than 3 million Afghan refugees in Pakistan. Where are the supporters for the Campaign for Nuclear Disarmament and all other do-gooders? Why do they not protest and go to Moscow? Why do they not go to Leningrad, Warsaw, Prague, Budapest and Afghanistan and put their arms around the Russian militarism? We should remember that there are no unilateralists in the Kremlin.

It is not a case of being better red than dead. The option is peace through deterrence and disarmament negotiations. In the Soviet Union a person could be red and dead – and I know it. Ask the Ukrainians, the Poles, Czechoslovakians, Hungarians, Latvians, Estonians, Lithuanians and Afghans the meaning of tyranny, barbarism and oppression, which are so brutally executed by the Soviet Marxist regime. If people in this great country of ours believe that the grass is greener in the Soviet Union, let them go there and find out for themselves.

There are apparatchiks and apologists for the Soviet Union, who would dearly like the Government to disarm the Army, sink the Navy, ditch the Air Force, and the Utopian state would be complete. That will not happen. The vast majority of the British people are too resilient to fall for that. Of course we must negotiate with the Soviets. Let us compromise if need be, but only when the compromise is on equal and realistic terms, without cheating.

The Pope speaks for peace, about multilateral, not unilateral, disarmament and about reduction of nuclear and conventional weapons. Where are the Christians in the CND? Why do they not listen and follow their leader? I do. They are misleading the public, especially the young generation who grew up in peace, protected by military strength. Let us negotiate not only for a reduction of military arsenals, but for their dismantling. Let us negotiate for the zero option. Let the Soviets make ploughs and tractors out of their military hardware so that they can plough the fields, sow the corn and reap the harvest to feed their people.

Mr Andropov said that when it comes to unilateral disarmament the Soviet people are not naive. I say to Mr Andropov that nor are the British. The British spirit of freedom is too strong and too resilient to be crushed by the tanks of tyrants. My regret is that some of the British who were born here take democracy for granted and play directly into the hands of our political enemies.

I am proud to be British and free to speak without fear, to worship God in my own way, to stand up for what I believe to be right and to oppose what I believe to be wrong and to choose who shall govern my country. I pledge to uphold this heritage of freedom for me, Britain, the oppressed nations and all mankind.

Appendix B

Letters following the Maiden Speech

From George Thomas, Lord Tonypandy.

13: 6: 83

My dear Stefan,

Sincere congratulations. You won a marvellous victory, and I wish you every happiness as the MP for my beloved Cardiff West. You will be a good House of Commons man I know, for you have a rich capacity for friendship. The House will love you if you show that you respect and honour its traditions.

I could not wish for a nicer person to whom I hand over the baton of responsibility. We have been good friends ever since we first met.

I am grateful to you for your generous tribute in the moment of your triumph. May God bless you in all that you try to do for our country.

I love the Commons. It has been my life for nearly four decades. I hope that you will find as much joy in serving there, as I did.

Bless you Stefan,
Ever Yours,
George.

P.S. My advice to you: <u>Always obey and support the speaker</u>.
George.

From The Rt. Hon. James Callaghan, MP.

Dear Stefan,

I am very sorry I did not know you were to make your maiden speech or I would have rearranged my engagements to be in the Chamber to listen.

I am sorry I missed it. Congratulations on a forthright statement that showed clearly enough that your first hard experience of Soviet rule is bound to mark you out as an enthusiastic upholder of the democratic way of life and of course I agree.

But I am also glad that despite your own experiences you proclaim the need for negotiation and compromise on a basis of equality. Coming from you that is very important.

Well done and congratulations,

Yours ever,
Jim Callaghan

Appendix C

Author's Ten Minute Rule Bill
24 March 1987

I beg to move, that leave be given to bring in a Bill to provide for the discontinuation of May Day bank holiday and to establish the Sir Winston Churchill National Day on or near to 10th May.

For the past forty-two years, the people of this country have enjoyed freedom and democracy and peace and tranquillity – in contrast to other parts opf the world where fighting and killing never stop, where poverty and slavery still exist and where freedom and democracy are never implemented. I have been privileged to share freedom, peace and democracy with the people of this country for the past thirty-nine years and that is due to the dedication, steadfastness, resilience, patriotism, and great sacrifices that the British people and their great leader, Sir Winston Churchill, made during the last world war. Sir Winston Churchill took Britain and its Allies through the greatest war in history, and Britain won.

When I was a small boy still living in the Ukraine before the Second World War, I remember so well my father telling me that in Britain there was a man called Winston Churchill who liked to smoke cigars and who had great courage, foresight and dedication and the determination of a great fighter, who believed in freedom and would never surrender. My father was right.

Sir Winston Churchill, throughout the Second World War, and for that matter throughout his political life, never gave up. He fought not only for life but for the value of life and the British people came to realize the truth of his loyalty and the bond he formed. They cheered him when he and Britain stood together, but not alone.

I experienced slavery and oppression under Marxism-Communism, and many millions of people still do. I experienced Nazism, having been taught at school that Stalin was my father and later that Hitler was my Führer, when I was a slave. It was political indoctrination that made me think that I would never experience freedom and democracy and even wonder whether such things ever existed.

When I arrived penniless to Britain in 1948, I realized that I had arrived in heaven on earth. I experienced for the first time freedom and democracy, and all that was possible because of a man called Winston Churchill and the resilience of the British people.

This House, the Mother of Parliaments, the cradle of democracy, still carries the scars of the Second World War. Hitler wanted to destroy it, but it was saved by brave men of Britain, and Sir Winston Churchill was one of them. They saved it for us all to speak, to debate, to agree and to disagree and to keep the light of freedom burning. I am further convinced that I would not be here today doing what I do and speaking as I do, nor would there be Right Hon. and Hon. Members of the House had it not been for Sir Winston Churchill who saved Britain from the Nazi holocaust and paved the way for the peace that we have all enjoyed over the past forty-two years.

The purpose of my Bill is to remind the people of this country time and again, the old and the young – especially the young – who do not know or who may have forgotten that, when Britain was in the grip of the iron fist of Nazism and was bombarded indiscriminately, a man called Winston Churchill, with his determination, courage and dedication, together with the British people, made it possible for us all to be free today.

I am not in the habit of creating more public holidays just for the sake of it, nor am I willing to do so. Some people say that we have too many holidays already, and I agree. My reason for seeking to discontinue the first Monday in May as a national holiday and nominating 10 May or as near to it, as Sir Winston Churchill national day is that that is the day when he became Prime Minister of Britain in 1940. Furthermore, it is my heartfelt desire to establish a permanent reminder to the British people, some of whom seem to take freedom and democracy for granted, that had it not been for a man called Winston Churchill who made it possible for them all to live in a free and democratic Britain, the alternative would have been tyranny, slavery, extermination, Auschwitz, Buchenwald, Treblinka, and Babi Yar.

I can almost remember Sir Winston Churchill saying that we had a rendezvous with destiny. Will we keep that rendezvous or spend our sunset years telling our children and grandchildren what it was like when men were free? What will our answers be when we are asked, 'Where were you when freedom was lost?' and, 'What did you find that was more precious to you than freedom?' ?

Nothing must be more precious to us than freedom. It is like fresh air: if one has not got it, one misses it. I know that. That is why I ask the leave of the House to give that Bill its full support and remind the people of this country, the old, the young and the generations still to come, of Sir Winston Churchill, his steadfastness and courageous leadership in the hour of this country's greatest peril. He captured the hearts and imagination of the people and saved Britain from Nazi slavery. In return we should give him a place in British history as the greatest freedom fighter in modern times.

Index

GKN, 212
Glücklich, Frau, 103, 106-7
Glücklich, Helga, 101-3
Glücklich, Herr, 103-5, 106-7, 108, 110, 112, 114, 117
Goldstone, David, 205
Gorbachev, Mikhail, 224, 225, 243, 251
Grand Hotel, Brighton, 242
Graz, 47, 68, 79, 81, 84, 87, 89, 93, 94, 101, 105, 117, 123, 124, 125, 126, 127, 128, 129, 135, 136
Grey, Sir Edward, 221
Gromyko, Andrei, viii, 230, 231, 243

Halychyna, 4, 7, 108
Hampton Court, 224
Harwich, 192, 217
Hawthorn Miners' Hostel, 197, 198
Heath, Ted, 211, 213
Heathrow Airport, 1, 231, 232, 242-3
Heimat Land, 166
Hitler, Adolf, 14, 19, 34, 38, 86, 89-90, 101, 104, 108, 160, 250, 254, 263
Holowatyj, Father, 5, 23
Hopkin Morgan, 198
Hotel Ukraine, Ivano-Frankiwsk, 247
House of Commons, 217, 226
Houses of Parliament, 240
Howe, Sir Geoffrey, later Lord Howe of Aberavon, viii, ix, 224, 230, 231, 241
HTV Wales, 253, 254, 256

International Monetary Fund (IMF), 210

Irkutsk, 2, 22, 230, 242
Ivano-Frankiwsk, xi, 5, 226
Ivanovich, Ivan, 204
Izvestia, 21

Jenkin, Patrick, 221
Jenkins, Roy, 215, 221, 223
Judenburg, 140

Kartuzka Bereza prison, 8
Kellerberg camp, 144
KGB, 2, 22, 203, 225, 237, 238, 243, 244, 245, 247, 248, 251
Khrushchev, Nikita, 220, 224, 251
Klagenfurt, 140, 144, 149, 160, 177, 179, 180
Kleter, Mr, 36, 39
Kleter, Mrs, 39
Köflach, 88, 130, 138
Komsomol, 21, 91-2
Kowaluk, Fedir, 30, 39, 60, 62, 63, 164-5
Kravchuk, Leonid, 251
Kuchma, Leonid, 251
Kupranec, Josef, 212

Labour, Ministry of, 62, 69, 71, 72, 74, 78, 79, 80
Lake Baikal, 230, 242
Lenin, Vladimir, 20, 21, 22, 38, 99, 104, 108, 160, 252
Lenkaran swamp, 239
Lieboch, 135
Lloyd George, David, 218, 223
London, 193, 240
Luhansk, see Voroshilovgrad
Lwiw, 45, 65
Lykhachova, Halyna, 247

Mackworth Hotel, Swansea, 200
Malo Polska 'Little Poland', 8, 15
Market Drayton, 193
Markov, Captain, 97-100, 102
Marks and Spencer, 198, 240
Marksman, 189
Marx, Karl, 18, 20, 104, 160
Metropolitan Archbishop of Lwiw, 23
Mikardo, Ian, 223
Millennium stadium, 252
Millfield School, 250
miners' strike, 241
Morgan, Rhodri, 228
Mortimer, Charlotte, 228
Mulroney, Brian, 223
Munich, 184, 188
Münster, 185, 187

NAAFI, 160, 161, 171, 172
Nadwirna, 35
NATO, 213, 220, 251
Newbridge, 195
Ninian Park, 206, 207
NKVD, 22, 23, 26, 27, 28, 29, 31, 33, 36, 52, 87, 91, 144, 165
Nyzhniw, 12, 19, 27
Nyzhniw High School, 20
Nyzhniw station, 42

Oakdale, 195
Oakdale Miners' Institute, 196
Odessa, 164
Oleshiw, 4, 7, 39, 65
Oleshiw brickworks, 9, 24
Orange Revolution, 251
Ostapowycz, Reverend, 20, 21-3